U•X•L ENCYCLOPEDIA OF WORLD BIOGRAPHY

Volume 1

A–Ba

Laura B. Tyle, Editor

Detroit • New York • San Diego • San Francisco • Cleveland • New Haven, Conn. • Waterville, Maine • London • Munich

U•X•L Encyclopedia of World Biography
Laura B. Tyle, Editor, Proof Positive/Farrowlyne Associates, Inc.

Project Editors
Lawrence W. Baker, Elizabeth Shaw Grunow

Editorial
Elizabeth Anderson, Sarah Hermsen

Permissions
Margaret Chamberlain

Imaging and Multimedia
Randy Bassett, Lezlie Light, Dave Oblender, Kelly A. Quin

Product Design
Tracey Rowens

Composition
Evi Seoud

Manufacturing
Rita Wimberley

For more information, contact:
The Gale Group, Inc.
27500 Drake Rd.
Farmington Hills, MI 48331-3535
Or you can visit our Internet site at
http://www.gale.com

LIBRARY OF CONGRESS CATALOGING-IN-PUBLICATION DATA

UXL encyclopedia of world biography / Laura B. Tyle, editor.
p. cm.
Summary: A collection of 750 biographies and portraits of notable historic and current figures in American and world history, literature, science and math, arts and entertainment, and the social sciences. Includes bibliographical references and index.
ISBN 0-7876-6465-0 (set hardcover : alk. paper)
1. Biography—Dictionaries—Juvenile literature. [1. Biography—Dictionaries.] I. Title: Encyclopedia of world biography. II. Tyle, Laura B.

CT103 .U95 2002
920.02—dc21
Revised
2002004316

ISBN 0-7876-6465-0 (set); 0-7876-6466-9 (v. 1); 0-7876-6467-7 (v. 2); 0-7876-6468-5 (v. 3); 0-7876-6469-3 (v. 4); 0-7876-6470-7 (v. 5); 0-7876-6471-5 (v. 6); 0-7876-6472-3 (v. 7); 0-7876-6473-1 (v. 8); 0-7876-6474-X (v. 9); 0-7876-6475-8 (v. 10)

Printed in the United States of America
10 9 8 7 6 5 4 3 2 1

contents

Volume 2: Be–Cap

Volume 3: Car–Da

Volume 4: De–Ga

Volume 5: Ge–I

Volume 6: J–L

Volume 7: M–Ne

Volume 8: Ni–Re

Volume 9: Rh–S

Volume 10: T–Z

African American

Albanian

American

Arabian

Argentine

Asian American

English

U•X•L Encyclopedia of World Biography features 750 biographies of notable historic and contemporary figures from around the world. Chosen from American history, world history, literature, science and math, arts and entertainment, and the social sciences, the entries focus on the people studied most often in middle school and high school, as identified by teachers and media specialists.

The biographies are arranged alphabetically across ten volumes. The two- to four-page entries cover the early lives, influences, and careers of notable men and women of diverse fields and ethnic groups. Each essay includes birth and death information in the header and concludes with a list of sources for further information. A contents section lists biographees by their nationality. Nearly 750 photographs and illustrations are featured, and a general index provides quick access to the people and subjects discussed throughout *U•X•L Encyclopedia of World Biography.*

Special thanks

Much appreciation goes to Mary Alice Anderson, media specialist at Winona Middle School in Winona, Minnesota, and Nina Levine, library media specialist at Blue Mountain Middle School in Cortlandt Manor, New York, for their assistance in developing the entry list. Many thanks also go to the following people for their important editorial contributions: Taryn Benbow-Pfalzgraf (proofreading), Jodi Essey-Stapleton (copyediting and proofing), Margaret Haerens (proofreading), Courtney Mroch (copyediting), and Theresa Murray (copyediting and indexing). Special gratitude goes to Linda Mahoney at LM Design for her excellent typesetting work and her flexible attitude.

Comments and suggestions

We welcome your comments on the *U•X•L Encyclopedia of World Biography.* Please write: Editors, *U•X•L Encyclopedia of World Biography,* U•X•L, 27500 Drake Road, Farmington Hills, MI 48331-3535; call toll-free: 1-800-877-4253; fax to 248-699-8097; or send e-mail via www.gale.com.

U•X•L ENCYCLOPEDIA OF WORLD BIOGRAPHY

HANK AARON

Born: February 5, 1934
Mobile, Alabama
African American baseball player

Hank Aaron is major league baseball's leading home run hitter, with a career total of 755 home runs from 1954 to 1976. He also broke ground for the participation of African Americans in professional sports.

Early life

Henry Louis Aaron was born in Mobile, Alabama, on February 5, 1934, the third of Herbert and Estella Aaron's eight children. His father was a shipyard worker and tavern owner. Aaron took an early interest in sports. Although the family had little money and he took several jobs to try to help out, he spent a lot of time playing baseball at a neighborhood park. Lacking interest in school because he believed he would make it as a ballplayer, Aaron transferred out of a segregated (restricted to members of one race) high school in his junior year to attend the Allen Institute in Mobile, which had an organized baseball program.

After high school graduation, Aaron played on local amateur and semi-pro teams, such as the Pritchett Athletics and the Mobile Black Bears, where he began to make a name

Hank Aaron.
Reproduced by permission of AP/Wide World Photos.

for himself. At this time Jackie Robinson (1919–1972) of the Brooklyn Dodgers was breaking the baseball color barrier by becoming the first African American player in the major leagues. At age seventeen, Aaron gained immediate success as a hard-hitting infielder. In 1951 the owner of the Indianapolis Clowns, part of the professional Negro American League, signed him as the Clowns' shortstop for the 1952 season.

Record breaker

Being almost entirely self-taught, Aaron batted cross handed in his early years, "because no one had told him not to," according to one of his biographers. Still, Aaron's sensational hitting with the Clowns prompted a Boston Braves scout to purchase his contract in 1952. Assigned to Eau Claire, Wisconsin, in the minor Northern League (where coaching corrected his batting style), Aaron batted .336 and won the league's rookie of the year award. The following year he was assigned to the Braves' Jacksonville, Florida team, in the South Atlantic (Sally) League. Even while enduring the taunting of fans and racial insults from fellow players in the segregated south, he went on to bat .362, with 22 homers and 125 runs batted in (RBIs). He was named the league's most valuable player in 1953.

During winter ball in Puerto Rico in 1953 and 1954 Aaron began playing positions in the outfield. In the spring of 1954 he trained with the major league Milwaukee Braves and won a starting position when the regular right fielder suffered an injury. Although Aaron was sidelined late in the season with a broken ankle, he batted .280 as a rookie that year. Over the next twenty-two seasons, this quiet, six-foot, right-handed All-Star established himself as one of the most durable and skilled hitters in major league history.

In fourteen of the seasons Aaron played for the Braves, he batted .300 or more. In fifteen seasons he hit 30 or more homers, scored 100 or more runs, and drove in 100 or more runs. In his long career Aaron led all major league players in RBIs with 2,297. He played in 3,298 games, which ranked him third among players of all time. Aaron twice led the National League in batting, and four times led the league in homers. His consistent hitting produced a career total of 3,771 hits, again ranking him third all-time. When Aaron recorded his three thousandth hit on May 7, 1970, he was the youngest player (at thirty-six) since Ty Cobb (1886–1961) to reach that milestone. Aaron played in twenty-four All-Star games, tying a record. His lifetime batting average was .305, and in two World Series he batted .364. He also held the record for hitting home runs in three straight National League playoff games, which he accomplished in 1969 against the New York Mets.

A quiet superstar

Although Aaron ranked among baseball's superstars, he received less publicity than other players. In part this was due to Aaron's quiet personality and the continuing prejudice against African American players in the majors. Moreover, playing with the Milwaukee Braves (who became the Atlanta Braves in 1966) denied Aaron the publicity received by major league players in cities like New York or Los Angeles. During Aaron's long career the Braves only won two National League pennants and one divisional title. The Braves won the World Series in 1957, the year Aaron's 44 homers helped him win his only Most Valuable Player award. The following year Milwaukee repeated as National League champions but lost the World Series.

Year after year Aaron ranked among the National League's leading home run hitters. It was not until 1970, however, that sportswriters and fans began noticing that Aaron was about to challenge Babe Ruth's (1895–1948) record total of 714 homers. By 1972 Aaron's assault on the all-time homer record was big news, and his $200,000 annual salary was the highest in the league. The following year Aaron hit 40 homers, falling one short of tying Ruth's mark. Early in the 1974 season Aaron hit the tying homer in Cincinnati, Ohio. Then, on the night of April 8, 1974, before a large crowd in Atlanta, Georgia, and with a national television audience looking on, Aaron hit his 715th homer off Dodgers pitcher Al Downing, breaking Ruth's record. It was the highlight of Aaron's career, although it was tempered by a growing number of death threats and racist letters that made Aaron fear for his family's safety.

A new career

After the 1974 season Aaron left the Braves and went to play for the Milwaukee Brewers until his retirement in 1976. At the time of his retirement as a player, the forty-two-year-old veteran had raised his all-time homer output to 755. When he left the Brewers he became a vice president and director of player development for the Braves, where he scouted new team prospects and oversaw the coaching of minor leaguers. He later went on to become a senior vice president for the Braves. Overall, his efforts contributed toward making the Braves one of the strongest teams in the National League. In 1982 Aaron was voted into the Baseball Hall of Fame at Cooperstown, New York, and in 1997 Hank Aaron Stadium in Mobile was dedicated to him.

Aaron received two honors in October 1999. Congress passed a resolution recognizing him as one of baseball's greatest players and praising his work with his Chasing the Dream Foundation, which helps children age nine through twelve pursue their dreams. Later that month, Aaron was named to major league baseball's All-Century Team, whose members were chosen by fans and a panel of baseball experts. In January 2002, Aaron was honored with one of the greatest tributes an athlete can receive: his picture appeared on a Wheaties cereal box.

For More Information

Aaron, Hank, with Lonnie Wheeler. *I Had a Hammer: The Hank Aaron Story.* New York: HarperCollins, 1991.

Rennert, Richard Scott. *Henry Aaron.* New York: Chelsea House, 1993.

Sweet, Kimberly Noel. *Hank Aaron: The Life of the Homerun King.* Montgomery, AL: Junebug Books, 2001.

Ralph Abernathy

Born: March 11, 1926
Linden, Alabama
Died: April 30, 1990
Atlanta, Georgia
African American civil rights activist

Civil rights leader Ralph Abernathy was the best friend and close assistant of Martin Luther King Jr. (1929–1968). He followed King as the president of the Southern Christian Leadership Conference (SCLC). The organization used nonviolent means to fight for civil rights for African Americans.

Family and youth

Ralph David Abernathy, one of twelve children, was born in Linden, Alabama, on March 11, 1926. His father, William, the son of a slave, first supported his family as a sharecropper (a farmer who pays some of his crops as rent to the land's owner). In time William Abernathy saved enough money to buy five hundred acres of his own and built a prosperous farm. William Abernathy eventually emerged as one of the leading African Americans in his county. William Abernathy became the county's first African American to vote and the first to serve on the grand jury (a jury that decides whether or not evidence supports a formal charge against a person for a crime). William Abernathy also served as a deacon (a nonclergy church member) in his church.

Ralph Abernathy went to Alabama State University and graduated with a degree in mathematics in 1950. He later earned a master's degree in sociology from Atlanta University in 1951. During this time he also worked as the first African American disc jockey at a white Montgomery, Alabama, radio station. While attending college he was elected president of the student council and led successful protests that called for better cafeteria conditions and better living quarters for students. This experience was the beginning of a career leading protests and working to improve the lives of others.

From an early age Ralph Abernathy wanted to become a preacher and was encouraged by his mother to pursue his ambition. As he later recalled, he had noticed that the preacher was always the person who was most admired in his community. Before finishing college Abernathy became a Baptist minister. After completing his education he served as minister at the Eastern Star Baptist church in Demopolis, Alabama, near his home town of Linden. At age twenty-six

Abernathy became a full-time minister at the First Baptist Church in Montgomery. Martin Luther King Jr. began preaching at another of Montgomery's leading African American churches, Dexter Avenue Baptist, three years later. During this time King and Abernathy became close friends.

Ralph Abernathy.
Reproduced by permission of Archive Photos, Inc.

Montgomery bus boycott

In 1955 an African American woman from Montgomery named Rosa Parks refused to give up her bus seat so that a white passenger could sit down. She was arrested for this action and was later fined. This event began an important historic phase of the civil rights movement. Local ministers and the National Association for the Advancement of Colored People (NAACP) began a boycott of the city buses to end segregation. At the time, the buses in Montgomery were segregated (people were required by law to sit in separate sections based on their race). Parks had been sitting in one of the front seats, which was in the "white" section. African Americans were required by law to give up their seats to white riders if other seats were not available. The ministers formed the Montgomery Improvement Association (MIA) to coordinate the boycott and voted Martin Luther King Jr. its president.

The MIA convinced African American cab drivers to take African American workers to their jobs for a ten-cent fare. This made it more affordable for African Americans to avoid riding the buses. After the city government declared the ten-cent cab rides illegal, people with cars formed car pools so that the boycotters would not have to return to the buses. After 381 days the boycott ended with the buses completely desegregated. The boycotters' victory over bus segregation was enforced by a United States district court.

During 1956 Abernathy and King had been in and out of jail and court as a result of their efforts to end the practice of separating people based on their race on buses. Toward the end of the bus boycott on January 10, 1957, Abernathy's home and church were bombed. By the time the boycott was over, it had attracted national and international attention. Televised reports of the MIA's activities inspired African American civil rights protesters all over the South.

Nonviolent civil rights movement

King and Abernathy's work together in the MIA was the beginning of years of partnership and friendship between them. Their friendship, as well as their joint efforts in the civil rights struggle, lasted until King's assassination in 1968. Soon after the bus boycott, they met with other African American clergymen in Atlanta, Georgia, to form the Southern Christian Leadership Conference (SCLC). The goal of the SCLC was to press for civil rights in all areas of life. King was elected president and Abernathy was named secretary-treasurer. The group began to plan for an organized, nonviolent civil rights movement throughout the South. Their aim was to end segregation and to push for more effective federal civil rights laws.

In the early 1960s the civil rights movement began to intensify. Students staged "sit-ins" by sitting in the "whites only" sections of lunch counters. Other nonviolent demonstrations and efforts to desegregate interstate buses and bus depots also continued. During this time Abernathy moved to Atlanta to become the pastor of West Hunter Baptist Church. In Atlanta, he would be able to work more closely with the SCLC and King, who was living in the city.

In the spring of 1963 SCLC leaders began to plan their efforts to desegregate facilities in Birmingham, Alabama. Publicity (of events shown on television) about the rough treatment of African American demonstrators directed the eyes of the world to that city's civil rights protest. Abernathy and King went to prison, while more than three thousand other African Americans in the city also endured periods of time in jail while working for equal rights. The Birmingham demonstrations were successful, and the demands for desegregation of public facilities were agreed upon. After the Birmingham demonstrations, desegregation programs began in over 250 southern cities. Thousands of schools, parks, pools, restaurants, and hotels were opened to all people, regardless of their race.

March on Washington

The success of the Birmingham demonstration also encouraged President John F. Kennedy (1917–1963) to send a civil rights bill to Congress. In order to stress the need for this bill, the leaders of all of the nation's major civil rights organizations agreed to participate in a massive demonstration in Washington, D.C. On August 28, 1963, this "March on Washington" attracted over 250,000 African American and white demonstrators from all over the United States. By the next summer the Civil Rights Act, which banned discrimination (treating people unequally because of their differences) based on race, color, religion, or national origin, had been signed into law. In 1965 the Voting Rights Act, which banned discrimination in voting, was passed.

Leadership of the SCLC

On April 4, 1968, King was assassinated in Memphis, Tennessee. Abernathy was named the new leader of the SCLC. His first project was to complete King's plan to hold a Poor People's Campaign in Washington during which poor whites, African Americans, and Native Americans would present their problems to President Lyndon B. Johnson (1908–1973) and the Congress. As a result of these protests, Abernathy once again found himself in jail. This time he was charged with unlawful assembly (an unlawful gathering of people for an illegal purpose). After the Poor People's Campaign, Abernathy continued to lead the SCLC, but the organization did not regain the popularity it had held under King's leadership.

Abernathy resigned from the SCLC in 1977. Later, he formed an organization that was designed to help train African Americans for better economic opportunities. He continued to serve as a minister and as a lecturer throughout the United States. In 1989 Abernathy published his autobiography, called *And the Walls Come Tumbling Down* (Harper, 1989). Abernathy died of a heart attack on April 30, 1990, in Atlanta.

For More Information

Abernathy, Ralph. *And the Walls Came Tumbling Down: An Autobiography.* New York: Harper & Row, 1991.

Oates, Stephen. *Let the Trumpet Sound.* New York: Harper & Row, 1982.

Reef, Catherine M. *Ralph David Abernathy (People in Focus Book).* Parsippany, NJ: Dillon Press, 1995.

BELLA ABZUG

Born: July 24, 1920
New York, New York
Died: March 31, 1998
New York, New York
American lawyer, politician, and civil rights activist

Bella Abzug worked for civil and women's rights as a lawyer and as a politician. Throughout her long political career, she used her sharp tongue and unusual style to advance the issues that were her deepest concern. As she wrote in her autobiography, "I'm going to help organize a new political coalition of the women, the minorities and the young people, along with the poor, the elderly, the workers, and the unemployed, which is going to turn this country upside down and inside out."

An early interest in women's rights

Bella Stavisky was born on July 24, 1920, in the Bronx, New York. She was the daughter of Emanuel and Esther Stavisky, Russian Jewish immigrants who owned a meat market. During her youth she worked in her father's store until it failed in the 1920s, and he turned to selling insurance. In 1930 her father died, leaving her mother to support the family with his insurance money and by taking jobs in local department stores.

Bella's interest in women's rights began at a young age. Her family was deeply religious. While attending synagogue (a place for Jewish worship of God) with her grandfather, she was offended that women were not treated the same as men. According to the rules of Orthodox Judaism (a branch of the Jewish faith that strictly follows customs and traditions), women were forced to sit in the back rows of the balcony in synagogues.

Making a difference

Bella Stavisky attended an all-female high school in the west Bronx, where she was elected president of her class. She then went

Bella Abzug.
Courtesy of the Library of Congress.

on to Hunter College, where she served as student-body president and graduated in 1942. She taught Jewish history and Hebrew on the weekends. She marched in protests against the harm being done to Jewish people in Europe and against British and American neutrality in the Spanish Civil War. (The war was a revolt led by the military against Spain's Republican government that lasted from 1936 to 1939). During World War II (1939–45) she was one of thousands of American women entering war production industries, working in a shipbuilding factory. In 1944 she married Maurice Abzug, a stockbroker and writer. The couple had two daughters.

Bella Abzug decided that she could do more to help people if she became a lawyer. She entered Columbia Law School, where she became editor of the *Columbia Law Review.* After graduating in 1947, she worked as a labor lawyer and represented civil rights workers. She became committed to helping poor people gain justice and a decent life in the days following World War II.

In the 1950s Abzug became deeply involved in the early civil rights movement. In 1950 she agreed to defend an African American man named Willie McGee. McGee was accused of raping a white woman with whom he had been having an affair, found guilty, and sentenced to death under the harsh laws in place in Mississippi during that time. Although she lost the case, Abzug succeeded in delaying the man's execution for two years by appealing the ruling twice to the Supreme Court.

In the late 1960s Abzug continued to do what she could to help ethnic minorities, women's groups, and the poor. During these years she became active in the Democratic Party. After the Chicago Democratic Convention in 1968 she joined with other like-minded Democrats to found the New Democratic Coalition. She also joined in the movement to ban nuclear testing, a movement that became more of an antiwar movement as the United States deepened its involvement in the Vietnam War (1955–75). In this war, the United States supported the anti-Communist government of South Vietnam in its fight against a takeover by the Communist government of North Vietnam.

Elected to office

In 1970, with the support of labor organizations and the Jewish population,

Abzug was elected to the U.S. House of Representatives from New York City's Nineteenth District. She quickly gained national attention for her bold ideas and for the wide hats she wore within the halls of Congress. On her first day on the job she introduced a bill calling for American troops to be pulled out of Vietnam by July 4, 1971. Although the bill was defeated within a week, Abzug had made a name for herself as a politician with a tough style who was unafraid of her opponents.

While in office she coauthored the 1974 Freedom of Information Act (a law that gives people in America the right to access otherwise secret information from government agencies) and the 1974 Privacy Act (a law that gives U.S. citizens and permanent residents the right to access many government files that contain information about them). She was the first to call for the impeachment (a process in which a public official is put on trial in Congress with the Senate acting as the judge) of President Richard Nixon (1913–1994) for his involvement in criminal activity. She also cast one of the first votes for the Equal Rights Amendment, a proposed amendment to the Constitution that if passed would have guaranteed equality of rights to both men and women.

In 1972 New York City changed the way its congressional districts were set up, eliminating Abzug's district. She decided to run against the popular William Fitts Ryan (1922–1972) in the Twentieth District. She lost the primary, but Ryan died before the general election in November. As a result, Abzug became the Democratic candidate in the general election. She won and went on to serve in the House until 1976, when she gave up her seat to run for the Senate, a race she lost to Daniel Patrick Moynihan (1927–). She then ran in the Democratic mayoral primary in New York but was defeated by Edward Koch (1924–). Never one to give up, she told reporters not to assume that she was finished with politics.

Continuing activism

Abzug continued to fight for peace and women's rights long after leaving office. President Jimmy Carter (1924–) appointed her as cochair, or joint leader, of the National Advisory Committee for Women. However, after the committee met with President Carter and pointed out that recent cuts in social services were having a negative effect on the nation's women, Abzug was dismissed from the committee. This led to the resignation of several other members, including the other cochair, and caused a massive public outcry against Carter.

Abzug devoted her energies to women's rights up to the final years of her life. As chair of New York City's Commission on the Status of Women, she directed a national campaign to increase the number of women in public office. Her presence at the United Nations 4th Women's Conference in Beijing, China, in 1991, attracted a great deal of attention. On March 31, 1998, after an operation on her heart, Abzug died in New York, bringing to an end a lifelong fight to improve the lives of women, minorities, and the poor.

For More Information

Abzug, Bella. *Bella.* Edited by Mel Ziegler. New York: Saturday Review Press, 1972.

Abzug, Bella, with Mim Kelber. *Gender Gap.* Boston: Houghton Mifflin, 1984.

Faber, Doris. *Bella Abzug.* New York: Lothrop, Lee & Shepard, 1976.

Chinua Achebe

Born: November 15, 1930
Ogidi, Nigeria
Nigerian novelist

Chinua Achebe is one of Nigeria's greatest novelists. His novels are written mainly for an African audience, but having been translated into more than forty languages, they have found worldwide readership.

Early life

Chinua Achebe was born on November 15, 1930, in Ogidi in Eastern Nigeria. His family belonged to the Igbo tribe, and he was the fifth of six children. Representatives of the British government that controlled Nigeria convinced his parents, Isaiah Okafor Achebe and Janet Ileogbunam, to abandon their traditional religion and follow Christianity. Achebe was brought up as a Christian, but he remained curious about the more traditional Nigerian faiths. He was educated at a government college in Umuahia, Nigeria, and graduated from the University College at Ibadan, Nigeria, in 1954.

Successful first effort

Achebe was unhappy with books about Africa written by British authors such as Joseph Conrad (1857–1924) and John Buchan (1875–1940), because he felt the descriptions of African people were inaccurate and insulting. While working for the Nigerian Broadcasting Corporation he composed his first novel, *Things Fall Apart* (1959), the story of a traditional warrior hero who is unable to adapt to changing conditions in the early days of British rule. The book won immediate international recognition and also became the basis for a play by Biyi Bandele. Years later, in 1997, the Performance Studio Workshop of Nigeria put on a production of the play, which was then presented in the United States as part of the Kennedy Center's African Odyssey series in 1999. Achebe's next two novels, *No Longer At Ease* (1960) and *Arrow of God* (1964), were set in the past as well.

By the mid-1960s the newness of independence had died out in Nigeria, as the country faced the political problems common to many of the other states in modern Africa. The Igbo, who had played a leading role in Nigerian politics, now began to feel that the Muslim Hausa people of Northern Nigeria considered the Igbos second-class citizens. Achebe wrote *A Man of the People* (1966), a story about a crooked Nigerian politician. The book was published at the very moment a military takeover removed the old political leadership. This made some Northern military officers suspect that Achebe had played a role in the takeover, but there was never any evidence supporting the theory.

Political crusader

During the years when Biafra attempted to break itself off as a separate state from Nigeria (1967–70), however, Achebe served as an ambassador (representative) to Biafra. He traveled to different countries discussing the problems of his people, especially the starving and slaughtering of Igbo children. He wrote articles for newspapers and magazines about the Biafran struggle and founded the Citadel Press with Nigerian poet Christopher Okigbo. Writing a novel at this time was out of the question, he said during a 1969 interview: "I can't write a novel now; I wouldn't want to. And even if I wanted to, I couldn't. I can write poetry—something short, intense, more in keeping with my mood." Three volumes of poetry emerged during this time, as well as a collection of short stories and children's stories.

After the fall of the Republic of Biafra, Achebe continued to work at the University of Nigeria at Nsukka, and devoted time to the Heinemann Educational Books' Writers Series (which was designed to promote the careers of young African writers). In 1972 Achebe came to the United States to become an English professor at the University of Massachusetts at Amherst (he taught there again in 1987). In 1975 he joined the faculty at the University of Connecticut. He returned to the University of Nigeria in 1976. His novel *Anthills of the Savanna* (1987) tells the story of three boyhood friends in a West African nation and the deadly effects of the desire for power and wanting to be elected "president for life." After its release Achebe returned to the United States and teaching positions at Stanford University, Dartmouth College, and other universities.

Chinua Achebe.
Reproduced by permission of AP/Wide World Photos.

Later years

Back in Nigeria in 1990 to celebrate his sixtieth birthday, Achebe was involved in a car accident on one of the country's dangerous roads. The accident left him paralyzed from the waist down. Doctors recommended he go back to the United States for good to receive better medical care, so he accepted a teaching position at Bard College, Annandale-on-Hudson, New York. In 1999, after a nine-year absence, Achebe visited his homeland, where his native village of Ogidi honored him for his dedication to the myths and legends of his ancestors. In 2000 Achebe's nonfiction book *Home and Exile,* consisting of three essays, was published by Oxford University Press.

For More Information

Carroll, David. *Chinua Achebe.* New York: St. Martin's Press, 1980.

Ezenwa-Ohaeto. *Chinua Achebe: A Biography.* Bloomington: Indiana University Press, 1997.

Innes, C. L. *Chinua Achebe.* New York: Cambridge University Press, 1990.

ABIGAIL ADAMS

Born: November 22, 1744
Weymouth, Massachusetts
Died: October 28, 1818
Quincy, Massachusetts
American political advisor and first lady

Though she believed her main role in life to be wife and mother, Abigail Adams also was a behind-the-scenes stateswoman. She used her talents to maintain her family during the many absences of her husband, John Adams, the second president of the United States, and to advise her husband about women's rights and slavery. Her detailed letters with her husband, family, and friends provide a historical record of the times and show her to have been a woman ahead of her time.

Early life

Abigail Smith was born in Weymouth, Massachusetts, on November 11, 1744, to William and Elizabeth Quincy Smith. Her well-educated father was the minister of the North Parish Congregational Church of Weymouth. Although many of Abigail's relatives were well-to-do merchants and ship captains, she was raised in a simple, rural setting. She was educated at home, learning domestic skills, such as sewing, fine needlework, and cooking, along with reading and writing. She took advantage of her father's extensive library to broaden her knowledge. Her lack of formal education became a lifelong regret. As an adult, she favored equal education for women. She once argued that educated mothers raise educated children.

On October 25, 1764, Abigail married John Adams, a struggling, Harvard-educated country lawyer nine years her senior. Although John Adams was not from a prominent family, the couple was well matched intellectually and the marriage was a happy one. He admired and encouraged Abigail's outspokenness and intelligence. She supported him by running the family farm, raising their children, listening to him, and trying to help him with his problems.

Early political years

During the first few years of their marriage, John Adams lived mostly in Boston, Massachusetts, building his law career and becoming involved with the growing political unrest. This political unrest was brought about by the English government's attempts to tighten control over its colonies through the passage of laws and new taxes that many colonists did not support. Abigail, however, remained at Braintree (later Quincy), Massachusetts, to run the family farm. Although women at that time did not normally handle business affairs, Abigail traded livestock, hired help, bought land, oversaw construction, and supervised the planting and harvesting. "I hope in time to have the reputation of being as good a Farmess as my partner has of being a good Statesman," she once wrote.

During the next few years, hostilities between the American colonies and Great Britain increased, forcing John Adams away from home more often. He was chosen as a delegate to the First Continental Congress. (The congress was a group of colonial representatives who met in Philadelphia, Pennsylvania, on September 5, 1774, and took a stand against the British government's policy of passing laws over the colonists without colonial representation.) He traveled constantly in addition to those duties, trying to earn as much money as he could practicing law. He tried to make these difficult times easier by writing long letters to Abigail, sometimes several a day. She, in turn, wrote to her husband of her own loneliness, doubts, and fears. She suffered from migraines and chronic insomnia. Despite her own bouts with illness, she gave birth to five children. One daughter, Susanna, born in 1768, lived for only a year.

Abigail Adams.
Courtesy of the National Portrait Gallery.

War affects the family

When the Revolutionary War (1775–83) began with the battles of Lexington and Concord in Massachusetts on April 17, 1775, John Adams was called back to the Continental Congress. On June 15, 1775, the Second Continental Congress made George Washington commander in chief of the American army. The Congress also set up a government for the colonies. A year later, on July 4, 1776, the Congress approved the Declaration of Independence, in which the American colonies declared their independence from the government of Great Britain. During the war Abigail provided meals and lodging to soldiers who stopped at the Adams' home at all hours of the day and night. In the fall of 1775, the inhabitants of Braintree suffered an epidemic of dysentery, an often-fatal bowel infection. Abigail had to nurse her sick relatives in addition to caring for her children. Her mother and five other members of her family eventually died from the illness.

As the fighting drew closer to Boston, Abigail Adams wrote many letters describing the events of the time. In a letter written in March 1776, she urged her husband to take women's rights into consideration if and when the colonies gained independence: "In the new code of laws which I suppose it will be necessary for you to make, I desire you would remember the ladies and be more generous and favorable to them than your ancestors . . . If particular care and attention is not paid to the ladies, we are determined to foment [promote] a rebellion, and will not hold ourselves bound by any laws in which we have no voice or representation."

John Adams is sent to Europe

As the war continued, John Adams was sent to Europe to work on treaties with other countries and to seek loans for the colonies. He took one or two of his sons on these assignments, which continued after the war ended, giving America its independence from Great Britain in 1883. These constant separations were difficult for Abigail Adams, but she supported her husband. She wrote that she "found his honor and reputation much dearer to [her] than [her] own present pleasure and happiness."

After five years, Abigail and her daughter, Nabby, joined her husband and sons in England. During the years in Europe, Abigail acted as hostess for both political and social gatherings and as an advisor to her husband. In April 1788, five years after Abigail's arrival, the family returned home.

John Adams is elected

After the American Revolution ended, the newly independent country of the United States needed a president. When the votes were counted in March 1789, George Washington (1732–1799) was the clear presidential winner. At the time, the person with the most votes became president, while the person with the next largest number became vice president. John Adams placed second and became vice president. Although Abigail Adams had been upset by her husband's earlier political assignments, which forced him to be away from home for years at a time, she fully supported his decision to accept the vice presidency. The family moved to Philadelphia, Pennsylvania, where the federal government was located at the time. Abigail assumed the role of hostess, welcoming visitors to the Adams's home. However, she returned to Braintree the next spring with her son, Thomas, who had fallen ill.

When Washington retired in 1797, John Adams ran for president and won the election. His wife joined him in Philadelphia in May. Abigail Adams quickly settled in as first lady; her husband discussed many important problems with her and often followed her advice. Abigail kept writing letters to friends and even continued managing the Quincy (formerly Braintree) farm through correspondence with her sister, Mary Cranch.

Whereas John Adams had never been in finer spirits, Abigail Adams became exhausted and ill with fever on a trip home to Quincy in the summer of 1797. This led to yet another separation when the president returned to Philadelphia in November. Abigail eventually recovered and returned to Philadelphia the next year, staying for the rest of her husband's term.

Retirement to Quincy

After losing his bid for reelection in 1800, John Adams retired to life on the farm. Abigail Adams continued to keep herself busy maintaining her home. The family remained plagued with illness. Both Mary Cranch and her husband died within days of each other. Nabby Adams had been diagnosed with cancer and underwent an operation. John Adams injured his leg in an accident and was unable to walk for several weeks. As always, Abigail Adams cared for them all.

In October of 1818, Abigail Adams suffered a stroke. She died quietly on October 28, 1818, surrounded by her family. John Adams lived several more years, passing away on July 4, 1826. Abigail Adams has the distinction of being the first woman in U.S. history to be the wife of one president (John Adams) and the mother of another (John Quincy Adams [1767–1848]).

For More Information

Akers, Charles W. *Abigail Adams.* New York: Longman, 2000.

Bober, Natalie S. *Abigail Adams.* New York: Atheneum Books for Young Readers, 1995.

Butterfield, L. H., et al., eds. *The Book of Abigail and John: Selected Letters of the Adams Family, 1762–1784.* Cambridge, MA: Harvard University Press, 1975.

Nagel, Paul C. *The Adams Women.* New York: Oxford University Press, 1987.

ANSEL ADAMS

Born: February 20, 1902
San Francisco, California
Died: April 22, 1984
Carmel, California
American photographer

Ansel Adams was a masterful photographer and a lifelong conservationist (a person who works to preserve and protect the environment) who encouraged understanding of, and respect for, the natural environment. Although he spent a large part of his career in commercial photography, he is best known for his photographs of landscapes.

Early life

Ansel Easton Adams, the only child of Charles Hitchcock and Olive Bray Adams, was born on February 20, 1902, in San Francisco, California, near the Golden Gate Bridge. In 1906 an aftershock from the famous earthquake of that year threw him to the floor and gave him a badly broken nose. His father, a successful businessman who owned an insurance agency and a chemical factory, sent him to private, as well as public, schools. Adams was shy and self-conscious about his nose and had problems in school. He received only an eighth-grade education, preferring to learn mainly through following his own interests. From a young age he enjoyed the outdoors, taking many long walks and exploring.

At age twelve Adams began playing the piano. He was serious about music and decided to pursue it as a career. But he was also interested in photography. A family trip to Yosemite National Park in 1916, where he made his first amateur photos, is said to have determined his direction in life. He then found a job as a photo technician for a commercial firm, which helped him learn more about his hobby. In 1919 he joined the Sierra Club, an organization devoted to protecting the wilderness of the Sierra Nevada. He spent

Ansel Adams.
Reproduced by permission of AP/Wide World Photos.

the next few summers working as a caretaker in the organization's headquarters in Yosemite Valley. Later in life, from 1936 to 1970, Adams was president of the Sierra Club, one of the many distinguished positions that he held.

In the 1920s Adams was spending as much time as he could in the Sierra Nevada, hiking, exploring, and taking photographs. He became friendly with leaders of the Sierra Club, had photos and writings printed in the club's official publication, and became more involved with the conservation movement. He even met his wife, Virginia Best, in Yosemite. They were married in 1928 and had two children.

Photography career

Ansel Adams gave up on the piano and decided to become a full-time professional photographer at about the time that some of his work was published in limited edition collections, such as *Parmelian Prints of the High Sierras* (1927) and *Taos Pueblo* (1930), with text written by Mary Austin. His first important one-man show was held in San Francisco in 1932 at the M. H. de Young Memorial Museum.

Adams went on to open the Ansel Adams Gallery for the Arts. He also taught, lectured, and worked on advertising assignments in the San Francisco area. During the 1930s he also began his extensive publications on methods of photography, insisting throughout his life on the importance of careful craftsmanship. In 1936 Alfred Stieglitz (1864–1946) gave Adams a one-man show in his New York gallery—only the second time the work of a young photographer was exhibited by Stieglitz.

In 1937 Adams moved to Yosemite Valley close to his major subject and began publishing a stream of volumes, including *Sierra Nevada: The John Muir Trail* (1938), *Illustrated Guide to Yosemite Valley* (1940), *Yosemite and the High Sierra* (1948), and *My Camera in Yosemite Valley* (1949).

New ideas on photography

In 1930 Adams met the famous photographer Paul Strand (1890–1976) while they were working in Taos, New Mexico, and the man and his work had a lasting effect on Adams's approach to photography. Strand encouraged Adams to change his approach from a soft expression of subjects to a much clearer, harder treatment, so-called "straight photography." This idea was further reinforced by his association with the short-lived, but important, group of photographers known as f/64 (referring to the lens opening which guarantees a distinct image), which included Edward Weston (1886–1958) and Imogen Cunningham (1883–1976). This group helped the development of photography as a fine art.

In one sense Ansel Adams's work is an extensive record of what is still left of the wilderness, the shrinking untouched part of the natural environment. Yet to see his work only as photographic images is to miss the main point that he tried to make: without a guiding vision, photography is not necessarily an important activity. The finished product, as Adams saw it, must be thought up before it can be executed. With nineteenth-century artists and philosophers (seekers of wisdom) he shared the belief that this vision must be inspired by life on earth. Photographs, he believed, were not *taken* from the environment but were *made* into something greater than themselves.

Ansel Adams died on April 22, 1984. During his life he was criticized for photographing rocks while the world was falling apart. He responded by suggesting that "the understanding of the . . . world of nature will aid in holding the world of man together."

For More Information

Adams, Ansel and Mary Street. *Ansel Adams: An Autobiography.* Boston: Little Brown, 1985.

Alinder, Mary Street. *Ansel Adams: A Biography.* New York: Holt, 1996.

JOHN ADAMS

Born: October 30, 1735
Braintree (now Quincy), Massachusetts
Died: July 4, 1826
Quincy, Massachusetts
American president, vice president, and politician

John Adams, the second president of the United States and the first vice president, also helped in the early years of the republic as a lawyer, writer, congressman, and public speaker. As president, he kept the country at peace when many were calling for war with France. Adams later described his peace decision as "the most splendid diamond in my crown."

Early life and education

John Adams was born in Braintree (now Quincy), Massachusetts, on October 30, 1735, the first of three children born to John Adams and Susanna Boylston Adams. His father was a modest but successful farmer and local officeholder. After some initial reluctance, Adams entered Harvard and received his bachelor's degree in 1755. For about a year he taught school in Worcester, Massachusetts.

Although he gave some thought to entering the ministry, Adams decided to study law instead. While developing his legal practice, he participated in town affairs and contributed essays to Boston newspapers. In 1764 he married Abigail Smith of Weymouth, Massachusetts, who was to provide him with important support and assistance during the full life that lay ahead.

John Adams.
Courtesy of the Library of Congress.

Early political career

By 1765 Adams had become known for his skills as a lawyer. After Great Britain passed the Stamp Act, which imposed taxes on printed materials in the American colonies that many viewed as unfair, he moved into the center of Massachusetts political life. He contributed an important series of essays to the Boston newspapers and prepared a series of anti-Stamp Act resolutions for the Braintree town meetings. These resolutions were copied widely throughout the province. In April 1768 Adams moved to Boston and eventually was elected the city's representative to the Massachusetts legislature.

In the spring of 1771, largely for reasons of health, Adams returned to Braintree, where he divided his attention between farming and law. Within a year, however, he was back in Boston. In 1774 he was one of the representatives from Massachusetts to the First Continental Congress. As a representative he helped write letters of protest to Great Britain. He also continued to write newspaper articles about the colonies and their disputes with Britain.

The war and colonial independence

After the battles of Lexington and Concord in Massachusetts on April 17, 1775, began the Revolutionary War (1775–83), Adams returned to Congress. At this time he believed that independence from Britain would probably be necessary for the American colonies. Congress, however, was not yet willing to agree, and Adams fumed while still more petitions were sent off to England. The best chance of promoting independence, he argued, was for the various colonies to adopt new forms of government. Many provinces sought his advice on setting up these new governments.

By February 1776 Adams was fully committed to American independence. In May, Congress passed a resolution stating that measures should be taken to provide for the "happiness and safety" of the people. Adams wrote the introduction that in effect spelled out the principle of independence. He contributed little to the actual content of the Declaration of Independence but served as "the pillar of its support on the floor of the Congress," according to Thomas Jefferson (1743–1826). On another committee Adams drew up a model treaty that encouraged Congress to enter into commercial alliances (business deals), but not political alliances, with European nations. Exhausted by his duties, he left Philadelphia in mid-October for Massachusetts. For the next year or so he traveled from Massachusetts to Philadelphia to serve in Congress.

Foreign assignments

In November 1777, Congress elected Adams commissioner to France, and in February he left Boston for what would prove to be an extended stay. Adams spent the next year and a half trying to secure badly needed loans for Congress. He sent numerous long letters to friends and family describing European affairs and observed the French court and national life. After coming home to Massachusetts, Adams was asked by Congress to return to Europe to help negotiate the terms of a peace agreement, which would mark the end of the American Revolution, and then to work on a commercial treaty with Great Britain. The treaty of peace was signed on September 3, 1783.

Before returning permanently to the United States, Adams spent three years as American minister to the Court of Saint James in London. He was unable to make much progress there because relations between the United States and Britain just after the American Revolution were so strained. He also did not have the full support of Congress. Adams eventually resigned and returned to Boston.

The presidency

Once back in Boston, Adams began the final stage of his political career. He was elected vice president in 1789 and served for two terms under President George Washington (1732–1799). Adams was unhappy in this post; he felt that he lacked the authority to accomplish much. In 1796, despite a strong challenge from Thomas Jefferson and the choice of his own Federalist Party (an early political party that supported a strong federal government) to run a candidate against him, Adams was elected as the second president of the United States.

Adams took office on March 4, 1797. From the beginning his presidency was a stormy one. His cabinet proved difficult to control, and many foreign policy problems arose. The French Revolution (1787–99) and fighting between England and France caused many Americans to take the sides of both those countries. Still others wanted the United States to remain neutral. Adams found himself caught in the middle.

Although anti-French feelings were running high, President Adams committed himself to a plan of peace with France. This decision enraged most of his opponents. The president's attempts to keep peace made sense; America was still young and not fully established, and entering into an unnecessary war could have been a disaster. Many members of his own Federalist Party were opposed to him, however, and in the end Adams lost the next election to Jefferson by a narrow margin. He was so disappointed over his rejection by the American people that he refused to stay to welcome his successor into office.

John Adams spent the remainder of his life at home on his farm. He retained a lively interest in public affairs, particularly when they involved the rising career of his son, John Quincy Adams (1767–1848), who would also become president. Adams divided his time between overseeing his farm and writing letters about his personal experiences as well as more general issues of the day. He died at the age of ninety–one in Quincy, Massachusetts, just a few hours after Jefferson's death, on July 4, 1826.

For More Information

Brookhiser, Richard. *America's First Dynasty: The Adamses, 1735–1918.* New York: Free Press, 2002.

Ferling, John E. *John Adams: A Life.* Knoxville: University of Tennessee Press, 1992.

McCullough, David G. *John Adams.* New York: Simon & Schuster, 2001.

SAMUEL ADAMS

Born: September 27, 1722
Boston, Massachusetts
Died: October 2, 1803
Boston, Massachusetts
American colonial leader

The colonial leader Samuel Adams was an influential figure in the years leading up to the American Revolution (1775–83). His newspaper articles and organizational activities helped inspire American colonists to rebel against the British government.

Early life and education

Samuel Adams was born on September 27, 1722, in Boston, Massachusetts, the son of a woman of strong religious beliefs and of a prosperous brewer who was active in local politics. For this reason Adams was familiar at a young age with Boston politics and politicians. As an adult he would play a strong role in Boston's political resistance to British rule.

The young Adams studied Greek and Latin in a small schoolhouse. He entered Harvard College at age fourteen. When he graduated in 1740 he was not sure what his career should be. He did not want to become a brewer like his father, nor did he want to enter the clergy. Although his father loaned him money to start his own business, Adams did not manage his funds well. As a result he went to work for his father's brewery after all. In 1749 he married Elizabeth Checkley.

For serveral years Adams struggled in his career. He worked as a tax collector in Boston, but he mismanaged funds and had to pay the difference when his accounts came up short. There seems to have been no charge that he was corrupt, only extremely inefficient. After his first wife died in 1757, he married Elizabeth Wells in 1764. Adams's second wife turned out to be a good manager. His luck had changed, for he was about to move into a political circle that would offer political opportunities unlike any in his past.

Political activities

Adams became active in politics, transforming himself from an inefficient tax gatherer into a leading patriot. As a member of the Caucus Club, one of Boston's local political organizations, Adams helped control local elections in 1764. When Britain began an attempt to tighten control over its American colonies by passing laws such as the Sugar Act (1764), Adams was influential in urging colonists to oppose these measures. The Sugar Act was a tax law imposed by the British aimed at increasing the prices Boston merchants paid for molasses. Urged on by radicals in the Caucus Club, Adams wrote instructions to local representatives attacking the Sugar Act as an unreasonable law. Adams argued that the law violated colonists' rights because it had not been imposed with the approval of an elected representative. He argued that there should be "no taxation without representation."

During the next decade Adams wrote essays about political ideas that were developing in Boston. Eager publishers hurried his writings into print. Meanwhile the British Parliament passed an even harsher tax law than the Sugar Act. This tax law was the Stamp Act of 1765, which placed a tax on printed materials throughout the American colonies.

Adams's fiery essays and continual activities helped solidify American opinion against the Stamp Act. His columns in the *Boston Gazette* newspaper sent a stream of abuse against the British government. Riding a wave of popularity, Adams was elected into the Massachusetts legislature.

Adams's next move was to protest the Townshend Acts of 1767, which placed customs duties on imported goods. His stand against the Townshend Acts placed him in the front ranks of the leading colonists and gained him the hatred of both British general Thomas Gage (1721–1787) and England's King George III (1738–1820). To protest the Townshend Acts, Adams and other radicals called for an economic boycott of British goods. Though the actual success of the boycott was limited, Adams had proved that an organized and skillful minority could effectively combat a larger but disorganized group.

In the series of events in Massachusetts that led up to the first battles of the Revolution, Adams wrote dozens of newspaper articles that stirred his readers' anger at the British. He appealed to American radicals and communicated with leaders in other colonies. In a sense, Adams was burning himself out. By the time of the battles of Lexington and Concord in Massachusetts on April 17, 1775, which marked the beginning of the Revolutionary War, his career as a revolutionary bandleader had peaked.

Samuel Adams.

Declining power

Adams served in the Continental Congress between 1774 and 1781. However, after the first session his activities lessened and his ties to other leaders cooled. He was uncertain about America's next steps and where he would fit into the scheme. Adams served in the 1779 Massachusetts constitutional convention, where he allowed his cousin, John Adams (1735–1826), to do most of the work. He attended the Massachusetts ratifying convention in 1788, but he contributed little to this meeting.

Although his political power had lessened, Adams served in political office for several more years. He was the lieutenant governor of Massachusetts from 1789 to 1793, when he became governor. He was reelected for three terms but did not seek reelection in 1797. Samuel Adams died in Boston on October 2, 1803.

For More Information

Alexander, John K. *Samuel Adams: America's Revolutionary Politician.* Lanham, MD: Rowman & Littlefield, 2002.

Fradin, Dennis B. *Samuel Adams: The Father of American Independence.* New York: Clarion Books, 1998.

Jones, Veda Boyd. *Samuel Adams: Patriot.* Philadelphia: Chelsea House, 2002.

JOY ADAMSON

Born: January 20, 1910
Troppau, Silesia, Austria
Died: January 3, 1980
Shaba Game Reserve, Kenya
Austrian naturalist, writer, and painter

Naturalist and wildlife preservationist Joy Adamson is best known for the books and films depicting her work in Africa, especially her inspirational book *Born Free.* Adamson spent almost forty years living on game reserves in Kenya, and became heavily involved in wildlife preservation activities.

An inspired childhood

Joy Adamson was born Friederike Victoria Gessner on January 20, 1910, in Troppau, Silesia, Austria, to a wealthy Austrian family. Her parents, Victor and Traute Gessner, divorced when Joy was ten years old. Her father worked as an architect and town planner. Hunting was a favorite sport on her family's estate but, after she shot a deer with the estate's gamekeeper as a teenager, Joy promised herself she would never kill for sport again. Growing up, Joy dreamed of becoming a concert pianist, but her hands were too small. So she turned to such varied fields as psychoanalysis (the study of the mental process), archaeology, and painting. She finally decided on medicine, but never completed her studies.

In 1935 Joy married Victor von Klarwill. Her new husband, a Jew, decided that the couple should move to Kenya to escape the rising Nazi movement in Austria. The Nazi movement started in Germany and aimed to "liquidate" or kill all Jews in Europe. Klarwill sent his young wife ahead to Africa. Unfortunately, on the voyage there, she met Peter Bally, a botanist (one who studies plants). When her husband arrived in Kenya, Joy announced her intention to divorce him. She married Bally shortly afterward, in 1938.

Bally traveled through Kenya, studying its plant life, and Joy accompanied him. She began to paint their findings, and eventually completed seven hundred paintings that were published in several books. Within only a few years, however, there was a second divorce, closely followed in 1943 by a third and final marriage for Joy. She had met and fallen in love with George Adamson, a game warden in an outlying area of Kenya. The couple spent the rest of their lives traveling through the Kenyan wilderness together.

Working with lions

George Adamson, as a game warden, often encountered lions and other wildlife during his travels. In 1956 he was forced to kill a lioness that attacked him while trying to protect her three cubs. Two of the cubs were sturdy enough to be sent to a zoo, but the Adamsons kept the third cub, a small female that they named Elsa. In her book, *Born Free,* Joy Adamson tells the story of how she and her husband raised the cub and then had to train it to fend for itself in the wilderness. After a great deal of work with Elsa, the Adamsons knew for certain that they had been successful when they left Elsa in the wild for a week and returned to find that she had killed a waterbuck, an African antelope. Elsa's story in *Born Free* ended with the news that the lioness had three cubs of her own.

In Adamson's two sequels to *Born Free*—*Living Free* and *Forever Free*—she writes about Elsa's cubs: Jespah, Gopa, and Little Elsa. In early 1961, Elsa became sick and died. She has a marker on her grave in the Meru Game Reserve in Kenya. The Adamsons then had to train her cubs, who were too young to be released into the wild, to become hunters. Eventually the cubs were released, but were never sighted again.

Joy Adamson.
Reproduced by permission of AP/Wide World Photos.

Elsa an inspiration to many

All three "Elsa" books were extremely popular, and films were made of each of them—the 1966 *Born Free* was the most popular. The stars of the film series, Virginia McKenna and her husband Bill Travers, were so moved by the Adamsons' work that they later founded the Born Free Foundation in England to support wildlife conservation. It is estimated that the "Elsa" series and other Adamson books have been translated into at least thirty-five languages. According to

Adrian House's biography, *The Great Safari: The Lives of George and Joy Adamson, Born Free* served as inspiration for zoologist Iain Douglas-Hamilton, a major activist working to protect the African elephant from extinction. House also notes that anthropologist Desmond Morris credits *Born Free* with affecting an entire generation's attitude towards animals.

After Elsa's death and the release of her cubs, Adamson adopted a young cheetah, Pippa, who had been the house pet of a British army officer. For several years, Pippa was also trained to survive in the wild. Her story is told in Adamson's *The Spotted Sphinx*. Adamson also studied and worked with a variety of other animals, including baby elephants, buffaloes, and colobus monkeys. However, not all of the Adamsons' work with wildlife was successful. One lion that had been returned to the wilderness was destroyed after it returned to areas where humans lived, attacked a child, and killed one of the Adamsons' servants.

Wildlife preservation

As is still the case, preservation of African wildlife was a serious problem in the 1960s and the 1970s. The Kenyan government did not place a high priority on saving wildlife. Even in protected reserves poaching (illegal hunting for profit) was a common event.

Adamson went on an international tour to speak about wildlife preservation in 1962, and became a founder of the World Wildlife Fund and the Elsa Wild Animal Appeal. The money earned from her books was used to set up animal reserves and to fund several preservation organizations. Adamson was also an early activist in the movement to boycott (to protest the selling and using of) clothing made from animal fur.

Mysteriously murdered in the wilderness

On January 3, 1980, the world heard the shocking news that Joy Adamson had been killed in the Shaba Game Reserve in northern Kenya, where she had been observing leopard behavior. Even more shocking was the original explanation for Adamson's death—that she had been attacked by a lion. Her body had been found on a road near her camp in Mawson, and it quickly became apparent to George Adamson and the authorities that human forces were responsible. Her injuries were caused by stabs from a sword-like weapon, not by a lion's fangs and claws. Plus, her tent had been opened, and the contents of a trunk had been scattered. Although authorities eventually convicted someone for the murder, the true story behind Joy Adamson's death remains a mystery.

A quiet funeral ceremony for Adamson was held near Nairobi, Kenya. Adamson had specified in her will that her ashes be buried in Elsa and Pippa's graves in the Meru Game Reserve. Her husband and several colleagues did just that. They took her ashes, divided them in half, and placed them in the graves of Adamson's two dear friends.

George Adamson carried on his work alone after his wife's murder. On August 20, 1989, George Adamson was also killed in the Kenyan wilderness, along with two coworkers. The murders were blamed on several shifta, or bandit-poachers, who were roaming the area. Nevertheless, the work of Joy and George Adamson lives on, through the books that Joy wrote and the organizations she founded.

For More Information

Adamson, Joy. *Born Free: A Lioness of Two Worlds.* New York: Pantheon, 1960.

House, Adrian. *The Great Safari.* New York: W. Morrow, 1993.

Neimark, Anne E. *Wild Heart.* San Diego: Harcourt Brace, 1999.

Jane Addams

Born: September 6, 1860
Cedarville, Illinois
Died: May 21, 1935
Chicago, Illinois
American reformer and social worker

Jane Addams was called the "beloved lady" of American reform. She was a social worker, reformer, and pacifist. One of her most important accomplishments was to create a settlement house, a center that provides services to members of a poor community. Addams founded the most famous settlement house in American history, Hull House, in Chicago, Illinois.

Family and education

Jane Addams was born in Cedarville, Illinois, on September 6, 1860. She was the eighth child of John Huy Addams, a successful miller, banker, and landowner. She did not remember her mother, who died when she was three years old. She was devoted to and deeply influenced by her father. He was an idealist and philanthropist who served as state senator of Illinois from 1854 to 1870.

Although Addams became an activist for the poor, she herself came from a prosperous family. As a young woman she attended Rockford Female Seminary in northern Illinois. There she was not only a fine student but also the class president for four years and the editor of the school magazine. Addams also developed an interest in the sciences, even though such studies were not stressed at the school. After her graduation in 1881 she entered the Women's Medical College in Philadelphia, Pennsylvania. However, after six months she was forced to end her studies to have a spinal operation. Addams was never quite free of illness throughout her life.

Finding a career

It took Addams a long time to recover from her operation. During this time she fell into a deep depression. This was partly because of her illness and partly because of her sensitivity to the way women of her status were expected to live in nineteenth-century America. Intelligent middle-class women like Addams were frequently well educated. However, they were expected to live simply as wives and mothers within homes dominated by men. Society discouraged women from putting their talents to use outside the home. Addams traveled in Europe between 1883 and 1885 and spent winters in Baltimore in 1886 and 1887. During this time she searched for comfort in religion. However, she did not find a satisfactory outlet for her abilities until she made a second trip to Europe in 1887. At this time she visited Toynbee Hall, the famous settlement house in London, England.

Jane Addams.
Courtesy of the Library of Congress.

Toynbee Hall was a social and cultural center in the slums of the East End neighborhood in London. It was designed to introduce young men who wanted to join the ministry to the world of England's urban poor. Addams thought it would be a good idea to provide a similar opportunity for young middle-class American women. She decided "that it would be a good thing to rent a house in a part of the city where many . . . needs are found." She especially wanted to provide opportunities for well-educated young women to "learn of life from life itself."

Creation of Hull House

Hull House was located in one of Chicago's poorest immigrant slums. Addams originally thought Hull House would provide a service to young women who wanted more than a homemaker's life, but it soon developed into a great center for the poor of the neighborhood. Hull House provided a home for working girls, a theater, a boys' club, a day nursery, and numerous other services.

Thousands of people visited Hull House each year. It became the source of inspiration for dozens of similar settlement houses in other cities. Its success also made Addams famous throughout the United States. She became involved in an attempt to reform Chicago's corrupt politics. She served on a commission to help resolve the Pullman railroad strike of 1894. Addams supported workers' rights to organize and spoke and wrote about nearly every reform issue of the day. Her topics ranged from the need for peace to women's right to vote.

Voice for reform

Addams served as an officer for countless reform groups. These groups included the Progressive political party and the Women's International League for Peace and Freedom. She served as this group's president in 1915 and attended international peace congresses in a dozen European cities. Addams gained a reputation as a pacifist (a person who is against conflict and war). She won the Nobel Peace Prize in 1931.

Addams also wrote books on a wide range of subjects. Her achievements gained her honorary degrees from several universities and made her an informal adviser to several American presidents. She died on May 21, 1935, in Chicago, Illinois.

For More Information

Addams, Jane. *Forty Years at Hull-House.* New York: Macmillan, 1935.

Davis, Allen F. *American Heroine.* New York: Oxford University Press, 1973.

Polikoff, Barbara Garland. *With One Bold Act.* Chicago: Boswell, 1999.

ALFRED ADLER

Born: February 7, 1870
Vienna, Austria
Died: May 28, 1937
Aberdeen, Scotland
Austrian psychiatrist

Austrian psychiatrist Alfred Adler was credited with developing several important theories on the motivation of human behavior. He founded the school of individual psychology, a comprehensive "science of living" that focuses on the uniqueness of the individual and a person's relationships with society.

Childhood and early career

Alfred Adler was born on February 7, 1870, in a suburb of Vienna, Austria. He was the second of seven children of a Hungarian-born grain merchant. The Adlers were a musical family and Alfred was known for his singing voice. Although he was encouraged to pursue a career in opera, in his childhood he suffered some illnesses and the death of a younger brother. These experiences contributed greatly to his early decision to become a physician, or medical doctor. He attended classical secondary school and received a degree from the University of Vienna Medical School in 1895. Later, he married Raissa Epstein, a Russian student.

Adler's early career was marked by enthusiasm for social reform (improvement), often expressed in articles in socialist newspapers. (Socialism is a social system where the goods and services are owned by the government and distributed among the people.) His first professional publication was a social-medicine monograph (pamphlet) on the health of tailors.

In 1902 famed Austrian psychiatrist Sigmund Freud (1856–1939) invited Adler to join a small discussion group, which became the famous Vienna Psychoanalytic Society. Adler was an active member but did not consider himself a pupil or follower of Freud. He could not agree with Freud's basic assumption that gender (male or female) was the main factor in the development of an individual's personality. Whereas Freud tried to explain man in terms of his similarity to machines and animals, Adler sought to understand and influence man in terms of what makes man different from machines and animals, such as concepts and values. This humanistic view characterized all the ideas of his theory. In 1911 Adler resigned from Freud's circle to found his own school.

Adler worked three years of hospital service during World War I (1914–18) when European forces fought for world domination. In 1919 he organized a child-guidance

Alfred Adler.
Reproduced by permission of Archive Photos, Inc.

clinic in Vienna, and also became a lecturer at the Pedagogical Institute. He was perhaps the first psychiatrist to apply mental hygiene (mental health) in the schools. Working with teachers in child-guidance clinics, he carried out his groundbreaking counseling before a small audience, dealing with the family and teacher as well as the child. This was probably the first "family therapy" and "community psychiatry" on record.

Beginning in 1926, Adler spent much time in the United States lecturing and teaching. When Adolf Hitler's (1889–1945) Nazi Party rose to power in Austria in 1932, Adler left with his wife and went to New York. On May 28, 1937, he died suddenly while on a lecture tour in Aberdeen, Scotland.

Adler's legacy

Adler left behind many theories and practices that very much influenced the world of psychiatry. Today these concepts are known as Adlerian psychology. His theories focused on the feelings of inferiority, and how each person tries to overcome such feelings by overcompensating (trying too hard to make up for what is lacking). Adler claimed that an individual's lifestyle becomes established by the age of four or five, and he stressed the importance of social forces, or the child's environment, on the development of behavior. He believed that each person is born with the ability to relate to other people and realize the importance of society as a whole.

As a therapist, Adler was a teacher who focused on a patient's mental health, not sickness. Adler encouraged self-improvement by pinpointing the error in patients' lives and correcting it. He thought of himself as an enabler, one who guides the patient through "self-determination," so that the patients themselves can make changes and improve their state. Adler was a pioneer in that he was one of the first psychiatrists to use therapy in social work, the education of children, and in the treatment of criminals.

For More Information

Grey, Loren. *Alfred Adler, the Forgotten Prophet: A Vision for the 21st Century.* Westport, CT: Praeger, 1998.

Hoffman, Edward. *The Drive for Self: Alfred*

Adler and the Founding of Individual Psychology. Reading, MA: Addison-Wesley, 1994.

Rattner, Josef. *Alfred Adler.* New York: F. Ungar, 1983.

AESCHYLUS

Born: 524 B.C.E.
Eleusis, Greece
Died: 456 B.C.E.
Gela, Italy
Greek playwright

The Greek playwright Aeschylus was the first European dramatist whose plays were preserved. He was also the earliest of the great Greek tragedians (writers of serious drama involving disastrous events), and was concerned with the common connection between man and the gods more than any of the other tragedians.

Early life

Aeschylus was born to a noble and wealthy Athenian family in the Greek town of Eleusis. His father was Euphorion, a wealthy man of the upper class. Aeschylus's education included the writings of Homer (Greek poet who lived during the 800s B.C.E. and wrote the *Iliad* and the *Odyssey*). In fact it was Homer who proved most inspiring to Aeschylus when he began to write as a teen. He entered his tragedies into the annual competition in Athens and won his first award as a young adult in 484 B.C.E. Aeschylus' writings were strongly Athenian and rich with moral authority. He carried home the first place award from the Athens competition thirteen times!

As a young man Aeschylus lived through many exciting events in the history of Athens. Politically the city underwent many constitutional reforms resulting in a democracy. Aeschylus became a soldier and took part in turning back a Persian invasion at the Battle of Marathon (490 B.C.E.). Nevertheless, Aeschylus's plays left a bigger mark in Greek history than any of his battle accomplishments.

Contributions, style, and philosophy

Because Aeschylus was writing for the Greek theater in its beginning stages, he is credited with having introduced many features that are now considered traditional. Formerly plays were written for only one actor and a chorus. Aeschylus added parts for a second and a third actor as well as rich costumes and dance.

Corresponding with his grand style were his grand ideas. Mighty themes and mighty men crossed his stage. Aeschylus has been described as a great theologian (a specialist in the study of faith) because of his literary focus on the workings of the Greek gods.

The plays

Modern scholarship has shown that the first of Aeschylus's plays was *The Persians.* It is also the only play on a historical subject that has survived in Greek drama. This play is seen from a Persian point of view. His theme sought to show how a nation could suffer due to its pride. Of his ninety plays only seven are still preserved.

Aeschylus.
Reproduced by permission of AP/Wide World Photos.

Prometheus Bound is perhaps Aeschylus' most well-known tragedy because of his depiction of the famous Prometheus, who is chained to a mountain peak and cannot move. He is being punished for defying the authority of the god Zeus by bringing fire to mankind. Zeus is depicted as a bully and Prometheus as a suffering but defiant rebel. Both are guilty of pride. Both must learn through suffering: Zeus to exercise power with mercy and justice, and Prometheus to respect authority.

Aeschylus' masterpiece is the *Oresteia,* the only preserved trilogy from Greek drama. The three plays are *Agamemnon, The Choephori, and The Eumenides.* Though they form separate dramas, they are united in their common theme of justice. King Agamemnon returns to his home after the Trojan War (490–480 B.C.E.; a war in which the Greeks fought against the Trojans and which ended with the destruction of Troy) only to be murdered by his scheming wife, Clytemnestra, and her lover. The king's children seek revenge that ultimately leads to their trial by the gods. The theme of evil compounding evil is powerfully written.

Albin Lesky has noted, "Aeschylean tragedy shows faith in a sublime [splendid] and just [fair] world order, and is in fact inconceivable [unthinkable] without it. Man follows his difficult, often terrible path through guilt and suffering, but it is the path ordained [designed] by god which leads to knowledge of his laws. All comes from his will."

According to legend, Aeschylus was picked up by an eagle who thought he was a turtle. The eagle had been confused by Aeschylus's bald head. Aeschylus was killed when the eagle realized its mistake and dropped him.

For More Information

Beck, Robert Holmes. *Aeschylus: Playwright, Educator.* The Hague: Nijhoff, 1975.

Herington, John. *Aeschylus.* New Haven: Yale University Press, 1986.

Spatz, Lois. *Aeschylus.* Boston: Twayne Publishers, 1982.

SPIRO AGNEW

Born: November 9, 1918
Baltimore, Maryland
Died: September 17, 1996
Ocean City, Maryland
American vice president and governor

Between the time of his nomination as Richard Nixon's running mate in August 1968 and his resignation in October 1973, Vice President Spiro Agnew was a leading spokesman for "The Silent Majority," a term used by Nixon to describe conservative, middle-class, white American voters. After being found guilty of tax evasion, Agnew became the second United States vice president to resign from office. (John Calhoun, Andrew Jackson's vice president, resigned in 1832.)

The early years

Spiro Theodore Agnew was born November 9, 1918, in Baltimore, Maryland. He was the son of Theodore S. Agnew and his Virginia-born wife, Margaret Pollard Akers. Spiro Agnew was, in his own words, a "typical middle class youth" who spoke and wrote very well and gained experience writing speeches for his father's many appearances before ethnic and community groups.

Agnew attended public schools in Baltimore before enrolling in Johns Hopkins University in 1937, where he studied chemistry. After three years he transferred to law school at the University of Baltimore, where he attended night classes. He supported himself by working for an insurance company, where he met Elinor (Judy) Isabel Judefind, his future wife.

The war years

In September 1941 Agnew was drafted into the army, three months before the United States entered World War II (1939–45). After the attack on Pearl Harbor, Agnew was sent to Fort Knox to train as a tank officer. He married Judy in 1942 before leaving for combat duty in Europe. Agnew commanded a tank company, was awarded a Bronze Star (a medal given for outstanding service performed under combat conditions), and was discharged with the rank of captain. After his army discharge, Agnew went back to the University of Baltimore Law School and graduated in 1947. He completed advanced law studies at the University of Maryland in 1949 and passed the Maryland Bar (an association that oversees the state's lawyers) exam. He could now practice law in the state of Maryland.

After spending a brief time with a Baltimore law firm, Agnew moved to Towson, a suburb of Baltimore, and opened his own law practice. When the Korean War (1950–53) broke out, he was recalled to active duty for a year. (During the Korean war, the United States supported the government of South Korea in its fight against a takeover by the communist government of North Korea.)

Early political career

After returning from active military duty, Agnew restarted his own law firm and became involved in Baltimore County's local politics. He joined the Republican Party in 1956 and began working for national and local campaigns.

Spiro Agnew.
Courtesy of the Library of Congress.

Agnew's first term in public office came in 1957 when he was appointed to a one-year term on the Baltimore County Zoning Board of Appeals. Agnew was reappointed for a three-year term in 1958 and eventually became the board chairman. He ran for associate circuit court judge in 1960, but lost, coming in fifth in a five-person race. Agnew then ran for chief county executive in 1962 and won. He was the first Republican executive elected in Baltimore County in seventy years.

From governor to vice president

Agnew's term as county executive was considered successful, and he became more popular. In 1966 he became the Republican candidate for governor of Maryland. His main opponent, George Mahoney, was strongly opposed to civil rights. Agnew defeated Mahoney and became the fifty-fifth governor of Maryland.

As governor, Agnew was known as a progressive leader with moderate civil rights beliefs. While in office he passed several tax reform laws, increased funding for antipoverty programs, repealed a law banning interracial marriage, spoke out against the death penalty, and drafted tough clean water legislation. However, by 1968 civil unrest had grown stronger throughout the United States. Protests had begun against the Vietnam War (a war in Vietnam fought from 1955 to 1975 in which the anti-Communist government of South Vietnam, supported by the United States, fought against a takeover by the Communist government of North Vietnam). Riots broke out in many major cities after the assassination of Martin Luther King Jr. (1929–1968). Governor Agnew ordered state police to arrest civil rights demonstrators, encouraged the use of military force to control civil disturbances, and spoke out harshly against Vietnam War protesters.

At the 1968 Republican Convention in Miami Beach, Florida, Richard M. Nixon (1913–1994) was nominated as the Republican presidential candidate. Nixon chose Agnew as his vice presidential running mate. As part of his acceptance speech, Agnew said, "I fully recognize that I am an unknown quantity to many of you." Those who considered Agnew unqualified for national office began saying "Spiro who?" In truth, as the governor of a relatively small southern state, he was relatively unknown within the party. Nixon chose Agnew because he wanted someone who was a southerner, an ethnic American, an experienced executive, a civil rights moderate, and a proven Republican vote-getter with appeal to Democrats.

The Nixon-Agnew victory over Hubert Humphrey (1911–1978) and Edmund S. Muskie (1914–1996) was close but clear cut, with a half million popular votes separating winners and losers. After the election, Agnew became the first vice president to have a White House office when Nixon gave him an office in the West Wing.

Controversial speeches and illegal activities

As vice president, Agnew began using attention-getting speeches to attack opponents of the Nixon administration. Patrick Buchanan (1938–), Cynthia Rosenwald, and William Safire (1929–) drafted many of his speeches. The vice president soon became known for his verbal attacks against college radicals, American permissiveness, and the media. At Ohio State University's graduation ceremonies in 1969, Agnew criticized the students' parents, calling their leadership a "sniveling hand-wringing power structure."

Nixon again chose Agnew as his running mate for the 1972 elections, and they overwhelmingly defeated their Democrat opponents, George McGovern (1922–) and R. Sargent Shriver (1921–). Early in his second term as vice president, Agnew came under investigation for crimes supposedly committed while he was an elected Maryland official. He was accused of accepting bribes from engineers who wanted contracts with the state of Maryland. He was also accused of failing to report campaign contributions as income. The situation became increasingly tense when Nixon came under attack for his alleged involvement in a break-in at the Democratic Party's headquarters in the Watergate complex. There were rumors that both the president and the vice president might be impeached (tried in Congress for charges of misconduct in office).

The end of a political career

On October 1, 1973, Agnew pleaded "no contest" in federal court to one misdemeanor charge of income tax evasion. He was fined $10,000 and put on probation for three years. He was also forced to resign from office. Agnew's friend Frank Sinatra (1915-1998) loaned him $160,000 to pay legal expenses, back taxes, and other fees. Agnew was disbarred (not allowed to work as a lawyer) by the state of Maryland in 1974.

After leaving politics, Agnew became an international business consultant and the owner of several properties in Palm Springs, California, and in Maryland. In his 1980 memoir, titled *Go Quietly or Else,* Agnew implied that Nixon and Alexander M. Haig (1924–), Nixon's chief of staff, planned to assassinate him if he refused to resign, and that Haig told him "to go quietly . . . or else." Agnew also wrote a novel, *The Canfield Decision* (1986), about a vice president who was "destroyed by his own ambition."

In 1981 Agnew was sued by three citizens of Maryland who sought to have the money he had reportedly received illegally from the state returned. After a few years the citizens won their case, and Agnew had to reimburse $248,735 to the state.

Agnew died of leukemia in Ocean City, Maryland, on September 17, 1996, at the age of 77.

For More Information

Agnew, Spiro T. *Go Quietly ... or Else.* New York: Morrow, 1980.

Cohen, Richard M, and Jules Witcover. *A Heartbeat Away; the Investigation and Resignation of Vice President Spiro T. Agnew.* New York: Viking Press, 1974.

ALVIN AILEY

Born: January 5, 1931
Rogers, Texas
Died: December 1, 1989
New York, New York
African American dancer and choreographer

Alvin Ailey founded the Alvin Ailey American Dance Theatre and won international fame as both a dancer and choreographer, a creator and arranger of dance performances.

Rough beginning

Alvin Ailey Jr. was born to Alvin and Lula Elizabeth Ailey on January 5, 1931, in Rogers, Texas. He was an only child, and his father, a laborer, left the family when Alvin Jr. was less than one year old. At the age of six, Alvin Jr. moved with his mother to Navasota, Texas. As he recalled in an interview in the *New York Daily News Magazine,* "There was the white school up on the hill, and the black Baptist church, and the segregated [only members of one race allowed] theaters and neighborhoods. Like most of my generation, I grew up feeling like an outsider, like someone who didn't matter."

In 1942 Ailey and his mother moved to Los Angeles, California, where his mother found work in an aircraft factory. Ailey became interested in athletics and joined his high school gymnastics team and played football. An admirer of dancers Gene Kelly (1912–1996) and Fred Astaire (1899–1987), he also took tap dancing lessons at a neighbor's home. His interest in dance grew when a friend took him to visit the modern dance school run by Lester Horton, whose dance company (a group of dancers who perform together) was the first in America to admit members of all races. Unsure of what opportunities would be available for him as a dancer, however, Ailey left Horton's school after one month. After graduating from high school in 1948, Ailey considered becoming a teacher. He entered the University of California in Los Angeles to study languages. When Horton offered him a scholarship in 1949 Ailey returned to the dance school. He left again after one year, however, this time to attend San Francisco State College.

Early career

For a time Ailey danced in a nightclub in San Francisco, California, then he returned to the Horton school to finish his training. When Horton took the company east for a performance in New York City in 1953, Ailey was with him. When Horton died suddenly, the young Ailey took charge as the company's artistic director. Following Horton's style, Ailey choreographed two pieces that were presented at the Jacob's Pillow Dance Festival in Becket, Massachusetts. After the works received poor reviews from the festival manager, the troupe broke up.

Despite the setback, Ailey's career stayed on track. A Broadway producer invited him to dance in *House of Flowers,* a musical based on Truman Capote's (1924–1984) book. Ailey continued taking dance classes while performing in the show. He also studied ballet and acting. From the mid-1950s through the early 1960s Ailey appeared in many musical productions on and off Broadway, among them: *The Carefree Tree; Sing, Man, Sing; Jamaica;* and *Call Me By My Rightful Name.* He also played a major part in the play *Tiger, Tiger, Burning Bright.*

In 1958 Ailey and another dancer with an interest in choreographing recruited dancers to perform several concerts at the 92nd Street Young Men's and Young Women's Hebrew Association in New York City, a place where modern dances and the works of new choreographers were seen. Ailey's first major piece, *Blues Suite,* was inspired by blues music. The performance drew praise. Ailey then scheduled a second concert to present his own works, and then a third, which featured his most famous piece, *Revelations.* Accompanied by the elegant jazz music of Duke Ellington (1899–1974), *Revelations* pulled the audience into African American religious life.

Alvin Ailey.
Reproduced by permission of AP/Wide World Photos.

Established own dance company

In 1959 Ailey established the Alvin Ailey American Dance Theater, a group of eight black dancers. One year later, the theater became the resident dance company at the Clark Center for the Performing Arts in New York City. By the mid-1960s Ailey, who struggled with his weight, gave up dancing in favor of choreography. He also oversaw business details as the director of his ambitious dance company. By 1968 the company had received funding from private and public organizations but still had money problems, even as it brought modern dance to audiences around the world. Ailey also had the leading African American soloist (a person who performs by oneself) of modern dance, Judith Jamison (1944–). Having employed Asian and white dancers since the mid-1960s, Ailey had also integrated (included people of different races) his company. In 1969 the company moved to Brooklyn, New York, as the resident dance company of the Brooklyn Academy of Music, an arts center with three theaters.

In the early 1960s the company performed in Southeast Asia and Australia as part of an international cultural program set up by President John F. Kennedy (1917–1963). Later the company traveled to Brazil, Europe, and West Africa. Ailey also choreographed dances for other companies, including *Feast of Ashes* for the Joffrey Ballet and *Anthony and Cleopatra* for the Metropolitan Opera at Lincoln Center in New York City. Ailey worked on projects with other artists, including one with Duke Ellington for the American Ballet Theater. For Ailey the decade peaked with the performance of *Masekela Language,* a dance based on the music of Hugh Masekela, a black South African trumpeter who lived in exile for speaking out against apartheid (South Africa's policy of separation based on race).

Ailey's Cry

By the late 1970s Ailey's company was one of America's most popular dance troupes. Its members continued touring around the world, with U.S. State Department backing. They were the first modern dancers to visit the former Soviet Union since the 1920s. In 1971 Ailey's company was asked to return to the City Center Theater in New York City after a performance featured Ailey's celebrated solo, *Cry.* Danced by Judith Jamison, she made it one of the troupe's best known pieces.

Dedicated to "all black women everywhere—especially our mothers," the piece depicts the struggles of different generations of black American women. It begins with the unwrapping of a long white scarf that becomes many things during the course of the dance, and ends with an expression of belief and happiness danced to the late 1960s song, "Right On, Be Free." Of this and of all his works Ailey told John Gruen in *The Private World of Ballet,* "I am trying to express something that I feel about people, life, the human spirit, the beauty of things. . . ."

Later years

Ailey suffered a breakdown in 1980 that put him in the hospital for several weeks. At the time he had lost a close friend, was going through a midlife crisis, and was experiencing money problems. Still, he continued to work, and his reputation as a founding father of modern dance grew during the decade.

Ailey received many honors for his choreography, including a *Dance* magazine award in 1975; the Springarn Medal, given to him by the National Association for the Advancement of Colored People (NAACP) in 1979; and the Capezio Award that same year. In 1988 he was awarded the Kennedy Center Honors prize. Ailey died of a blood disorder on December 1, 1989. Thousands of people flocked to the memorial service held for him at the Cathedral of St. John the Divine.

For More Information

Ailey, Alvin, with A. Peter Bailey. *Revelations: The Autobiography of Alvin Ailey.* Secaucus, NJ: Carol Pub. Group, 1995.

Dunning, Jennifer. *Alvin Ailey: A Life in Dance.* Reading, MA: Addison-Wesley, 1996.

Probosz, Kathilyn Solomon. *Alvin Ailey, Jr.* New York: Bantam Books, 1991.

MADELEINE ALBRIGHT

Born: May 15, 1937
Prague, Czechoslovakia
Czech-born American businessperson, speaker, and secretary of state

On January 23, 1997, when Madeleine Albright was sworn in as the United States secretary of state, she became the first woman to hold this position. Albright's impressive career highlights a combination of scholarly research and political activity.

Family background and education

Madeleine Korbel Albright was born Marie Jana Korbel on May 15, 1937, in Prague, Czechoslovakia (now in the Czech Republic). Her grandmother gave her the nickname "Madeleine" when she was young, and her name was legally changed when she was an adolescent. Her father, Josef Korbel, was a member of the Czechoslovakian diplomatic service (a person who deals with international relations). Her mother, Anna, was a homemaker. Between 1937 and 1948 her family lived in Prague, Czechoslovakia; Belgrade, Yugoslavia; and London, England.

In 1948, while working for the United Nations, Madeleine's father lived in India while the rest of the family lived in New York. When the Communists overthrew the Czechoslovakian government, her father was sentenced to death. Madeleine was eleven years old when her family was given political asylum, or a safe place to live, in the United States. Albright was strongly influenced by her father and credits his influence for her own view of the world.

After becoming a U.S. citizen, Albright pursued an academic career. Her education reflects her interest in politics. She studied political science at Wellesley College and graduated in 1959. Albright then went on to earn advanced degrees in international affairs from the Department of Public Law and Government at Columbia University.

Albright married Joseph Medill Patterson Albright three days after graduating from Wellesley. She and her husband lived in Chicago, Illinois, and Long Island, New York, before moving to Washington, D.C. She and her husband had three daughters before they divorced.

Early political career

Albright began her political career by working for the unsuccessful presidential campaign in 1976 of Senator Edmund S. Muskie (1914–1996). She then served as Senator Muskie's chief legislative assistant from 1976 to 1978.

In 1978 Albright was asked by one of her former professors at Columbia University, Zbigniew Brzezinski (1928–), National Security Adviser under President Jimmy Carter (1924–), to be a legislative liaison for the National Security Council. She remained in this position until 1981. Albright spent the following year writing *Poland, the Role of the Press in Political Change,* about the role played by the press during a time of unusual political change in Poland during the 1980s.

Albright's next important career milestone came in 1982, when she joined the faculty of Georgetown University. At George-

Madeleine Albright.
Reproduced by permission of Archive Photos, Inc.

town she became a research professor of international affairs and the director of women students enrolled at the university's School of Foreign Service.

Albright became advisor to presidential candidate Walter Mondale (1928–) and his running mate, Geraldine Ferraro (1935–), during their 1984 presidential race. She was senior policy advisor to Michael S. Dukakis (1933–) during his 1988 presidential campaign. In 1989, Albright became president of the Center for National Policy, a nonprofit research organization. Over the next few years she was appointed to the boards of several institutions, including Wellesley College, the Black Student Fund, and the Washington Urban League.

Ambassador to the United Nations

When Bill Clinton (1946–) sought the presidential nomination in 1992, Albright supported him. She served as his senior foreign policy advisor during his campaign. In the transition period she served as foreign policy liaison, or the person who is responsible for communicating information about foreign policy, in the White House. Then, Clinton chose Albright to be the U.S. ambassador to the United Nations (UN).

Albright immediately became a major force at the UN. She was familiar with world politics and she represented the United States, the UN's largest contributor to its activities and budget. As a UN ambassador, Albright learned to balance the needs of three different groups: the Clinton administration, the UN delegates, and the American public. She was involved in debates over UN peacekeeping activities and the direction of American foreign policy.

First woman to serve as Secretary of State

In 1996 Clinton nominated Albright for secretary of state and the U.S. Senate unanimously confirmed her nomination. On January 23, 1997, Madeleine Albright was sworn in as secretary of state. She became the highest-ranking female within the United States government.

Shortly after her confirmation, Albright's cousin, Dasha Sima, revealed to reporters at the *Washington Post* that Albright's family had been Czechoslovakian Jews, not Catholics as she had believed, and that three of her grandparents had died in concentration camps.

Before World War II (1939–45) the Nazi government in Germany had set up concentration camps to hold people who they saw as enemies of the state. Eventually minority groups, including Jews, were forced into these camps, where many people died during the course of the war. (Albright was quoted in Newsweek as saying, "I have been proud of the heritage that I have known about and I will be equally proud of the heritage that I have just been given." A few months later, Albright flew to Prague and was honored by Czech Republic president Vaclav Havel (1936–).

Albright began a peace mission in the Middle East in the fall of 1997, first meeting with Israeli Prime Minister Benjamin Netanyahu (1949–), then with Palestinian leader Yasir Arafat (1929–), Syrian President Hafez al-Assad (1930–2000), Egyptian President Hosny Mubarak (1928–), King Fahd ibn Abdul Aziz of Saudi Arabia (1922–), and King Hussein of Jordan (1935–1999). Albright condemned terrorist activities, urged Netanyahu to make some concessions to the Palestinians, and then vowed not to meet with Israeli and Palestinian leaders again until they were "ready to make the hard decisions." In July 2000 Albright returned to the Middle East. This time, talks between the new Israeli Prime Minister Ehud Barak (1942–) and Arafat ended when Barak said he was taking time out from the peace process.

Albright made history with her October 23, 2000, visit to North Korea's leader Kim Jong Il (1941–). She became the first U.S. secretary of state to visit North Korea.

Another career

After Albright's term as secretary of state ended in January 2001, she became chairman of the board for the National Democratic Institute. Albright is also a well-known public speaker. According to the Washington Speakers Bureau, "Madeleine Albright speaks with humor, insight, and eloquence about her life and career . . . she provides audiences with a unique, no-holds-barred account of service at the highest levels of the American government."

In spring 2001 Albright became the Michael and Virginia Mortara Distinguished Professor in the Practice of Diplomacy. In a comment about her new teaching position Albright said, "I am very pleased . . . to have the opportunity to teach, and be inspired by, inquiring students."

For More Information

Blackman, Ann. *Seasons of Her Life: A Biography of Madeleine Korbel Albright.* New York, NY: Scribner, 1998.

Dobbs, Michael. *Madeleine Albright: A Twentieth-Century Odyssey.* New York: H. Holt and Co., 1999.

LOUISA MAY ALCOTT

Born: November 29, 1832
Germantown, Pennsylvania
Died: March 6, 1888
Boston, Massachusetts
American writer

Louisa May Alcott is one of America's best-known writers of juvenile (intended for young people) fiction.

Louisa May Alcott.
Reproduced by permission of Archive Photos, Inc.

She was also a reformer who worked to gain the right to vote for women and who opposed the drinking of alcohol.

Early poverty

Louisa May Alcott was born in Germantown, Pennsylvania, on November 29, 1832. She was one of four daughters of Bronson Alcott, an educator and philosopher (one who seeks an understanding of the world and man's place in it), and Abigail May Alcott. Her father was unsuited for many jobs and also unwilling to take many of them, and as a result he was unable to support his family. The Alcotts were very poor. Her father moved the family to Boston, Massachusetts, in 1834 and founded the Temple School, in which he planned to use his own teaching methods. The school failed, and the family moved to Concord, Massachusetts, in 1840.

Alcott's father was a strong supporter of women's rights and an early abolitionist (opponent of slavery), and his friends were some of the most brilliant and famous men and women of the day. His friends included Henry David Thoreau (1817–1862), Ralph Waldo Emerson (1803–1882), Margaret Fuller (1810–1850), and Theodore Parker (1810–1860). Alcott and her sisters became friends with these visitors as well, and were even tutored by them at times. This combination of intellectual richness and actual poverty helped Alcott develop her sense of humor.

Alcott soon realized that if she and her sisters did not find ways to bring money into the home, the family would be doomed to permanent poverty. In her early years she worked at a variety of tasks to make money to help her family, including teaching, sewing, and housework. At sixteen she wrote a book, *Flower Fables* (not published for six years), and she wrote a number of plays that were never produced. By 1860 her stories and poems were being published in the *Atlantic Monthly.* During the Civil War (1861–65; a war fought in the United States between the states in the North and the states in the South mainly over the issue of slavery), Alcott served as a nurse until her health failed. Her description of the experience in *Hospital Sketches* (1863) brought her work to the attention of many people.

Success arrives

The attention seemed to die out, however, when she published her first novel, *Moods,* in 1865, and she was glad to accept a job in 1867 as the editor of the juvenile magazine *Merry's Museum.* The next year she produced the first volume of *Little Women,* a cheerful and attractive account of her childhood. The character Jo represented Alcott herself, and Amy, Beth, and Meg represented her sisters. The book was an instant success, and a second volume followed in 1869. The resulting sales accomplished the goal she had worked toward for twenty-five years: the Alcott family had enough money to live comfortably.

After *Little Women* set the direction, Alcott continued producing similar works. She wrote *An Old-fashioned Girl* (1870), *Little Men* (1871), and *Work* (1873), an account of her early efforts to help support the family. During this time she took an active role in speaking out about the danger of drinking alcohol, and she also campaigned for women's suffrage (right to vote). She also toured Europe. In 1876 she produced *Silver Pitchers,* a collection containing "Transcendental Wild Oats," a description of her father's failed attempts to found a communal group (where people live together and share ownership and use of property) in Fruitlands, Massachusetts. In later life she produced a book almost every year and maintained a loyal following of readers.

Alcott died on March 6, 1888, in Boston, Massachusetts. She seems never to have become bitter about the struggles of her early years or her father's flaws. She did give some indication of her feelings about him, however, when she said that a philosopher was like a man up in a balloon: he was safe, as long as three women held the ropes on the ground.

For More Information

Ruth, Amy. *Louisa May Alcott.* Minneapolis: Lerner, 1999.

Saxton, Martha. *Louisa May Alcott: A Modern Biography.* New York: Farrar, Straus, and Giroux, 1995.

Stern, Madeleine B. *Louisa May Alcott.* Norman: University of Oklahoma Press, 1950.

ALEXANDER II

Born: April 17, 1818
Moscow, Russia
Died: March 1, 1881
St. Petersburg, Russia
Russian emperor

Alexander II was emperor of Russia from 1855 to 1881. He is called the "czar liberator" because he freed the serfs (poor peasants who lived on land owned by nobles) in 1861. Alexander's reign is famous in Russian history and is called the "era of great reforms."

Alexander as a young man

Alexander II, the oldest son of Emperor Nicholas I (1796–1855), was born in Moscow, Russia, on April 17, 1818. Because he would become emperor one day, Alexander was taught many different subjects. Vasili Zhukovski (1783–1852), a famous Russian poet, was his principal tutor, or private

Alexander II.
Reproduced by permission of Archive Photos, Inc.

teacher. Alexander learned to speak Russian, German, French, English, and Polish. He gained a knowledge of military arts, finance, and diplomacy, or the study of dealing with foreign countries. From an early age he traveled widely in Russia and in other countries. For example, in 1837 he visited thirty Russian provinces, including Siberia (a frigid, northern region of Russia) where no member of the royal family had ever visited. Unlike his father, Alexander had various military and government jobs throughout his younger days. In fact during Nicholas's absence Alexander was given the duties of the czar, or Russian emperor.

Freeing the serfs

Before he became czar, Alexander did not believe that freeing the serfs was a good idea. He changed his mind because he believed that freeing the serfs was the only way to prevent them from revolting. However, freeing the more than forty million serfs was not an easy task. In 1861 Alexander created an emancipation, or freedom, law, which said that serfs could now marry, own property, and argue court cases. Each landowner had to determine the area of land owned by the serfs. Landowners also had to pay the serfs for the work they did. Each peasant family received their house and a certain amount of land. Land usually became the property of the village government, which had the power to distribute it among the families. Peasant families had to make payments for the land for more than forty–nine years. The original landowner kept only a small portion of the land.

The emancipation law of 1861 has been called the greatest single law in history. It gave the serfs a more dignified life. Yet there were many problems. In many cases the serfs did not receive enough land and they were overcharged for it. Since they had to pay for the land, they could not easily move. Still, overall it was a good law for the Russian people.

Reforms at home

Because the serfs were now free citizens, it was necessary to reform the entire local system of government. A law in 1864 created local assemblies, which handled local finances, education, agriculture, medical care, and maintenance of the roads. A new voting system provided representation to the peasants in these assemblies. Peasants and their former landowners were brought together to work out problems in their villages.

During Alexander's reign other reforms were also started. Larger cities were given governmental assemblies similar to those of the villages. The Russian court system was reformed, and for the first time in Russian history, juries, or panels of citizens called together to decide court cases, were permitted. Court cases were debated publicly, and all social classes were made equal before the law. Censorship (or the silencing of certain opinions) was eased, which meant that people had more freedom of speech. Colleges were also freed from the rules imposed on them by Alexander's father Nicholas I.

Foreign policy

Alexander also had success in foreign relations. In 1860 he signed a treaty with China that ended a land dispute between the two nations. Russia successfully ended an uprising in Poland in 1863. Then in 1877 Alexander led Russia to war against Turkey in support of a group of Christians in the areas of Bosnia, Herzegovina, and Bulgaria.

A violent end

Despite the many reforms Alexander II made to improve the lives of the Russian people, in 1866 he became the target of revolutionaries, or people who fight for change. Terrorists, or people who use violence to achieve their goals, acted throughout the 1870s. They wanted constitutional changes, and they were also upset over several peasant uprisings that the government violently put down. A member of a terrorist group murdered Alexander II on March 1, 1881, in St. Petersburg, Russia.

For More Information

Almedingen, E.M. *The Emperor Alexander II.* London: Bodley Head, 1962.

Mosse, W. E. *Alexander II and the Modernization of Russia.* Rev. ed. New York: Collier, 1962.

Van der Kiste, John. *The Romanovs, 1818–1959: Alexander II of Russia and His Family.* Stroud, Gloucestershire, England: Sutton, 1998.

ALEXANDER THE GREAT

Born: September 20, 356 B.C.E.
Pella, Macedonia
Died: June 13, 323 B.C.E.
Babylon
Macedonian king

Alexander the Great was one of the best-known rulers in ancient history. By the time of his death at thirty-two, he ruled the largest Western empire of the ancient world.

Education by tutors

Alexander was born in 356 B.C.E. to King Philip II of Macedon (382–336 B.C.E.) and Queen Olympias (375–316 B.C.E.). Growing up, Alexander rarely saw his father, who was usually involved in long military campaigns. Olympias, a fierce and possessive mother, dominated her son's youth and filled him with a deep resentment of his father. Nonetheless, their son's education was important to both parents.

Alexander the Great.

One of Alexander's first teachers was Leonidas, a relative of Olympias, who struggled to control the defiant boy. Philip hired Leonidas to train the youth in math, archery, and horsemanship (the training and care of horses). Alexander's favorite tutor was Lysimachus. This tutor devised a game in which Alexander impersonated the hero Achilles. Achilles was a heroic Greek warrior from a famous ancient poem called the *Iliad.* Achilles became the model of the noble warrior for Alexander, and he modeled himself after this hero. This game delighted Olympias because her family claimed the hero as an ancestor.

In 343 Philip asked Aristotle (384–322 B.C.E.), the famous Greek philosopher and scientist, to tutor Alexander. For three years in the rural Macedonian village of Mieza, Aristotle taught Alexander philosophy, government, politics, poetry, drama, and the sciences. Aristotle wrote a shortened edition of the *Iliad,* which Alexander always kept with him.

Beginnings of the soldier

Alexander's education at Mieza ended in 340 B.C.E.. While Philip was away fighting a war, he left the sixteen-year-old prince as acting king. Within a year Alexander led his first military attack against a rival tribe. In 338 he led the cavalry (troops who fight battles on horseback) and helped his father smash the forces of Athens and Thebes, two Greek city-states.

Alexander's relationship and military cooperation with his father ended soon after Philip took control of the Corinthian League. The Corinthian League was a military alliance made up of all the Greek states except for Sparta. Philip then married another woman, which forced Alexander and Olympias to flee Macedon. Eventually Philip and Alexander were reunited.

Alexander as king

In the summer of 336 B.C.E. at the ancient Macedonian capital of Aegai, Alexander's sister married her uncle Alexander. During this event Philip was assassinated by a young Macedonian noble, Pausanias. After his father's death Alexander sought the approval of the Macedonian army for his bid for kingship. The generals agreed and proclaimed him king, making Alexander the ruler of Macedon. In order to secure his throne, Alexander then killed everyone who could have a possible claim to the kingship.

Although he was the king of Macedon, Alexander did not automatically gain control of the Corinthian League. Some Greek states rejoiced at Philip's murder, and Athens wanted to rule the League. Throughout Greece independence movements arose. Immediately Alexander led his armies to Greece to stop these movements. The Greek states quickly recognized him as their leader, while Sparta still refused to join. The League gave Alexander unlimited military powers to attack Persia, a large kingdom to the east of Greece.

Asian campaign

In October 335 B.C.E. Alexander returned to Macedon and prepared for his Persian expedition. In numbers of troops, ships, and wealth, Alexander's resources were inferior to those of Darius III (380–330 B.C.E.), the king of Persia. In the early spring of 334 Alexander's army met Darius's army for the first time. Alexander's army defeated the Persians and continued to move west. Darius's capital at Sardis fell easily, followed by the cities of Miletus and Halicarnassus. The territories Alexander conquered formed the foundations of his Asian empire.

By autumn 334 Alexander had crossed the southern coast of Asia Minor (now Turkey). In Asia Minor, Alexander cut the famous Gordian Knot. According to tradition, whoever undid the intricate Gordian Knot would become ruler of Asia. Many people began to believe that Alexander had godlike powers and was destined to rule Asia.

Then in 333 Alexander moved his forces east and the two kings met in battle at the city of Issus. Alexander was outnumbered but used creative military formations to beat Darius's forces. Darius fled. Alexander then attacked the Persian royal camp where he gained lots of riches and captured the royal family. He treated Darius's wife, mother, and three children with respect. With Darius's army defeated, Alexander proclaimed himself king of Asia.

As a result of the defeat, Darius wanted to sign a truce with Alexander. He offered a large ransom for his family, a marriage alliance, a treaty of friendship, and part of his empire. Alexander ignored Darius's offer because he wanted to conquer all of Asia.

Campaign in Egypt

Alexander then pushed on into Egypt. Egypt fell to Alexander without resistance, and the Egyptians hailed him as their deliverer from Persian domination. In every country, Alexander respected the local customs, religions, and citizens. In Egypt he sacrificed to the local gods and the Egyptian priesthood recognized him as pharaoh, or ruler of ancient Egypt. They hailed Alexander as a god. Alexander then worked to bring Greek culture to Egypt. In 331 B.C.E. he founded the city of Alexandria, which became a center of Greek culture and commerce.

More fighting in Persia

In September 331 B.C.E. Alexander defeated the Persians at the Battle of Gaugamela. The Persian army collapsed, and again Darius fled. Instead of chasing after him, Alexander explored Babylonia, which was the region that Darius had abandoned. The land had rich farmlands, palaces, and treasures. Alexander became "King of Babylon, King of Asia, King of the Four Quarters of the World."

Alexander next set out for Persepolis, the capital of the Persian Empire. To prevent an uprising, Alexander burned Persepolis. In the spring of 330 he marched to Darius's last capital, Ecbatana (modern Hamadan). There Alexander set off in pursuit of Darius.

By the time Alexander caught up with Darius in July 330, Darius's assistants had assassinated him. Alexander ordered a royal funeral with honors for his enemy. As Darius's successor, Alexander captured the assassins and punished them according to Persian law. Alexander was now the king of Persia, and he began to wear Persian royal clothing. As elsewhere, Alexander respected the local customs.

Iran and India

After defeating Darius, Alexander pushed eastward toward Iran. He conquered the region, built cities, and established colonies of Macedonians. In the spring of 327 B.C.E. he seized the fortress of Ariamazes and captured the prince Oxyartes. Alexander married Oxyartes's daughter Rhoxana to hold together his Eastern empire more closely in a political alliance.

In the summer of 327 Alexander marched toward India. In northern India, he defeated the armies of King Porus. Impressed with his bravery and nobility, Alexander allowed Porus to remain king and gained his loyalty.

By July 325 the army continued north to the harsh and barren land in the Persian Gulf. The hardship and death that occurred after arriving brought disorganization to the army. It was also at this time that disorder began to spread throughout the empire. Alexander was greatly concerned with the rule of his empire and the need for soldiers, officers, and administrators.

In order to strengthen the empire, Alexander then made an attempt to bind the Persian nobility to the Macedonians to create a ruling class. To accomplish this goal, he ordered eighty of his Macedonian companions to marry Persian princesses. Alexander, although married to Rhoxana, married Stateira, a daughter of Darius, to solidify his rule.

When Alexander incorporated thirty thousand Persians into the army, his soldiers grumbled. Later that summer, when he dismissed his aged and wounded Macedonian soldiers, the soldiers spoke out against Alexander's Persian troops and his Persian manners. Alexander arrested thirteen of their leaders and executed them. He then addressed the army and reminded his soldiers of their glories and honors. After three days the Macedonians apologized for their criticism. In a thanksgiving feast the Persians joined the Macedonians as forces of Alexander.

Alexander's death

In the spring of 323 B.C.E. Alexander moved to Babylon and made plans to explore the Caspian Sea and Arabia and then to conquer northern Africa. On June 2 he fell ill, and he died eleven days later.

Alexander's empire had been a vast territory ruled by the king and his assistants. The empire fell apart at his death. The Greek culture that Alexander introduced in the East had barely developed. In time, however, the Persian and Greek cultures blended and prospered as a result of his rule.

For More Information

Briant, Pierre. *Alexander the Great.* New York: Harry N. Abrams, 1996.

Green, Peter. *Alexander of Macedon, 356–323 B.C.* Rev. ed. Harmondsworth, England: Penguin, 1974.

O'Brien, John Maxwell. *Alexander the Great.* New York: Routledge, 1992.

Muhammad Ali

Born: January 17, 1942
Louisville, Kentucky
African American boxer

Muhammad Ali was the only professional boxer to win the heavyweight championship three times. He provided leadership and an example for African American men and women around the world with his political and religious views.

Early life

Muhammad Ali was born Cassius Marcellus Clay Jr. on January 17, 1942, in Louisville, Kentucky, the first of Cassius Marcellus Clay Sr. and Odessa Grady Clay's two sons. His father was a sign painter who also loved to act, sing, and dance; his mother worked as a cleaning lady when money was tight. Ali began boxing at the age of twelve. His bicycle had been stolen, and he reported the theft to a policeman named Joe Martin, who gave boxing lessons in a local youth center. Martin invited Ali to try boxing and soon saw that he had talent.

Martin began to feature Ali on his local television show, "Tomorrow's Champions," and he started Ali working out at Louisville's Columbia Gym. An African American trainer named Fred Stoner taught Ali the science of boxing. Among the many things Ali learned was how to move with the grace and ease of a dancer. Although his schoolwork suffered, Ali devoted all of his time to boxing and improved steadily.

"Float like a butterfly, sting like a bee"

As a teenager Ali won both the national Amateur Athletic Union (AAU) and Golden Gloves championships. At the age of eighteen he competed in the 1960 Olympic games held in Rome, Italy, winning the gold medal in the lightheavyweight division. This led to a contract with a group of millionaires called the Louisville Sponsors Group. It was the biggest contract ever signed by a professional boxer. Ali worked his way through a series of professional victories, using a style that combined speed with great punching power. He was described by one of his handlers as having the ability to "float like a butterfly, and sting like a bee."

Ali's unique style of boasting, rhyming, and expressing confidence brought him considerable media attention as he moved toward a chance to fight for the world heavyweight boxing championship. When he began to write poems predicting his victories in different fights he became known as "The Louisville Lip." Both the attention and his skill as a fighter paid off. In February 1964, when he was only twenty-two years old, he fought and defeated Sonny Liston for the heavyweight championship of the world.

Muhammad Ali.
Reproduced by permission of Hulton/Archive by Getty Images.

Religious change

Inspired by Muslim spokesman Malcolm X (1925–1965), Ali began to follow the Black Muslim faith (a group that supports a separate black nation) and announced that he had changed his name to Cassius X. This was at a time when the struggle for civil rights was at a peak and the Muslims had emerged as a controversial (causing disputes) but important force in the African American community. Later the Muslim leader Elijah Muhammad (1897–1975) gave him the name Muhammad Ali, which means "beloved of Allah." (Allah is the god worshipped by Muslims.) In his first title defense in May 1965 Ali defeated Sonny Liston with a first-round knockout. (Many called it a phantom punch because it was so fast and powerful that few watching the fight even saw it.) Ali successfully defended his title eight more times.

In April 1967 Ali was drafted into military service during the Vietnam War (1957–75; a war fought in an unsuccessful attempt to stop Communist North Vietnam from overtaking South Vietnam). He claimed that as a minister of the Black Muslim religion he was not obligated to serve. The press criticized him as unpatriotic, and the New York State Athletic Commission and World Boxing Association suspended his boxing license and stripped him of his heavyweight title. Ali told *Sports Illustrated,* "I'm giving up my title, my wealth, maybe my future. Many great men have been tested for their religious beliefs. If I pass this test, I'll come out stronger than ever." Ali was finally sentenced to five years in prison but was released on appeal, and his conviction was thrown out three years later by the U.S. Supreme Court.

Back in the ring

Ali returned to the ring and beat Jerry Quarry in 1970. Five months later he lost to Joe Frazier (1944–), who had replaced him as heavyweight champion when his title had been stripped. Ali regained the championship for the first time when he defeated George Foreman (1949–), who had beaten Frazier for the title, in a fight held in Zaire in 1974. Ali referred to this match as the "Rumble in the Jungle." Ali fought Frazier several more times, including a fight in 1974 staged in New York City and a bout held in the Philippines in 1975, which Ali called the

"Thrilla in Manila." Ali won both matches to regain his title as the world heavyweight champion. In 1975 *Sports Illustrated* magazine named Ali its "Sportsman of the Year."

Ali now used a new style of boxing, one that he called his "rope-a-dope." He would let his opponents wear themselves down while he rested, often against the ropes; he would then be strong and lash out in the later rounds. Ali successfully defended his title ten more times. He held the championship until Leon Spinks defeated him in February 1978 in Las Vegas, Nevada. Seven months later Ali regained the heavyweight title by defeating Spinks in New Orleans, Louisiana, becoming the first boxer in history to win the heavyweight championship three times. At the end of his boxing career he was slowed by a condition related to Parkinson's disease (a disease of the nervous system that results in shaking and weakness of the muscles). Ali's last fight (there were sixty-one in all) took place in 1981.

Role as statesman

As Ali's boxing career ended, he became involved in social causes and politics. He campaigned for Jimmy Carter (1924–) and other Democratic political candidates and took part in the promotion of a variety of political causes addressing poverty and the needs of children. He even tried to win the release of four kidnapped Americans in Lebanon in 1985. As a result, his image changed and he became respected as a statesman. At the 1996 Summer Olympic Games in Atlanta, Georgia, the world and his country honored Ali by choosing him to light the Olympic torch during the opening ceremonies.

Ali remains in the public eye even as he continues to suffer from the effects of Parkinson's disease. In 1998 he announced he was leaving an experimental treatment program in Boca Raton, Florida, claiming that the program's leader was unfairly using his name to gain publicity. In 1999 Ali became the first boxer to ever appear on a Wheaties cereal box. Later that year he supported a new law to clean up the business side of boxing. After the terrorist attacks on the United States on September 11, 2001, Ali agreed to record sixty-second announcements for airing in Muslim countries to show that the United States remained friendly to those of the Muslim faith. Among many documentaries and books about Ali, a film version of his life, *Ali,* was released in December 2001.

For More Information

Myers, Walter Dean. *The Greatest: Muhammad Ali.* New York: Scholastic Press, 2001.

Remnick, David. *King of the World: Muhammad Ali and the Rise of an American Hero.* New York: Random House, 1998.

WOODY ALLEN

Born: December 1, 1935
Brooklyn, New York
American filmmaker, actor, author, and comedian

Woody Allen is one of America's most prominent filmmakers. He has made many comedies and serious films that deal with subjects that have always interested him—the relationships of men and women, death, and the meaning of life.

The early years

Woody Allen was born Allen Stewart Konigsberg on December 1, 1935, in the Flatbush area of Brooklyn, New York, into a family that he described as "typical noisy ethnic." His father, Martin, held a variety of jobs including bartending, and his mother, Nettie, worked as a bookkeeper. His only sibling is a sister. As a teenager Woody did not show much intellectual or social interest and spent long hours in his bedroom practicing magic tricks. He started using the name Woody Allen at age seventeen when he began submitting jokes to a local newspaper. People noticed his jokes and asked him to write for other comedians.

After Allen graduated from high school, he enrolled in New York University as a motion picture major and, later, in the night school at City College, but he was unhappy. He dropped out of both schools to pursue his career as a comedy writer.

Before Allen turned twenty he had sold twenty thousand gags (short jokes) to the New York newspapers. By the time he turned twenty-three he was writing for one of television's biggest comedy stars, Sid Caesar (1922–). He also hired a tutor from Columbia University to teach him literature and philosophy (the study of knowledge).

Allen began performing his own material in a small New York City nightclub in 1960. He worked six nights a week and learned how to work with an audience. He began to be noticed and started to appear on network television. Unlike other comics who favored political humor, Allen made jokes about his own comic character whom he had invented, a little guy tormented by the big questions about life issues and his hard luck with women. Success in clubs and on television led to a comedy album that was nominated for a Grammy (a recording industry award) in 1964.

Begins film career

Allen had long been a lover of movies, American and foreign, but the first one he wrote and acted in, *What's New, Pussycat?* (1965), turned out to be a very bad experience for him. He was so unhappy that he said he would never do another movie unless he was given complete control of the cast and how it looked in the end. Fortunately, *What's New, Pussycat?* was so successful that Allen was given his wish for future movies.

Allen was successful in writing and directing films such as *Take the Money and Run* (1969), and *Bananas* (1971). His Broadway play *Don't Drink the Water* was also made into a movie in 1969, although Allen neither directed it nor acted in it. His success continued with *Play It Again, Sam* (1972) (also based on a play he wrote), *Sleeper* (1973), and *Love and Death* (1975).

First serious film

Allen made his first serious film, *Annie Hall,* in 1977. It was a bittersweet (having both pleasure and pain) comedy about a romance that ends sadly. The movie won four Academy Awards (Oscars) including Best Screenplay (script) for Allen. He followed *Annie Hall* with *Interiors* (1978) and *Manhattan* (1979), both of which were more serious than comedic. His career as a serious filmmaker had definitely been recognized.

Annie Hall also marked the beginning of a nine-picture collaboration with movie cameraman Gordon Willis. Allen continued to use different filmmaking techniques to create a new style for each new film. He imitated the style of Italian director Federico Fellini (1920–1993) in his next film, *Stardust Memories* (1980). In that movie he plays a filmmaker who does not like his fans. During an interview with *Esquire* magazine in 1987, Allen said, "The best film I ever did, really, was *Stardust Memories.*"

Woody Allen.
Reproduced by permission of AP/Wide World Photos.

Leading ladies

Allen has been married to or has been romantically involved with the women who have starred in his movies. These include Louise Lasser (1939–), Diane Keaton (1946–), and Mia Farrow (1945–). Lasser acted in several of Allen's earlier films. Keaton appeared not only in *Annie Hall,* but also in *Bananas; Play It Again, Sam; Sleeper; Love and Death; Interiors; Manhattan;* and *Radio Days* (1987). Each relationship ended unhappily, but each actress received very favorable recognition for her roles in Allen's films.

In 1982 Allen began working with his new off-screen partner, actress Mia Farrow, in a film that was loosely based on Shakespeare's (1564–1616) *A Midsummer's Night Dream.* Farrow also starred in *Zelig* (1983), *Broadway Danny Rose* (1984), and *The Purple Rose of Cairo* (1985). Hollywood gave three Oscars to the next movie they made, *Hannah and Her Sisters* (1986). They worked on several more films but ended their personal life together in 1992.

Later work

Allen continued to write and direct many films, including *Manhattan Murder Mystery* (1993), which reunited (brought together again) him with Diane Keaton. It was pure comedy. *Bullets Over Broadway* (1994) was a critically-acclaimed (liked by reviewers) comedy and melodrama (a play or film relying on highly sensational events) set on Broadway in the 1920s.

Allen continued with another comedy in 1995, making *Mighty Aphrodite,* a modern story that includes scenes parodying (comically imitating) Greek tragedy. The next release, *Everyone Says I Love You,* (1996) marked Allen's first attempt at a musical. Reports said that he waited until two weeks after the film's stars signed their contracts to mention that he was making a musical. On purpose he chose actors who were not necessarily musically trained in order to get more honest emotion in the songs. (Allen himself is a very accomplished musician. He plays clarinet in the style of old New Orleans jazz every week at a club in New York City and has performed music for several of his own films.)

Woody Allen's most recent films are *Small Time Crooks* (2000), *The Curse of the Jade Scorpion* (2001), and *Hollywood Ending* (2002). Most of Allen's films have been made on modest budgets in New York City. Of the many film writers and directors, he is one of the few who has complete control of his films.

Woody Allen has grown beyond his beginnings as a comedian. Today he is regarded as one of the most versatile (capable of doing many things) movie makers in America.

For More Information

Baxter, John. *Woody Allen: A Biography.* New York: Carroll & Graf, 2000.

Lax, Eric. *Woody Allen: A Biography.* New York: Knopf, 1991.

Meade, Marion. *The Unruly Life of Woody Allen: A Biography.* New York: Scribner, 2000.

ISABEL ALLENDE

Born: August 2, 1942
Lima, Peru
Chilean novelist, journalist, and dramatist

The author of several novels and a collection of short fiction, as well as plays and stories for children, Chilean author Isabel Allende has received international praise for her writing. Many of her books are noted for their feminine point of view and dramatic qualities of romance and struggle. Her first novel, *The House of the Spirits,* was made into a film in 1994.

Early years in Chile

Isabel Allende was born on August 2, 1942, in Lima, Peru. Her parents, Tomás (a Chilean government representative) and Francisca (Llona Barros) Allende divorced when she was three. After the divorce Isabel traveled with her mother to Santiago, Chile, where she was raised in her grandparents' home. Her grandmother's interest in fortune telling and astrology (the study of the influence of the stars on human behavior), as well as the stories she told, made a lasting impression on Allende. The house was filled with books, and she was allowed to read whatever she wanted.

Allende graduated from a private high school at the age of sixteen. Three years later, in 1962, she married her first husband, Miguel Frías, an engineer. Allende also went to work for the United Nations Food and Agricultural Organization in Santiago, where she was a secretary for several years. Later she became a journalist, editor, and advice columnist for *Paula* magazine. In addition she worked as a television interviewer and newscaster.

Exile in Venezuela

When her uncle, Chilean president Salvador Allende (1908–1973), was assassinated in 1973 as part of a military takeover of the government, Isabel Allende's life changed greatly. At first she did not think that the new government would last, but later she came to realize that it was too dangerous to stay in Chile. As a result she, her husband, and their two children fled to Venezuela. Although she had established a successful career as a journalist in Chile, she had a difficult time finding similar work in Venezuela.

During her life in exile Allende was inspired to write her debut novel, *The House of the Spirits* (1982), which became a best seller in Spain and West Germany. Based on Allende's memories of her family and the political change in her native country, the book describes the personal and political conflicts in the lives of several generations of a family in a Latin American country. These events are communicated through the memories of the novel's three main characters: Esteban and Clara, the father and mother of the Trueba family, and Alba, their granddaughter who falls into the hands of torturers during a military takeover. *The House of the Spirits* earned the Quality Paperback Book Club New Voice Award nomination. The novel was adapted by the Danish writer and director Bille August and was released as a film in the United States in 1994.

The House of Spirits was followed by *Of Love and Shadows,* which concerns the switching at birth of two infant girls. One of the babies grows up to become the focus of a journalist's investigation, and the revelation of the woman's assassination compels the reporter and her photographer to go into exile. The novel received a *Los Angeles Times* Book Prize nomination.

Isabel Allende.
Reproduced by permission of Ms. Isabel Allende.

While on a lecture tour in San Jose, California, to promote the publication of *Of Love and Shadows* in the United States, Allende met William Gordon, a lawyer, who was an admirer of her work and with whom she fell in love. Having been divorced from her first husband for about a year, she married Gordon in 1988 and has lived with him in Marin, California, ever since.

Became powerful storyteller

As she became more popular, Allende decided to devote all of her time to writing and quit her job as a school administrator. Her next book, *Eva Luna* (1988), focused on the relationship between Eva, an illegitimate (born to unmarried parents) writer and storyteller, and Rolfe Carlé, an Austrian filmmaker haunted by the knowledge of his father's criminal past. The novel received positive reviews and was voted One of the Year's Best Books by *Library Journal.* Allende followed up this novel with *The Stories of Eva Luna* (1991), in which Eva relates several stories to her lover Carlé.

The Eva Luna stories were followed by *The Infinite Plan* (1993) that, unlike her other books, features a male hero in a North American setting. Gregory Reeves is the son of a traveling preacher who settles in the Hispanic section of Los Angeles after becoming ill. Local gang members torment Reeves, as he is the only Caucasian (white) boy in the district. Eventually he finds his way out of the neighborhood, serves in the army, and goes on to study law. *The Infinite Plan* received less praise than Allende's previous books. Still, as novelist Jane Smiley pointed out in her *Boston Globe* review, "Not many [authors from foreign countries] have even attempted writing a novel from the point of view of a native of the new country."

Allende's next work, *Paula* (1995), was a heartbreaking account of the circumstances surrounding the long illness and death of her daughter in 1991. Published in 1999 *Daughter of Fortune* is the story of Eliza Sommers, a girl who breaks with nineteenth-century Chilean tradition to follow her lover to California. In September 1996 Allende was honored at the Hispanic Heritage Awards for her contributions to the Hispanic American community. In 1998 she received the Dorothy and Lillian Gish Prize for excellence in the arts. Another novel, *Portrait in Sepia,* was published in 2001.

For More Information

Bloom, Harold, ed. *Isabel Allende.* Philadelphia: Chelsea House, 2002.

Correas de Zapata, Celia. *Isabel Allende: Life and Spirits.* Houston: Arte Público Press, 2002.

Levine, Linda Gould. *Isabel Allende.* New York: Twayne Publishers, 2002.

JULIA ALVAREZ

Born: March 27, 1950
New York, New York
American novelist and poet

Julia Alvarez is a writer whose most notable work is *How the Garcia Girls Lost Their Accents,* a discussion of her life in the Dominican Republic and in the United States and the hardships members of her family faced as immigrants. Many of her works examine the conflicts and benefits that go along with living as both a Dominican and an American.

Background in the Dominican Republic

Julia Alvarez was born on March 27, 1950, in New York, New York, but she spent her early years in the Dominican Republic. She and her sisters were brought up along with their cousins, and were supervised by her mother, maids, and many aunts. Her father, a doctor who ran a nearby hospital, had met her mother while she was attending school in the United States. Alvarez's family was highly influenced by American attitudes and goods. Alvarez and her sisters attended an American school, and, for a special treat, they ate ice cream from an American ice cream parlor. The entire extended family had respect and admiration for America; to the children, it was a fantasy land.

When Alvarez was ten years old, her father became involved with a plot to overthrow the dictator (military ruler) of the Dominican Republic, Rafael Leonidas Trujillo Molina. His plans were discovered, however. With the help of an American agent, he was able to get his family out of the country before being arrested or killed. The Alvarez family returned to New York. Describing the scene in *American Scholar* as their plane landed in the United States, Alvarez wrote, "All my childhood I had dressed like an American, eaten American foods, and befriended American children. I had gone to an American school and spent most of the day speaking and reading English. At night, my prayers were full of blond hair and blue eyes and snow. . . . All my childhood I had longed for this moment of arrival. And here I was, an American girl, coming home at last."

Julia Alvarez.
Reproduced by permission of Mr. Jerry Bauer.

American experiences

Alvarez's homecoming was not what she had expected it to be. Although she was thrilled to be back in America, she would soon face homesickness and the feeling of not fitting in. She missed her cousins, her family's large home, and the respect her family had in the Dominican Republic. Alvarez, her parents, and her sisters squeezed themselves and their possessions into a tiny apartment in Brooklyn, New York. Alvarez became a devoted reader, spending all of her free time with books and, eventually, writing.

Alvarez went on to college. In 1971 she earned her undergraduate degree at Middlebury College in Vermont, and in 1975 she went on to receive her master's degree in creative writing at Syracuse University. She became an English professor at Middlebury College and published several collections of poetry, including *Homecoming,* which appeared in 1984. By 1987 she was working on a collection of stories.

Success arrives

When Alvarez published *How the Garcia Girls Lost Their Accents* in 1991, the novel received considerable attention. Rather than a straight narrative, the book is a series of fifteen connected stories told in reverse order detailing the lives of four sisters and their parents. A comparison with Alvarez's article in *American Scholar* suggests that these stories are based on her own experience. Like her family, the Garcia family is Dominican and displaced in America. Like Alvarez and her sisters, the Garcia girls struggle to adapt to their new environment and the American culture. The praise Alvarez received for her first novel outweighed the criticism that a new novelist often encounters. She received grants from the National Endowment for the Arts and The Ingram Merrill Foundation, in addition to receiving a PEN Oakland/Josephine Miles Award for excellence in multicultural literature.

Alvarez's second novel, *In the Time of Butterflies,* was published in 1994. This work recounts the lives of the Mirabel sisters—Patria, Minerva, and Maria Terese (Mate)—who were assassinated after visiting their imprisoned husbands during the last days under the Trujillo government in the Dominican Republic. Each sister in turn relates her own part of the narrative, beginning with her childhood and gradually revealing how she came to be involved in the movement against the government. Their story is completed by that of the surviving sister, Dedé, who adds her own tale of suffering to the memory of her sisters. *In the Time of Butterflies* received a favorable reaction from reviewers, some of whom admired Alvarez's ability to express the wide range of feelings brought on by the revolution. The novel was a finalist for the National Book Critics Award in 1994.

A collection of poems entitled *The Other Side/El Otro Lado* was published in 1995. It deals with the similar themes of power of language and having ties to two cultures. In the book's title poem Alvarez is commanded by a spirit conjurer (a kind of magician or psychic) to serve her own people in the Dominican Republic. But in the end she returns "to the shore I've made up on the other side, to a life of choice, a life of words." Her next work, *Yo!,* published in 1997, is based on Yolanda, one of her characters from *How the Garcia Girls Lost Their Accents.* Each section of the novel is told from the point of view of a different character, all of whom describe Yolanda as they see her. *Something to Declare,* published in 1998, collects a series of Alvarez's essays about her experiences growing up and finding her voice as a Latin American writer.

Alvarez gave up her teaching position at Middlebury in 1997 in order to devote all of her time to writing. She continues to stay in touch with her roots by visiting the Dominican Republic four or five times a year, partly to check on the coffee bean farm she and her husband own. Profits from the farm will be used to create a learning center for Dominican children. *In the Name of Salome,* which tells the story of Dominican poet Salome Urea and her daughter, Camila, was published in 2000.

For More Information

Alvarez, Julia. *Something to Declare.* Chapel Hill, NC: Algonquin Books of Chapel Hill, 1998.

Sirias, Silvio. *Julia Alvarez: A Critical Companion.* Westport, CT: Greenwood Press, 2001.

American Horse

Born: early nineteenth century
Died: September 7, 1876
Sioux Native American tribal leader and warrior

American Horse was a Sioux chief during the Lakota Wars of the 1860s and 1870s. His capture and death was one in a series of defeats for the Sioux after the historic Battle of the Little Bighorn (1876).

The son of Old Smoke becomes a shirt-wearer

American Horse, also known as Iron Shield, was the son of Old Smoke, leader of the Smoke People. The Smoke People were also referred to as the Bad Faces. Historians are not sure about when American Horse was born. Little is known about American Horse's early life as a Lakota, but sources show that his cousin Red Cloud (1822–1909) and another Lakota, Crazy Horse (1844–1877), were lifelong friends. (The Sioux Nation is made of Lakotas, Nakotas, and Dakotas.)

In 1865 four warriors, including American Horse and Crazy Horse, were made shirt-wearers. Shirt-wearers were young warriors who had proved themselves to be strong, brave, and generous. During a ceremonial feast, each warrior was given a shirt made from the hides of two bighorn sheep and decorated with feathers, quillwork (decoration using porcupine quills or the shafts of bird feathers), and scalps. Although shirt-wearers were not considered chiefs by their people, they were looked upon as leaders. They were expected to lead warriors in peace as well as in war, keeping the peace and respecting the rights of the weak.

Fort Laramie treaties

The 1851 Fort Laramie Treaty set aside an area in northern Wyoming for Lakota hunting grounds. The treaty called for peace among the northern tribes, promised safety to the Sioux, and approved roads and military posts. In 1862, however, Congress passed the Homestead Act in 1862, and three hundred thousand settlers crossed the Plains. In addition, gold was discovered in Montana. In 1862, John M. Bozeman (1835–1867) made a trail across the Lakota Territory. From 1863 to 1864, the Bozeman Trail was the main route to the Montana gold fields. The Lakotas attacked travelers on the trail. This was the start of the Lakota Wars.

In 1865, the southern Lakota signed a new peace treaty. When attacks along the Bozeman Trail continued, the government realized the northern Lakota leaders had not agreed to the treaty. The commander at Fort Laramie was ordered to have all Lakota sign a new treaty in 1868. The Fort Laramie Treaty of 1868 promised that the Lakota, Cheyenne, and Arapaho groups could travel the buffalo grounds of the upper Missouri as long as the buffalo herds survived. The treaty also required their children to attend Christian missionary schools and promised that Fort Phil Kearney would be burnt to the ground.

In the summer of 1870, American Horse joined Red Cloud and other Lakota leaders on a trip to Washington, D.C. On their journey, the Lakota leaders saw how many people lived in the East. Several of the leaders then

American Horse.
Reproduced by permission of Archive Photos, Inc.

agreed to move their people to reservations. Others, including Sitting Bull (1831–1890), American Horse, and Crazy Horse, refused.

The Black Hills

In 1874, while on a scouting mission in the Black Hills, Lieutenant Colonel George Armstrong Custer (1839–1876) discovered gold. This discovery brought a new wave of miners into the Black Hills. A Senate commission then met with Red Cloud and other chiefs and offered to buy their land. Seven thousand Lakota came to a special council meeting in September 1875. Red Cloud said he would not accept payment of less than seventy million dollars and beef herds to last seven generations. Others called for war and vowed to protect their sacred land.

In December 1875, in the middle of a bitter Plains winter, the U.S. Interior Department ordered all Sioux to the Dakota reservations. Those who did not report by January 31, 1876, would be considered hostile. Because it was winter, when no one moved around on the northern plains, the Indians remained where they were. Unfamiliar with the area and the tribal customs, the Interior Department ordered the military to drive the Lakota onto the reservations. General George Crook (1828–1898) led his troops to the region to carry out the military's orders.

Little Bighorn

On March 17, 1876, a group of Crook's soldiers surprised a small Lakota camp, destroying all the tepees and winter food stores. The following month, Sitting Bull held a council to talk of war. As Sitting Bull prepared for war, many of the reservation Indians joined him. There were several minor skirmishes between soldiers and Lakotas before summer that year. By June, the Indians made camp at the Little Bighorn in the Bighorn Mountains.

Depending on who tells the story, either Custer surprised Sitting Bull's camp or Sitting Bull ambushed the Seventh Cavalry. Whichever version actually occurred, 189 soldiers, 13 officers, and 4 civilians died on June 25, 1876, at the Little Bighorn, according to official military records. Hundreds of warriors had overwhelmed the Seventh Cavalry. After their victory celebration, Sitting Bull's forces broke into smaller groups and began their summer buffalo hunt.

The Battle of Slim Buttes

General Crook and other military leaders began searching for the Sioux. By September 1876, Crook's troops had run out of supplies. He sent a small group of soldiers, led by Captain Anson Mills (1834–1924), for supplies. Mills's scout found signs of a Lakota camp, and on the morning of September 9, 1876, the soldiers stampeded the tribe's horses through the sleeping camp. A private saw Custer's Seventh Cavalry guidon, or pennant, hanging on American Horse's tepee. Mills's troops also found uniforms, guns, ammunition, a letter addressed to a Seventh Cavalry soldier, and other supplies. This was considered proof that American Horse had taken part in the Battle at the Little Bighorn in June. Later, other Lakota said American Horse had not taken part in Little Bighorn and that these things had been brought into his camp by other Native Americans. No historical evidence has ever been found to prove American Horse took part in the Little Bighorn battle.

When the soldiers attacked, many Lakota escaped into the surrounding bluffs and started firing back. A small group of Lakota managed to kill some of Mills's pack mules and held off the soldiers from inside a gulch. Mills sent a message to Crook asking for help.

After two hours of exchanging shots, Crook ordered the shooting stopped. Thirteen women and children surrendered. Crook asked the women to return to the gulch to tell the remaining holdouts they would be treated well if they surrendered. A young warrior helped American Horse out of the gulch along with nine more women and children. Two warriors, one woman, and a child were left behind, dead. Cyrus Townsend Brady in *The Sioux Indian Wars from the Powder River to the Little Big Horn* said, " Even the women had used guns, and had displayed all the bravery and courage of the Sioux."

The death of American Horse

American Horse had been shot in the gut. When he came out of the gulch he was holding his wound and biting down on a piece of wood to keep from crying out. He handed Crook his gun and sat down by one of the fires. American Horse died that night. It was the first of many defeats for the Lakota.

In *Crazy Horse: The Strange Man of the Oglalas,* Marie Sandoz reported that American Horse said, "It is always the friendly ones who are struck," before he died. Other writers indicate American Horse said nothing before he died. In any event, American Horse is remembered as a brave Sioux fighter and leader who defended his people, the land, and the Sioux way of life.

For More Information

Biographical Dictionary of Indians of the Americas. Newport Beach, CA: American Indian Publishers, 1991.

IDI AMIN

Born: c. 1925
Koboko, West Nile Province, Uganda
Ugandan president

As president of Uganda from 1971 to 1979, Idi Amin (c. 1925–) became well known for his terrible violations of human rights, for causing the collapse of the country's economy, and for causing social disorganization. Amin is remembered best as the tyrant of Uganda who was responsible for a reign filled with mass killings and disorder.

Early life

Idi Amin Dada was born sometime between 1925 and 1927 in Koboko, West Nile Province, in Uganda. His father was a Kakwa, a tribe that exists in Uganda, Zaire (now Congo), and Sudan. As a boy, Amin spent much time tending goats and working in the fields. He embraced Islam and attained a fourth-grade education. He was brought up by his mother, who abandoned his father to move to Lugazi, Uganda.

As Amin grew he matched the qualifications for military service desired by the British at that time. He was tall and strong. He spoke the Kiswahili language. He also lacked a good education, which implied that he would take orders well. Joining the army as a private in 1946, Amin impressed his superiors by being a good swimmer, rugby player, and boxer. He won the Uganda heavyweight boxing championship in 1951, a title he held for nine years. He was promoted to corporal in 1949.

Friendship with Obote

During the 1950s Amin fought against the Mau Mau African freedom fighters, who were opposed to British rule in Kenya. Despite his cruel record during the uprisings, he was promoted to sergeant in 1951, lance corporal in 1953, and sergeant-major and platoon commander in 1958. By 1961 Amin had become one of the first two Ugandan officers with the rank of lieutenant.

In 1962 Amin helped stop cattle rustling, or stealing, between neighboring ethnic groups in Karamoja, Uganda, and Turkana, Kenya. Because of the brutal acts he committed during these operations, British officials recommended to Apolo Milton Obote (1924–), Uganda's prime minister, that he be brought to trial as a criminal. Obote instead publicly criticized him, deciding it would have been politically unwise to put on trial one of the two African officers just before Uganda was to gain independence from Britain on October 9, 1962. Thereafter Amin was promoted to captain in 1962 and major in 1963. He was selected to participate in the commanding officers' course at Wiltshire school of infantry in Britain in 1963. In 1964 he was made a colonel.

Amin's close association with Obote apparently began in 1965. Obote sympathized with the followers of the murdered prime minister of the Congo, Patrice Lumumba (1925–1961). Obote asked Amin for help in establishing military training camps. Amin also brought coffee, ivory, and gold into Uganda from the Congo so that the rebels there could have money to pay for arms. The opponents of Obote wanted an investigation into the illegal entry of gold and ivory into Uganda. Obote appointed a committee to look into the issue. He promoted Amin to chief of staff in 1966, and to brigadier and major-general in 1967.

Amin seizes control

By 1968 the relationship between Obote and Amin had gone sour. An attempted assassination of Obote in 1969, and Amin's suspicious behavior thereafter, further widened the gap between the two men. It is unclear why Obote promoted Amin in 1970 to become chief of general staff, a position that gave him access to every aspect of the armed forces. Amin overthrew Obote's government on January 25, 1971.

Ugandans joyfully welcomed Amin. He was a larger-than-life figure and yet simple enough to shake hands with common people and participate in their traditional dances. He was charming, informal, and flexible. Amin was thought to be a nationalist (a person who supports his or her country above all else). His popularity increased when he got rid of Obote's secret police, freed political prisoners, and told Ugandans that he would hand power back to the people.

During this period, Amin's other personality began to emerge: that of a merciless, unpredictable, cunning liar. His "killer squads" murdered Obote's supporters and two Americans who were investigating massacres (large-scale killings). It was becoming clear that Amin's seeming friendliness and clowning were only a mask to hide his brutality.

Idi Amin.
Reproduced by permission of AP/Wide World Photos.

In 1972 he savagely attacked the Israelis and the British, with whom he had been friendly. He did not like that these countries would not sell him weapons. Once Mu'ammar al-Qaddafi (1942–) of Libya agreed to help, Amin immediately threw Israelis and fifty thousand Asians out of Uganda. Uganda's economy was wrecked because Asian traders were suddenly forced to leave. The action also earned Amin a poor international image.

Between 1972 and 1979 Amin's policy was to stay in power at any cost. Though he seemed brave, Amin was a coward. He was, for example, terrified in 1978 when a story circulated that a "talking tortoise" had predicted his downfall. He constantly changed bodyguards, traveling schedules and vehicles, and sleeping places. He controlled the army through frequent reorganization. He also kept his army happy by giving them tape recorders, expensive cars, rapid promotions, and businesses that had been owned by Asian traders.

Trying to stay in power

Amin used violence and terror to eliminate his real and imaginary enemies. The human cost of Amin's rule was huge—not only in terms of the loss of thousands of Ugandans, but also because of its dehumanizing (making people feel less than human) effects. Human life had become less important than wealth.

Most government funds were devoted to the armed forces and to Amin's safety. Health, transport, production of food and cash crops (easily marketable crops), industrial and manufacturing sectors, and foreign investments were neglected. Despite his growing poor reputation, Amin was elected chairman of the Organization of African Unity (OAU), an organization of African nations, on July 28, 1975. In 1977 African countries blocked a United Nations resolution that would have condemned Amin for his gross violation of human rights.

By the late 1970s Amin's luck was running out. The economy was getting worse. Arabs were concerned about Amin's failure to show how Uganda was becoming an Islamic nation but also concerned about his killing of fellow Muslims. It was becoming difficult for Amin to import luxury goods for his army. To distract attention from the country's internal crises, Amin ordered an invasion of Tanzania in October 1978, supposedly because the latter planned to overthrow his government. Amin's army was forced back. Tanzanians and exiled Ugandan soldiers then invaded Uganda and continued their pursuit of Amin until his government was overthrown on April 11, 1979.

Amin fled to Libya, but he later moved to Jidda, Saudi Arabia. There he spends his time reciting the Koran (the holy book of Islam), reading books, playing an accordion, swimming, fishing, and watching television—especially sports programs and news channels. He follows events in his homeland closely.

For More Information

Grahame, Iain. *Amin and Uganda: A Personal Memoir.* London: Granada, 1980.

Gwyn, David. *Idi Amin: Deathlight of Africa.* Boston: Little, Brown, 1977.

Kyemba, Henry. *A State of Blood: The Inside Story of Idi Amin.* New York: Grosset & Dunlap, 1977.

HANS CHRISTIAN ANDERSEN

Born: April 2, 1805
Odense, Denmark
Died: August 4, 1875
Copenhagen, Denmark
Danish writer, author, and novelist

Hans Christian Andersen was the first Danish author to emerge from the lowest class. He enjoyed fame as a novelist, dramatist, and poet, but his fairy tales are his greatest contribution to world literature.

Early life

Hans Christian Andersen was born on April 2, 1805, in Odense, Denmark. His father was a shoemaker, and his mother earned money washing other people's clothes. His parents spoiled him and encouraged him to develop his imagination. At the age of fourteen, Andersen convinced his mother to let him try his luck in Copenhagen, Denmark, rather than studying to become a tailor. When she asked what he planned to do in Copenhagen, he replied, "I'll become famous! First you suffer cruelly, and then you become famous."

For three years Andersen lived in one of Copenhagen's most run-down areas. He tried to become a singer, a dancer, and an actor, but he failed. When he was seventeen, a government official arranged a scholarship for him in order to give him a second chance to receive an education. But he was a poor student and was never able to study successfully. He never learned how to spell or how to write in Danish. As a result his writing style remained close to the spoken language and still sounds fresh today, unlike the work of other writers from the same era.

After spending seven years at school, mostly under the supervision of a principal who seems to have hated him, Andersen celebrated the passing of his university exams in 1828 by writing his first narrative. The story was a success, and it was quickly followed by a collection of poems. Andersen's career as an author had begun, and his years of suffering were at an end.

Hans Christian Andersen.
Reproduced by permission of the Corbis Corporation.

Literary career

In 1835 Andersen completed his first novel, *The Improvisatore,* and he published his first small volume of fairy tales, an event that attracted little attention at the time. *The Improvisatore,* like most of Andersen's novels, was based on his own life. It was a success not only in Denmark but also in England and Germany. He wrote five more novels, but as a writer of drama, Andersen failed almost completely. Many of his poems are still a part of popular Danish literature, however, and his most lasting contributions, after the fairy tales, are his travel books and his autobiography (the story of his own life).

A lifelong bachelor, Andersen was frequently in love (with, among others, the singer Jenny Lind). He lived most of his life as a guest at the country homes of wealthy Danish people. He made many journeys abroad, where he met and in many cases became friends with well-known Europeans, among them the English novelist Charles Dickens (1812–1870).

Fairy tales

Andersen began his fairy-tale writing by retelling folk tales he had heard as a child from his grandmother and others. Soon, however, he began to create his own stories. Most of his tales are original. The first volumes written from 1835 to 1837 contained nineteen stories and were called *Fairy Tales Told for Children.* In 1845 the title changed to *New Fairy Tales.* The four volumes appearing with this title contained twenty-two original tales and are considered Andersen's finest works. In 1852 the title was changed to *Stories,* and from then on the volumes were called *New Fairy Tales and Stories.* During the next years Andersen published a number of volumes of fairy tales. His last works of this type appeared in 1872. Among his most popular tales are "The Ugly Duckling," "The Princess and the Pea," and "The Little Mermaid."

At first Andersen was not very proud of his fairy-tale writing, and, after talks with friends and Danish critics, he considered giving them up. But he later came to believe that the fairy tale would be the "universal poetry" (poetry that exists in all cultures) of which so many romantic writers dreamed. He saw fairy tales as the poetic form of the future, combining folk art and literature and describing both the tragic and the comical elements of life. Andersen's tales form a rich, made-up world. While children can enjoy most of the tales, the best of them are written for adults as well. The tales also take on different meanings to different readers, a feat only a great poet can accomplish. Andersen died in Copenhagen, Denmark, on August 4, 1875.

For More Information

Bredsdorff, Elias. *Hans Christian Andersen.* New York: Scribner, 1975.

Wullschläger, Jackie. *Hans Christian Andersen: The Life of a Storyteller.* New York: Knopf, 2001.

Carl David Anderson

Born: September 3, 1905
New York, New York
Died: January 11, 1991
San Marino, California
American physicist

The American physicist Carl David Anderson opened up the entire field of particle physics, the study of the atom, the smallest unit of matter. Because of his discoveries of the positron (positive electron) and the meson (similar to the negative electron), two particles that make up the atom, Anderson was awarded the Nobel Prize in Physics in 1936.

Childhood and education

On September 3, 1905, Carl David Anderson was born in New York, New York. He was the only child of Swedish parents, Carl and Emma Anderson. When he was a child Anderson wanted a career in athletics, as a high jumper. The Anderson family moved to Los Angeles, where Carl David attended Los Angeles Polytechnic High School and first became interested in science. In 1924 he entered the California Institute of Technology (Cal Tech), with which he would remain associated throughout his life. In 1927 Anderson received his bachelor's degree. He then continued his education in graduate school on a research grant, centering his graduate work on physics and mathematics.

As a teacher Anderson obtained a doctorate degree with honors in 1930 under the physicist R. A. Millikan (1868–1953), who was awarded the Nobel Prize in 1923 for his work in physics. After working with Millikan at Cal Tech as a researcher for three years, Anderson was promoted to assistant professor in 1933. He eventually worked his way to chairman of the Division of Physics, Mathematics, and Astronomy in 1962.

Carl David Anderson.
Reproduced by permission of AP/Wide World Photos.

Discovery of the positron

In the years immediately after Anderson received his degree, he discovered the positron, or positive electron—a revolutionary discovery, because the positron became the first known antiparticle (the oppositely charged particles of an atom) and the first known positively charged particle other than the proton. Anderson made his discovery during his and Millikan's quest to determine the nature of cosmic rays (positive particles from outer space) by allowing the rays to pass through a Wilson cloud chamber (a device used to detect elementary particles) in a strong magnetic field. By 1931 he had found evidence indicating that the rays produced charged particles whose tracks were very similar to those produced by ordinary electrons, except that they were bent by the magnetic field in the opposite direction. His famous photograph taken on August 2, 1932, clearly displayed a positron crossing a lead plate placed in the cloud chamber.

The following spring P. M. S. Blackett (1897–1974) and G. P. S. Occhialini were working independently at the Cavendish Laboratory in England. They produced a number of cloud chamber photographs indicating that a gamma-ray photon (electromagnetic energy) interacting with the intense electromagnetic field surrounding a nucleus, the center part of an atom, can create a positron-electron pair—that is, matter (anything that has mass and occupies space). They also recognized, as Anderson at the time had not, that Anderson's positron was the same particle that had been predicted by P. A. M. Dirac's (1902–1984) 1928 relativistic quantum-mechanical theory of the electron, a theory that described the structure of the atom. (Many physicists had believed Dirac's theory to be imperfect because it used the yet-undiscovered positron.) Work by Anderson and others established beyond doubt the proper experimental conditions for the creation and destruction of positrons.

In 1936 Anderson made a second important experimental discovery: the existence of a charged particle in cosmic radiation (rays from the sun) with a mass (an amount of matter) of about 200 electron masses, or of about one-tenth the mass of a proton. Anderson named these particles mesotrons (later shortened to mesons). He believed them to be identical to the nuclear particle H. Yukawa (1907–1981) had theoretically predicted less than two years earlier. It was later realized, however, that Anderson's meson is actually the mu meson (or muon), and Yukawa's meson is actually the pi meson (or pion). After World War II (1939–45) Anderson continued to develop the field of particle physics, which his groundbreaking 1932 discovery had opened up for research.

Later life

Anderson received many honors, beginning at just thirty-one years of age with the Nobel Prize for Physics in 1936, which he shared with V. F. Hess (1883–1964). Anderson received several honorary doctoral degrees and became a member of the National Academy of Sciences.

In 1946 he married Lorraine Elvira Bergman. The Andersons had two sons, Marshall and David. Anderson maintained his research and teaching activities until his retirement in 1976. He died in San Marino, California on January 11, 1991, at the age of eighty-five.

For More Information

Heathcote, Niels H. de V. *Nobel Prize Winners in Physics, 1901–1950.* New York: H. Schuman, 1953.

Weiss, Richard J., ed. *The Discovery of Anti-Matter: The Autobiography of Carl David Anderson, the Youngest Man to Win the Nobel Prize.* River Edge, NJ: World Scientific Pub. Co, 1999.

ELIZABETH GARRETT ANDERSON

Born: 1836
Aldeburgh, Suffolk, England
Died: December 17, 1917
Aldeburgh, Suffolk, England
English physician and activist

Elizabeth Garrett Anderson was the first woman officially approved to practice medicine in Great Britain, and was a pioneer in opening education in medicine to women. She made great sacrifices and struggled to create new pathways for women in British medicine.

Childhood and schooling

Elizabeth Garrett was the second of ten children (four sons and six daughters) born to Newson Garrett, a successful businessman of Aldeburgh, Suffolk, England, and his wife, Louisa Dunnell Garrett. Her parents had not always been wealthy, and Garrett's father was eager to make sure his children's circumstances would improve. Believing that all his children—girls as well as boys—should receive the best education possible, Elizabeth's father saw to it that she and her sister Louie were taught at home by a governess (a live-in, female tutor). In 1849 they were sent to the Academy for the Daughters of Gentlemen, a school in Blackheath, England, run by the aunts of famous poet Robert Browning (1812–1889). Garrett would later shudder when she recalled the "stupidity of the teachers" and the school's lack of instruction in science and mathematics. Nonetheless the school's rule requiring students to speak French proved to be a great benefit.

On her return to Aldeburgh two years later, Garrett studied Latin and mathematics with her brothers' tutors. Garrett's friend, the educator Emily Davies (1830–1921), encouraged her to reject the traditional life of the well-to-do English lady. Davies believed that women should be given the opportunity to obtain a better education and prepare themselves for a profession, especially medicine. But Davies herself did not feel suited to becoming a pioneer in medicine and encouraged Garrett to take on this role.

Elizabeth Garrett Anderson.
Reproduced by permission of the Corbis Corporation.

An important meeting

In 1859 Garrett met Elizabeth Blackwell, the first woman in America to graduate from a regular medical school. Blackwell was delivering a series of lectures in London, England, on "Medicine as a Profession for Ladies." Blackwell compared what she considered the useless life of the well-to-do lady with the services that female doctors could perform. She stressed the contributions female doctors could make by educating mothers on nutrition (proper diet) and childcare, as well as working in hospitals, schools, prisons, and other institutions. Blackwell was enthusiastic about Garrett's interest and potential, and she helped fuel Garrett's interest in becoming a fully accredited physician (a physician who is recognized as having met all of the official requirements needed to practice medicine).

Although Garrett's father at first found the idea of a woman physician "disgusting," he went with Garrett as she visited well-known physicians, seeking advice on how to pursue her goal. The doctors told Garrett and her father that it was useless for a woman to seek a medical education, because a woman's name would not be placed on the Medical Register, an official list of approved doctors. Unless a person's name was listed on the Medical Register, that person could not legally practice medicine in England.

Struggle for education

Eventually, Garrett began a "trial period" of work as a surgical nurse (a nurse who assists during surgeries) at London's Middlesex Hospital. She used the opportunity to attend surgical procedures and gain some of the training given to medical students. At the end of her three-month trial period, she unofficially became a medical student. She visited patients, worked in the dispensary (a unit where medical supplies and treatments are given out), and helped with emergency patients. The hospital staff accepted her as a guest, but would not officially accept her as a student.

Despite further rejections from Oxford and Cambridge universities and the University of London, Garrett would not be held back. Determined to earn a qualifying diploma in order to place her name on the Medical Register, she decided to pursue the degree of Licentiate of the Society of Apothecaries (L.S.A.). Apothecaries were pharmacists—that is, they prepared and gave out medications. Although the L.S.A. degree was not as impressive as the M.D. (Doctor of Medicine) degree, people with L.S.A.s were officially recognized as physicians. A person had to work for five years under the guidance of a doctor, take certain required lecture courses, and pass an examination to qualify. Although Britain's organization for apothecaries was not at all an advocate of equal opportunity for women, its charter stated that it would examine "all persons" who had satisfied the regulations.

Garrett tried to study at St. Andrews University in Scotland, but the school refused to allow a woman to graduate from its programs. She was finally able to piece together the required courses she needed. But when Garrett presented her qualifications to the Society of Apothecaries in the fall of 1865, they refused to allow her to take the examination that would qualify her for an L.S.A. degree. After Garrett's father threatened to take them to court, they changed their minds. Garrett passed the qualifying examination and her name was listed in the Medical Register one year later.

Opening a women's hospital

Garrett's goal was to establish a hospital for women staffed by women. Thus in 1866 she opened the St. Mary's Dispensary for Women in London. The dispensary (which was not a full-fledged hospital, but was a place where aid and supplies were distributed) filled a great need, and soon found it necessary to expand its services. In 1872, with a ward (unit) of ten beds, the dispensary became the New Hospital for Women and Children.

Garrett maintained a strong interest in the reform of education. At the time free basic education was becoming a reality for poorer children, and the working men of the district in which she practiced medicine asked her to run for election to the school board. She was elected to the London School Board in 1870, the same year she obtained her M.D. degree from the University of Paris. In 1869 Garrett applied for a position at the Shadwell Hospital for Children in London. One of the members of the hospital board of directors who interviewed her was James George Skelton Anderson, her future husband. They were married in 1871.

The New Hospital for Women provided a demonstration of what trained professional women could accomplish. In 1878 Garrett became the first woman in Europe to successfully perform an ovariotomy (removal of one or both ovaries, the female reproductive glands that produce eggs). Garrett did not enjoy operating, however, and was perfectly willing to turn this part of hospital work over to other women surgeons on her staff. The hospital moved to a larger site in 1899, nearly twenty years before it was renamed the Elizabeth Garrett Anderson Hospital.

Later accomplishments

In 1874 Garrett helped establish the London School of Medicine for Women, where she taught for twenty-three years. Two years after its founding, the school was placed on the list of recognized medical schools, guaranteeing its graduates access to a medical license. In 1877 the school was attached to the Royal Free Hospital, and was permitted to grant the degrees that were required for enrollment on the British Medical Registry.

In 1902 the Andersons moved to Aldeburgh, England, and six years later Garrett became the town's first female mayor. It was one of many "firsts" in a life full of them. Anderson was England's first female doctor, the first female M.D. in France, the first female member of the British Medical Association (Britain's leading association of doctors), the first female dean of a medical school, and Britain's first female mayor. Her distinguished life came to an end on December 17, 1917, when she died in Aldeburgh.

For More Information

Garrett Anderson, Louisa. *Elizabeth Garrett Anderson, 1836–1917*. London: Faber & Faber, 1939.

Hume, Ruth Fox. *Great Women of Medicine*. New York: Random House, 1964.

Manton, Jo. *Elizabeth Garrett Anderson*. New York: Dutton, 1965.

Marian Anderson

Born: February 27, 1897
Philadelphia, Pennsylvania
Died: April 8, 1993
Portland, Oregon
African American opera singer

Marian Anderson is remembered as one of the best American contraltos (women with lower singing voices) of all time. She was the first African American singer to perform at the White House and the first African American to sing with New York's Metropolitan Opera.

Anderson's early years

Marian Anderson was born in Philadelphia, Pennsylvania, on February 27, 1897. She was educated in the public schools. She displayed a remarkable skill for singing when she was very young, and she loved singing for her church choir. When she could not afford singing lessons, her fellow choir members raised the money that allowed her to study with a famous singing teacher.

When Anderson was twenty-three years old, she entered a competition and won first place over three hundred other singers. The

Marian Anderson.
Reproduced by permission of the Corbis Corporation.

prize was the opportunity to sing with the New York Philharmonic orchestra. Further sponsorships enabled her to continue her studies in both the United States and in Europe.

Following Anderson's debuts (first performances on stage in a particular city) in Berlin, Germany, in 1930 and London, England, in 1932, she performed in Scandinavia (northern Europe), South America, and the Soviet Union. In Salzburg, Austria, she gave a sensational performance. The famous conductor Arturo Toscanini (1867–1957) was in the audience. After hearing her sing, Toscanini said she had "a voice heard but once in a century."

Return to the United States

At the end of Anderson's European tour, she was signed to a contract for fifteen concerts in the United States. On December 30, 1935, she opened her American tour at New York's Town Hall. She performed pieces by European classical composers as well as several African American spirituals (traditional religious songs). The performance was a great success. Critics welcomed her as a "new high priestess of song." In the words of a writer for the *New York Times,* the concert established her as "one of the great singers of our time."

Over the next several years Anderson sang for U.S. president Franklin Delano Roosevelt (1882–1945) at the White House and for Great Britain's King George VI (1895–1952) during his 1939 visit to the United States. She made several cross-country tours and soon was booking engagements (scheduling jobs) two years in advance. In one year she traveled twenty-six thousand miles. It was the longest tour in concert history. She gave seventy concerts in five months. After World War II (1939–45; a war fought between Great Britain, France, the Soviet Union, and the United States against Germany, Italy, and Japan) ended, she performed in major European cities again. By 1950 it was estimated that she had performed before nearly four million listeners.

Victory over racial discrimination

Anderson was a pioneer in winning recognition at home and abroad for African American artists. In 1939 an incident involving the Daughters of the American Revolution (DAR) helped focus public attention on racism. The DAR denied Anderson use of their Constitution Hall in Washington, D.C., for an April concert. First Lady Eleanor Roosevelt resigned from the DAR in protest and had the U.S. government allow Anderson to perform at the Lincoln Memorial. Her concert there, on Easter morning, drew a live audience of seventy-five thousand, and millions more heard it over the radio.

In 1948 Anderson underwent a dangerous throat operation for a growth that threatened to damage her voice. For two months she was not permitted to use her voice. She was not sure if she would ever be able to sing again. When she was finally allowed to rehearse, her voice returned free of damage. Following her recovery, Anderson made her first post–World War II tour of Europe, including stops in Scandinavia, Paris (France), London (England), Antwerp (Belgium), Zurich (Switzerland), and Geneva (Switzerland).

Operatic debut

In 1955, and again in 1956, Anderson sang in an opera at New York's Metropolitan Opera House. This was the first time an African American had sung with the Metropolitan since it opened in 1883. Over the years Anderson continued to add to her accomplishments. She sang at the presidential inaugurations of Dwight D. Eisenhower (1890–1969) and John F. Kennedy (1917–1963). In 1957 Anderson made a concert tour of India and the Far East for the U.S. State Department. In 1958 President Eisenhower appointed her a delegate (representative) to the Thirteenth General Assembly of the United Nations (UN). She was awarded the UN Peace Prize in 1977. Anderson gave her farewell concert (last public performance) at Carnegie Hall in New York on Easter Sunday in 1965. She died on April 8, 1993, in Portland, Oregon.

A *New York Times* music critic wrote about Anderson this way: "Those who remember her at her height ... can never forget that big resonant voice, with those low notes almost visceral [having to do with basic emotions] in nature, and with that easy, unforced ascent to the top register. A natural voice, a hauntingly colorful one, it was one of the vocal phenomena [rare event] of its time."

For More Information

Broadwater, Andrea. *Marian Anderson: Singer and Humanitarian.* Berkeley Heights, NJ: Enslow, 2000.

Keiler, Allan. *Marian Anderson: A Singer's Journey.* New York: Scribner, 2000.

Tedards, Anne. *Marian Anderson.* New York: Chelsea House Publishers, 1988.

FRA ANGELICO

Born: c. 1400
Vicchio, Italy
Died: c. 1455
Rome, Italy
Italian painter and artist

The Italian painter Fra Angelico combined the religious style of the Middle Ages (a period in European history from around 500 to around 1500) with the Renaissance's (a period of revived interest

Fra Angelico.
Courtesy of the Library of Congress.

in Greek and Roman culture that began in Italy during the fourteenth century) concern for representing mass, space, and light.

Early years

Not much is known about Fra Angelico's early life. He was born around 1400 and was named Guido di Pietro. Around 1418 he and his brother Benedetto took vows to become monks in the Order of Dominican Preachers in Fiesole, Italy, near Florence. Fra Angelico's religious name was Fra Giovanni da Fiesole. The titles Fra Angelico and Beato Angelico came into use only after his death, as a way of honoring his religious life and work.

In the early 1420s Fra Angelico and Fra Benedetto began operating a painter's workshop and a room for copying documents in Fiesole. Many of Fra Angelico's early works were created at the monastery (a house for persons who have taken religious vows) of San Domenico in Fiesole. The *Annunciation* of about 1430 and the *Linaiuoli Altarpiece (Madonna of the Linen Guild)* reveal the directions of Fra Angelico's art. His gentle people are modeled in chiaroscuro (the arrangement or treatment of light and dark parts), and these saints and angels stand out from the rest of the picture. Numerous large altarpieces (works of art that decorate the space above and behind an altar) were ordered from Fra Angelico and his popular shop in the 1430s.

Other projects

From 1438 to 1445 Fra Angelico worked on frescoes (paintings done on moist plaster with water-based colors) and altarpieces for the Dominican monastery of San Marco in Florence. The church and monks' quarters were newly rebuilt at this time under the supervision of Cosimo de' Medici, with Michelozzo as architect for the project. The frescoes by the master and his assistants were placed throughout the corridors, chapter house, and rooms. In the midst of the traditional subjects from the life of Christ, figures of Dominican saints meditate (focus all their thoughts) upon the sacred events. At the same time the dramatic effect is increased by the inclusion of architectural details of San Marco itself in some of the scenes.

A masterpiece of panel painting created at the same time as the San Marco project was the *Deposition* altarpiece, requested by the Strozzi family for the Church of Sta Trinita. The richly colored and shining figures, the wide views of the Tuscan landscape serving as a backdrop to Calvary, and the division into sacred and nonreligious people reveal Fra Angelico as an artist in tune with the ideas and methods of the Renaissance. Yet all of the accomplishments in representation do not lessen the air of religious happiness.

Later years

The final decade of Fra Angelico's life was spent mainly in Rome (c. 1445–49 and c. 1453–55), with three years in Florence (c. 1450–52), as prior (second in command of a monastery) of San Domenico at Fiesole. His main surviving works from these final years are the frescoes of scenes from the lives of Saints Lawrence and Stephen in the Chapel of Pope Nicholas V in the Vatican, Rome. The dramatic figure groupings serve to sum up the highlights of the long tradition of fourteenth-and early fifteenth-century Florentine fresco painting. In the strict construction and rich detail of the architectural backgrounds, the dignity and luxury of a Roman setting are shown.

In spite of the fact that Fra Angelico's life unfolded in a monastic environment, his art stands as an important link between the first and later generations of Renaissance painting in Florence.

For More Information

Pope-Hennessy, John. *Fra Angelico.* 2nd ed. Ithaca, NY: Cornell University Press, 1974.

Spike, John T. *Fra Angelico.* New York: Abbeville Press, 1996.

MAYA ANGELOU

Born: April 4, 1928
St. Louis, Missouri
African American author, poet, and playwright

Maya Angelou—author, poet, playwright, stage and screen performer, and director—is best known for *I Know Why the Caged Bird Sings* (1970), the story of her early life, which recalls a young African American woman's discovery of her self-confidence.

Eventful early life

Maya Angelou was born Marguerite Johnson on April 4, 1928, in St. Louis, Missouri. After her parents' marriage ended, she and her brother, Bailey (who gave her the name "Maya"), were sent to rural Stamps, Arkansas, to live with their grandmother, who owned a general store. Although her grandmother helped her develop pride and self-confidence, Angelou was devastated when she was raped at the age of eight by her mother's boyfriend while on a visit to St. Louis. After she testified against the man, several of her uncles beat him to death. Believing that she had caused the man's death by speaking his name, Angelou refused to speak for approximately five years. She attended public schools in Arkansas and later California. While still in high school she became the first ever African American female streetcar conductor in San Francisco, California. She gave birth to a son at age sixteen. In 1950 she married Tosh Angelos, a Greek sailor, but the marriage lasted only a few years.

Maya Angelou.
Reproduced by permission of AP/Wide World Photos.

Later Angelou studied dance and drama and went on to a career in theater. She appeared in *Porgy and Bess,* which gave performances in twenty-two countries. She also acted in several plays on and off Broadway, including *Cabaret for Freedom,* which she wrote with Godfrey Cambridge. During the early 1960s Angelou lived in Cairo, Egypt, where she was the associate editor of *The Arab Observer.* During this time she also contributed articles to *The Ghanaian Times* and was featured on the Ghanaian Broadcasting Corporation programming in Accra, Ghana. During the mid-1960s she became assistant administrator of the School of Music and Drama at the University of Ghana. She was the feature editor of the *African Review* in Accra from 1964 to 1966. After returning to the United States civil rights leader Dr. Martin Luther King, Jr. (1929–1968) requested she serve as northern coordinator for the Southern Christian Leadership Conference.

Success as an author

I Know Why the Caged Bird Sings (1970), the first in a series of Angelou's autobiographical (telling the story of her own life) works, was a huge success. It describes Angelou's life up to age sixteen, providing a child's point of view about the confusing world of adults. The book concludes with Angelou having regained her self-esteem and caring for her newborn son. In addition to being a sharp account of an African American girl's coming of age, this work offers insights into the social and political climate of the 1930s.

Her next autobiographical work, *Gather Together in My Name* (1974), covers the period immediately after the birth of her son Guy and describes her struggle to care for him as a single parent. *Singin' and Swingin' and Gettin' Merry Like Christmas* (1976) describes Angelou's experiences on the stage and concludes with her return from the international tour of *Porgy and Bess. The Heart of A Woman* (1981) shows the mature Angelou becoming more comfortable with her creativity and her success. *All God's Children Need Traveling Shoes* (1986) recalls her four-year stay in Ghana. Angelou wrote about other subjects as well, including a children's book entitled *Kofi and His Magic* (1996).

Other works and awards

Angelou had been writing poetry since before her novels became popular. Her collections include: *Just Give Me A Cool Drink of Water 'Fore I Diiie* (1971); *Oh Pray My Wings Are Going to Fit Me Well* (1975); *And Still I Rise* (1976), which was made into an Off-Broadway production in 1979; *Shaker, Why Don't You Sing* (1983); *Life Doesn't Frighten Me,* illustrated by celebrated New York artist Jean Michel Basquiat (1993); *Soul Looks Back in Wonder* (1994); and *I Shall Not Be Moved* (1997). Angelou's poetry, with its short lyrics and jazzy rhythms, is especially popular among young people, but her heavy use of short lines and her simple vocabulary has turned off several critics. Other reviewers, however, praise Angelou's poetry for discussing social and political issues that are important to African Americans. For example Angelou's poem "On the Pulse of the Morning," which she recited at the 1993 swearing in of President Bill Clinton (1946–), calls for a new national commitment to unity and social improvement.

Angelou has received many awards for her work, including a nomination for National Book Award, 1970; a Pulitzer Prize nomination, 1972; a Tony Award nomination from the League of New York Theatres and Producers, 1973, for her performance in *Look Away;* a Tony Award nomination for best supporting actress, 1977, for *Roots;* and the North Carolina Award in Literature, 1987. In the 1970s she was appointed to the Bicentennial Commission by President Gerald Ford (1913–) and the National Commission on the Observance of International Women's Year by President Jimmy Carter (1924–). She was also named Woman of the Year in Communications by *Ladies' Home Journal,* 1976, and one of the top one hundred most influential women by *Ladies' Home Journal,* 1983. Angelou has also taught at several American colleges and universities, including the University of California at Los Angeles, the University of Kansas, Wichita State University, and California State University at Sacramento.

Television and movies

Angelou also worked in television as a writer-producer for 20th Century-Fox, from which her full-length feature film *Sister, Sister* received critical praise. In addition she wrote the screenplays *Georgia, Georgia* and *All Day Long* along with television scripts for *Sister, Sister* and the series premiere of *Brewster Place.* She wrote, produced, and hosted the National Educational Television series *Blacks! Blues! Black!* She also costarred in the motion picture *How to Make an American Quilt* in 1995. Angelou made her first attempt at film directing with the feature length movie *Down in the Delta* (1998). The film told the story of a seventy-year-old woman and her personal journey. Angelou found directing to be a much different experience from writing because with directing you have "ninety crew and the cast and the sets and lights and the sound."

Although Angelou is dedicated to the art of autobiography—a sixth volume, *A Song Flung Up to Heaven,* was published in 2002—in her seventies she remains a force in several different fields. Since the early 1980s she has been Reynolds Professor and writer-in-residence at Wake Forest University. In the year 2000 she was honored by President Clinton with the National Medal of Arts, and in 2002 Hallmark introduced The Maya Angelou Life Mosaic Collection, a series of greeting cards containing her verse. She also has plans to write a cookbook and direct another feature film.

For More Information

Kite, L. Patricia. *Maya Angelou.* Minneapolis: Lerner Publications, 1999.

Loos, Pamela. *Maya Angelou.* Philadelphia: Chelsea House, 2000.

Shapiro, Miles. *Maya Angelou.* New York: Chelsea House, 1994.

KOFI ANNAN

Born: April 8, 1938
Kumasi, Ghana
Ghanian-born international diplomat

International diplomat Kofi Annan of Ghana is the seventh secretary-general of the United Nations (UN), the multinational organization created to, among other things, maintain world peace. He is the first black African to head that organization and was awarded the Nobel Prize. Noted for his cautious style of diplomacy, Annan is sometimes criticized for his soft-spokenness, which some say may be mistaken for weakness.

A worldly scholar

Kofi Atta Annan was born in Kumasi, in central Ghana, Africa, on April 8, 1938. Since 1960 Ghana has been a republic within the British Commonwealth, a group of nations dependent on Great Britain. Named for an African empire along the Niger River, Ghana was ruled by Great Britain for 113 years as the Gold Coast. Annan is descended from tribal chiefs on both sides of his family. His father was an educated man, and Annan became accustomed to both traditional and modern ways of life. He has described himself as being "atribal in a tribal world."

After receiving his early education at a leading boarding school in Ghana, Annan attended the College of Science and Technology in the capital of Kumasi. At the age of twenty, he won a Ford Foundation scholarship for undergraduate studies at Macalester College in St. Paul, Minnesota, where he studied economics. Even then he was showing signs of becoming a diplomat, or someone skilled in international relations. Annan received his bachelor's degree in economics in 1961. Shortly after completing his studies at Macalester College, Annan headed for Geneva, Switzerland, where he attended graduate classes in economics at the Institut Universitaire des Hautes Etudes Internationales.

Early career

Following his graduate studies in Geneva, Annan joined the staff of the World Health Organization (WHO), a branch of the United Nations. He served as an administrative officer and as budget officer in Geneva. Later UN posts took him to Addis Ababa, Ethiopia, and New York City, New York. Annan always assumed that he would return to his native land after college, although he was disturbed by the unrest and numerous changes of government that occurred there during the 1970s.

Annan became the Alfred P. Sloan fellow at the Massachusetts Institute of Technology. At the end of his fellowship in 1972, he was awarded a master of science degree in management. Rather than return to Ghana upon graduation, he accepted a position at the UN headquarters in New York City.

Work with the UN

In 1974 he moved to Cairo, Egypt, as chief civilian personnel officer in the UN Emergency Force. Annan briefly changed careers in 1974 when he left the United Nations to serve as managing director of the Ghana Tourist Development Company.

Annan returned to international diplomacy and the United Nations in 1976. For the next seven years, he was associated with the Office of the United Nations High Commissioner for Refugees in Geneva. He returned to the UN headquarters in New York City in 1983 as director of the budget in the financial services office. Later in the 1980s, he filled the post of assistant secretary-general in the Office of Human Resources Management and served as security coordinator for the United Nations. In 1990, he became assistant secretary-general for another department at the United Nations, the Office of Program Planning, Budget, and Finance. In fulfilling his duties to the United Nations, Annan has spent most of his adult life in the United States, specifically at the UN headquarters in New York City.

Annan had by this time filled a number of roles at the United Nations, ranging from peacekeeping to managerial, and the 1990s were no different. In 1990 he negotiated the release of hostages in Iraq following the invasion of Kuwait. Five years later, he oversaw the transition of the United Nations Protection Force (UNPROFOR) to the multinational Implementation Force (IFOR), a UN peacekeeping organization. In this transfer of responsibility, operations in the former Yugoslavia were turned over to the North Atlantic Treaty Organization (NATO).

Kofi Annan.
Reproduced by permission of Archive Photos, Inc.

In recognition of his abilities, Annan was appointed secretary-general, the top post of the UN, by the UN General Assembly in December 1996. He began serving his four-year term of office on January 1, 1997. Joining him was his second wife, former lawyer Nane Lagergren of Sweden. She is the niece of the diplomat Raoul Wallenberg (1912–c. 1947), who saved thousands of European Jews from the German Nazis during World War II (1939–45), when American-led forces fought against Germany, Italy, and Japan.

Annan and Lagergren were married in 1985. The couple has one child.

Heading the United Nations

The post of secretary-general of the United Nations has been called one of the world's "oddest jobs." According to the United Nations web site, "Equal parts diplomat and activist . . . the Secretary-General stands before the world community as the very emblem of the United Nations." The secretary-general is the boss of ten thousand international civil servants and the chief administrator of a huge international parliamentary system (a governing body with representation from many nations).

In this post, Annan is expected to coordinate, although he does not control, the activities of such groups as the WHO and the United Nations Educational, Scientific, and Cultural Organization (UNESCO). He is also expected to practice "preventive diplomacy," meaning he and his staff must try to prevent, contain, or stop international disputes. Above all, Annan must try to maintain world peace.

In an address to the National Press Club, Annan declared, "If war is the failure of diplomacy, then . . . diplomacy . . . is our first line of defense. The world today spends billions preparing for war; shouldn't we spend a billion or two preparing for peace?"

Questioning his role

Almost immediately after Annan's election to secretary-general came the question: Is this man just too nice a person for the job? His reputation for "soft-spokenness," according to *U.S. News & World Report,* could be mistaken for weakness. Another factor that made people question Annan's toughness was his involvement in the UN efforts at peacekeeping in Bosnia from 1992 to 1996. Despite the United Nations's presence, Bosnia remained the site of an ethnic war (a war between religious or cultural groups), in which thousands died. Sir Marrack Goulding, head of peacekeeping, once commented that Annan never expressed his doubts about the UN policy in a forceful manner. Annan disagreed, saying that he always pressed the involved countries—the United States, Britain, France, and Russia—to rethink their policy on sending soldiers to the peacekeeping force. Not one to raise his voice in anger, Annan favored diplomacy. In a press conference in Baghdad, Iraq, in 1998, Annan noted, "You can do a lot with diplomacy, but of course you can do a lot more with diplomacy backed up by fairness and force."

All eyes turned to Annan and his handling of the touchy situation with Iraq in 1998. Early in that year, threats of war seemed all too real. Saddam Hussein (1937–), president of Iraq, became once again a threatening presence by refusing to let UN observers into certain areas of his country, as had been previously agreed upon, to check for illegal possession of chemical-warfare items and the like. Then-president Bill Clinton (1946–) hinted strongly at the use of force to make Hussein agree to let in the UN officials. In his role as secretary-general, Annan went to Iraq in February of 1998 to meet with the Iraqi leader. After talking with Annan, Hussein agreed to what he had refused before—unlimited UN access to the eight sites that he had previously called completely off-limits. Because of Annan's intervention, war was avoided.

Annan in a new world

Annan's code of soft-spoken diplomacy was given a boost by the outcome of his talks with Saddam Hussein in 1998. UN observers wait to see how additional crises will be handled by the gentle but determined man from Ghana.

In the summer of 2001, the United Nations unanimously appointed Kofi Annan to his second five-year term as secretary-general. On October 12, 2001, the Nobel Peace Prize was awarded jointly to the United Nations and Kofi Annan. The Nobel citation pointed out that Annan had brought new life to the peacekeeping organization, highlighted the United Nations's fight for civil rights, and boldly taken on the new challenges of terrorism and acquired immune deficiency syndrome (AIDS; a disease of the immune system).

For More Information

Tessitore, John. *Kofi Annan: The Peacekeeper.* New York: Franklin Watts, 2000.

SUSAN B. ANTHONY

Born: February 15, 1820
Adams, Massachusetts
Died: March 13, 1906
Rochester, New York
American women's rights activist, abolitionist, and women's suffrage leader

Susan B. Anthony was an early leader of the American women's suffrage (right to vote) movement and a pioneer in the struggle to gain equality for women. As an active abolitionist, or opponent of slavery, she campaigned for the freedom of slaves.

Early influences

Susan Brownwell Anthony was born on February 15, 1820, in Adams, Massachusetts. She was the second of seven children born to Daniel and Lucy Read Anthony. Her father, the owner of a cotton mill, was a religious man who taught his children to show their love for God by working to help other people. Susan began attending a boarding school in Philadelphia, Pennsylvania, in 1837. She left and began working as a teacher after growing debt forced her father to sell his business and move the family to a farm near Rochester, New York.

Anthony continued teaching to help her family pay the bills until 1849, when her father asked her to come home to run the family farm so that he could spend more time trying to develop an insurance business. Many famous reformers, such as Frederick Douglass (1817–1895), William Lloyd Garrison (1805–1879), and Wendell Phillips (1811–1884), came to visit Anthony's father during this time. Hearing their discussions helped Susan form her strong views on slavery, women's rights, and temperance (the avoidance of alcohol).

Women's rights

Although her family attended the first women's rights convention held in Seneca Falls and Rochester, New York, in 1848,

Susan B. Anthony.
Reproduced by permission of Archive Photos, Inc.

Anthony did not take up the cause until 1851. Until that time, she had devoted most of her time to the temperance movement. However, when male members of the movement refused to let her speak at rallies simply because she was a woman, she realized that women had to win the right to speak in public and to vote before they could accomplish anything else. Her lifelong friendship and partnership with Elizabeth Cady Stanton (1815–1902), who had proposed a resolution giving women the right to vote, also began in 1851.

Anthony attended her first women's rights convention in 1852. From that first convention until the end of the Civil War (1861–65), she campaigned from door-to-door, in legislatures, and in meetings for the two causes of women's rights and the abolition of slavery. The passage of the New York State Married Woman's Property and Guardianship Law in 1860, which gave married women in New York greater property rights, was her first major legislative victory.

Formation of suffrage movement

The Civil War was fought between northern and southern states mainly over the issues of slavery and the South's decision to leave the Union to form an independent nation. With the outbreak of the Civil War, Anthony focused her attention on ending slavery. She organized the Women's National Loyal League, which gathered petitions to force passage of the Thirteenth Amendment to the Constitution to end slavery. When the war ended, she increased her efforts to gain the right to vote for women as well as for African American males. However, her former male allies from the antislavery movement were unwilling to help her fight for the first cause, saying the time was not yet right for women's suffrage.

Saddened by this defeat but refusing to give up the fight, Anthony worked solely for women's suffrage from this time to the end of her life, organizing the National Woman Suffrage Association with Stanton. The association's New York weekly, *The Revolution,* was created in 1868 to promote women's causes. After it went bankrupt in 1870, Anthony traveled across the country for six years giving lectures to raise money to pay the newspaper's ten-thousand-dollar debt.

In 1872 Susan B. Anthony and fifteen

supporters from Rochester became the first women ever to vote in a presidential election. That they were promptly arrested for their boldness did not bother Anthony. She was eager to test women's legal right to vote under the Fourteenth Amendment by taking the case to the U.S. Supreme Court. Free on bail of one thousand dollars, Anthony campaigned throughout the country with a carefully prepared legal argument: "Is It a Crime for a U.S. Citizen to Vote?" She lost her case in 1873 in Rochester following some questionable rulings by the judge and was barred from appealing the result to the Supreme Court.

Later years

Susan B. Anthony spent the rest of her life working for the federal suffrage amendment—an exhausting job that took her not only to Congress but to political conventions, labor meetings, and lecture halls in every part of the country. After she noticed that most historical literature failed to mention any women, in 1877 she and her supporters sat down to begin writing the monumental and invaluable *History of Woman Suffrage* in five volumes. She later worked with her biographer, Ida Husted Harper, on two of the three volumes of *The Life and Work of Susan B. Anthony.* The material was drawn mainly from the scrapbooks she had kept throughout most of her life, which are now in the Library of Congress, and from her diaries and letters.

Anthony remained active in the struggle for women's suffrage until the end of her life. She attended her last suffrage convention just one month before her death. She closed her last public speech with the words, "Failure is impossible." When she died in her Rochester home on March 13, 1906, only four states had granted women the right to vote. Fourteen years later the Nineteenth Amendment, which gave women the right to vote, was added to the U.S. Constitution.

For More Information

Barry, Kathleen. *Susan B. Anthony: A Biography of a Singular Feminist.* New York: New York University Press, 1988.

Harper, Judith E. *Susan B. Anthony: A Biographical Companion.* Santa Barbara, CA: ABC-CLIO, 1998.

Sherr, Lynn. *Failure Is Impossible: Susan B. Anthony in Her Own Words.* New York: Times Books, 1995.

Virginia Apgar

Born: June 7, 1909
Westfield, New Jersey
Died: August 7, 1974
New York, New York
American medical researcher and educator

Virginia Apgar forever changed the field of perinatology (the care of infants around the time of birth). She was the creator of the Apgar Newborn Scoring System, a method of evaluating the health of infants minutes after birth in order to make sure they receive proper medical care. Her lifetime of energetic work resulted in standard medical procedures for mothers and babies that have prevented thousands of infant deaths.

Virginia Apgar.
Reproduced by permission of AP/Wide World Photos.

Going into medicine

Virginia Apgar was born on June 7, 1909, in Westfield, New Jersey. Her father, a businessman, and other members of the family shared a love of music, and Apgar played the violin during family concerts. Apgar's childhood home also contained a basement laboratory, where her father built a telescope and pursued scientific experiments with electricity and radio waves (electromagnetic waves in the range of radio frequencies). Perhaps due to this atmosphere of curiosity and investigation, Apgar decided she wanted a scientific career in the field of medicine. After graduating from high school, where she played in the school orchestra and participated in athletics, she entered Mount Holyoke College with the plan of becoming a doctor. Although she had to take a number of jobs to support herself through college, she graduated with a bachelor's degree in 1929.

Apgar's financial situation did not improve when she enrolled at the College of Physicians and Surgeons at Columbia University in New York City the following September. The United States would soon be severely affected by the Great Depression (1929–39), a period of nationwide economic crisis. Determined to stay in school, Apgar borrowed money in order to complete her classes. She emerged in 1933 with a medical degree and a fourth-place rank in her graduating class, but also with a large financial debt. She began to consider how she could best support herself in the medical profession. She saw that even male surgeons were having trouble finding work in New York City. As a woman in what was then a male-dominated profession, she realized that her chances of success were slim. She felt that she was more likely to be successful in the field of anesthesiology, the study or practice of giving patients anesthesia. Administered by physicians called anesthesiologists, anesthetics are drugs or gas that numbs the pain of medical procedures or causes patients to lose consciousness before a procedure is performed.

Traditionally nurses had been responsible for administering anesthesia, but at that time doctors had also begun entering the field. Women physicians in particular were encouraged to pursue medical anesthesiology, perhaps because it was still considered a female area. Therefore in 1935 Apgar began a two-year program of study and work in anesthesiology. During this time she studied not only at Columbia, but also at the University of Wisconsin in Madison and at Bellevue Hospital in New York.

Apgar's choice of career allowed her to realize her goal of securing a job. She was hired as director of the anesthesia division at Columbia University in 1938. Her new position, however, proved to be a challenging one. She struggled to get surgeons to recognize the anesthesiologist as a fellow doctor who was their equal, not their inferior. She eventually increased the number of physicians in the anesthesiology division, however, and in 1941 won adequate funding for the division and its employees after threatening to quit her post if the school refused her requests. A few years later Columbia University created a separate department of anesthesia for training physicians and conducting research. When the head of the new department was selected in 1949, however, Apgar was passed over in favor of a man. Instead she was named a full professor in the department, making her the first woman to reach such a level at Columbia.

The Apgar Newborn Scoring System

It was in this position as a teacher and researcher that Apgar would make her greatest contributions to medicine over the next ten years. She began to focus her work in the area of anesthesia used during childbirth. Apgar realized that the period just after a baby is born is an extremely important time for many infants. At the time babies were not usually evaluated (assessed in regard to their health) carefully at birth by doctors, who were often more concerned with the health of the mother. Because of this lack of an organized examination, many life-threatening conditions were not identified in infants. To provide a quick and efficient way to decide which babies required special care, Apgar created a five-part test that scored a child's heart rate, respiration (breathing), muscle tone, color, and reflexes. The test, known as the Apgar Newborn Scoring System, was to be performed one minute after birth. This later expanded to five and ten minutes as well. Developed in 1949, Apgar's system eventually became a worldwide standard among physicians for determining a child's chance of survival and rate of development.

Another victory for infant health was won with Apgar's research into the effects of anesthesia given to mothers during childbirth. During the time she researched these effects, Apgar found that the anesthesia called cyclopropane had a noticeable negative effect on a baby's overall condition. She immediately stopped using this anesthesia for mothers in labor, and other doctors across the country quickly did so also after Apgar published a report on her research.

Birth defect research

After a more than twenty-year career at Columbia, Apgar left her post as professor to earn a master of public health degree at Johns Hopkins University. Her new career took her to the March of Dimes organization, an organization that provides services and support to children and pregnant women. In 1959 she was hired as the head of the division on congenital birth defects (physical or developmental abnormalities that are caused before birth). In 1969 she became the head of the March of Dimes research program, and during her time in this role she changed the foundation's focus so that it concentrated on trying to prevent birth defects. In an effort to educate the public about this topic, she also gave many lectures and cowrote a book titled *Is My Baby All Right?* in 1972. Later, as a professor at Cornell University, she became the first U.S. medical professor to specialize in birth defects.

During her lifetime Apgar made significant contributions to science not only in the laboratory, but also in the classroom. She instructed hundreds of doctors and left a lasting mark on the field of neonatal care (the care of newborns). Apgar received a number of awards recognizing her role in medicine, including the Ralph Waters Medal from the American Society of Anesthesiologists; the Gold Medal of Columbia University; and *Ladies' Home Journal* named her Woman of the Year in 1973. In addition she was the recipient of four honorary degrees, the American Academy of Pediatrics founded a prize in her name, and an academic chair was created in her honor at Mount Holyoke College.

On August 7, 1974, Apgar died in New York City at the age of sixty-five. She was remembered as an honest and encouraging teacher who inspired numerous doctors in their practice of medicine and research. The modern fields of anesthesiology and neonatal care owe much to her pioneering work.

For More Information

Apgar, Virginia, and Joan Beck. *Is My Baby All Right?: A Guide to Birth Defects.* New York: Trident Press, 1972.

Calmes, Selma. "Virginia Apgar: A Woman Physician's Career in a Developing Specialty." *Journal of the American Medical Women's Association* (November/December 1984): 184–188.

Diamonstein, Barbaralee. *Open Secrets: Ninety-four Women in Touch with Our Time.* New York: Viking Press, 1972.

BENIGNO AQUINO

Born: November 27, 1932
Tarlac Province, Luzon, Philippines
Died: August 21, 1983
Manila, Philippines
Filipino politician

Benigno Aquino of the Philippines was a leading opponent of the rule of President Ferdinand Marcos (1917–1989), who governed the Philippines from 1966 to 1986. Aquino's opposition ended in August 1983 when, after living in the United States for three years, he returned to the Philippine capital of Manila and was assassinated (killed) at the airport. Aquino's death touched off massive demonstrations against President Marcos.

Youthful accomplishments

Benigno "Ninoy" Aquino was born on November 27, 1932, in Tarlac Province, on the island of Luzon, to a prominent family. He was the grandson of a general and the son of a Philippine senator who was also a wealthy landowner. His ambition and energy stood out early when, at age seventeen, he was sent by the *Manila Times* newspaper to report on the Korean War (1950–53). The war was between the Democratic People's Republic of Korea (North Korea) and the Republic of Korea (South Korea), and was a war in which the United States and China eventually joined.

At age twenty-two Aquino became the Philippines' youngest mayor in his hometown of Concepcion. Just six years later he became governor of Tarlac province (a position similar to governing a state). In 1967 Aquino once again made history when he became the youngest senator ever elected in the Philippines. Meanwhile he married Corazon Cojoangco, with whom he eventually raised five children.

A fallen leader

Aquino became famous for his gifts as a public speaker and for his brilliant mind, as well as his great ambition. He became the leading candidate for the presidency in 1973, when President Marcos was scheduled to leave office after completing the maximum two terms as president. Aquino's ambition to be president was never realized, however, because President Marcos declared martial law (a state of emergency in which military authorities are given temporary rule). At the same time Marcos dissolved the constitution, claiming supreme power and jailing his political opponents, including Aquino. Aquino was charged with murder, subversion (intention to undermine legal authority), and illegal possession of firearms. Although he denied the charges, Aquino was found guilty and was convicted by a military tribunal, or military court, and spent over seven years in prison. In 1980 he was allowed to go to the United States for a heart bypass operation. He remained in the United States as a refugee until returning to the Philippines in 1983. Upon arriving at the Manila airport he was shot and killed.

Benigno Aquino.
Reproduced by permission of AP/Wide World Photos.

Following the assassination President Marcos was pressured to appoint a five-person, politically neutral investigative board, led by Judge Corazon Agrava. Marcos and the military stated that a lone gunman who had been hired by the Communist Party had carried out the assassination. The alleged gunman, who had been shot at the airport immediately following the shooting of Aquino, could not be cross-examined. The military carried out its own investigation, and reported that no military personnel were involved in the death.

The official commission's majority report found that Aquino was not slain by the alleged gunman, as Marcos and the military claimed, but was the victim of a "criminal conspiracy" by the military led by General Fabian C. Ver, who was the armed forces chief of staff. He was also a close friend and cousin of President Marcos. The commission's findings were astonishing, although from the beginning most Filipinos doubted the official version of the assassination. No proof was ever presented that directly showed Marcos was involved, but almost no one in the Philippines believed that military generals would order the execution of Aquino on their own. Those who suspected Marcos's involvement noted that Aquino posed a threat as someone who might unite the opposition and who had been the president's main rival for decades.

Aquino's legacy

As it turned out the democratic opposition to Marcos was strongest after its leader's death. As Marcos lost the trust of his people, the Philippine economy also fell apart. By 1985 the nation was in political and economic chaos, with Marcos under attack by the press and by the strengthened political opposition, which did well in elections.

In December 1985 the court proclaimed that General Ver and the others charged with Aquino's murder were not guilty. Marcos promptly returned Ver to his former position. Popular unrest with Marcos's rule grew steadily, however. Within weeks a political movement formed around Aquino's widow, Corazon. She was elected president of the Philippines in 1986, unseating Marcos.

For More Information

Hill, Gerald N. and Kathleen Thompson. *Aquino Assassination: The Story and Analysis of the Assassination of Philippine Senator Benigno S. Aquino.* Sonoma, CA: Hilltop Pub. Co., 1983.

White, Mel. *Aquino.* Dallas: Word Pub., 1989.

YASIR ARAFAT

Born: October 24, 1929
Cairo, Egypt
Palestinian political leader, military leader, and president

Yasir Arafat was elected chairman of the Palestine Liberation Organization (PLO) in 1969. Though originally in favor of an all-out war to end Israel's occupation of Arab lands in the Middle East, from 1974 on he and the PLO claimed to be interested in a peaceful resolution to the Palestinian problem.

Background

Yasir Arafat was born Abdel-Rahman Abdel-Raouf Arafat al-Qudwa al-Husseini on October 24, 1929, to a Palestinian family living in Cairo, Egypt. His father was a merchant. Arafat's youth was spent in Cairo and Jerusalem. At that time, in the decades following World War I (1914–18), the British ruled Palestine. Many Jewish people from Europe sought to build a Jewish homeland there, but many Muslim and Christian Arabs who lived in Palestine opposed Jewish immigration because they were afraid it would upset the cultural balance there.

While still in his teens Arafat became involved with a group seeking independence for Palestinian Arabs. When the British moved out of Palestine in 1948 and the Jewish state of Israel was created on a piece of Palestinian land, fighting broke out between the Jewish and Arab communities. The Jews were easily able to beat the Palestinians. As a result approximately one million Palestinians were forced to flee their homeland and seek refuge in neighboring Arab nations. Thus two-thirds of pre-war Palestine then became Israel. The rest came under the control of two Arab neighbors, Egypt and Jordan.

Yasir Arafat.
Reproduced by permission of Archive Photos, Inc.

Fatah and the PLO

After the Palestinians' 1948 defeat, Arafat went to Cairo, where he studied engineering and founded a student union. By the end of the 1950s, he helped to found al-Fatah which became one of the main groups in the new Palestinian independence movement. Arafat was one of Fatah's most important founders and sat on the group's central committee. Fatah members argued that Palestinians should seek to regain their country by their own efforts, including guerrilla warfare (independent acts of war and terrorism) against Israel. This armed struggle was launched in 1965. The attacks did not damage the Jewish military, but they did increase Arafat's popularity. Meanwhile, in 1964, Palestinian freedom fighters in Arab countries had created their own confederation, which they called the Palestine Liberation Organization (PLO).

In 1967 the Israelis defeated the Arabs in the Six-Day War. Israel took over the rest of Palestine, along with sections of Egypt and Syria. The Arab states were embarrassed by this defeat. Fatah members were able to assume control of the PLO, with Arafat elected chairman of the executive committee. Guerrilla camps were set up in Jordan along the border with Israel. In September 1970 Jordan's King Hussein (1935–1999) sent his army into the camps, killing many Palestinians in what became known as Black September. The PLO began to engage in terrorist acts, including the murder of eleven Israeli athletes at the Olympic Games in Munich, Germany, in 1972.

Endless peace talks

In 1973 Egypt and Syria attacked Israel in the Yom Kippur War, an attempt to regain lands Israel occupied six years earlier. This led to efforts by the United States to seek peace in the region. In 1974 the PLO voted to be included in any settlement. It also called for the creation of a Palestinian national authority in two areas the Israelis occupied in 1967, the West Bank and the Gaza Strip. Participating in a debate on the Middle East at the United Nations General Assembly, Arafat said, "I have come bearing an olive branch and a freedom fighter's gun. Do not let the olive branch fall from my hand." The Israelis and the Americans refused to have any dealings with the PLO until it recognized a United Nations resolution regarding Israel's right to exist. Arafat and the PLO would not satisfy this condition.

Arafat and the PLO also opposed peace agreements proposed by Egyptian president Anwar Sadat (1918–1981) in 1977–79. These agreements were known as the Camp David Accords, because they had been drawn up in Maryland at the U.S. presidential retreat of that name. Egypt, Israel, and the United States signed them in 1978. They called for the establishment of Palestinian self-government in the West Bank and Gaza, but the plan never went into effect. The PLO continued its demand for an independent Palestinian state in the area. Arafat worked to make peace with Jordan and Egypt throughout the 1980s, and sought help from the United States in setting up a confederation between Jordan and a Palestinian entity that would be established in the West Bank and Gaza. King Hussein broke off talks with Arafat, however, saying that the PLO refused to compromise.

In 1993 Arafat and Israeli Prime Minister Yitzhak Rabin (1922–1995) signed the Oslo Accords. The following year the two men and Israeli foreign minister Shimon Peres shared the Nobel Peace Prize for their efforts. The Oslo Accords placed the city of Jericho, the Israeli-occupied Gaza Strip, and eventually the remainder of the West Bank under Palestinian self-rule. In January 1996 Arafat was elected president of the Palestinian National Authority (PNA), the area's new governing body. Later that same year an agreement was reached to remove Israelis from the last occupied city in the West Bank. In return Arafat promised to amend the portion of the Palestinian National Charter calling for the destruction of Israel.

Same old situation

Israel's decision to build homes in Jerusalem started up the terrorism campaign once again in the Middle East, placing peace efforts on very shaky ground. In July 2000 peace talks between Arafat, U.S. president Bill Clinton (1946–), and Israeli Prime Minister Ehud Barak (1942–) at Camp David did not lead to any agreement. Arafat had said that he would declare a Palestinian state on September 13, 2000, with or without an agreement with Israel. He finally agreed to wait in the hopes that more talks might lead to a settlement.

Unfortunately, outbreaks of violence began between Palestinians and Israeli security forces. In October 2000 Arafat, Barak, and Clinton met and came up with a "statement of intent" to end the violence, but neither side was completely satisfied. Nearly one hundred people, almost all of them Palestinians, had been killed in the clashes between Israeli security forces and Palestinians. In November 2000 Arafat told Fatah activists to cease firing on Israelis. Steady gunfire followed news of Arafat's announcement, however, with Palestinians shooting at Israeli positions from an apartment building. Israeli forces returned fire with machine guns.

Though Arafat was offered a peace proposal designed by Clinton and approved by Barak in January 2001, the leader found it unsatisfactory (it did not allow displaced Palestinians the right to return to their homeland), and the Arab-Israeli violence in the Middle East continued. After the attacks on the United States on September 11, 2001, the U.S. government increased the pressure on the Israelis and the Palestinians to reach a settlement. The United States hoped to involve Arab nations in the fight against terrorism. Despite Arafat's demands for it to stop, there seemed to be no end to the violence, however. In December 2001 the Israeli government severed all ties to the PNA, leaving little hope of a resolution anytime soon. And on two occasions in 2002, the Israeli army took over the majority of Arafat's compound, essentially making him a prisoner in his own home.

For More Information

Aburish, Saïd K. *Arafat: From Defender to Dictator.* London: Bloomsbury, 1998.

Wallach, Janet, and John Wallach. *Arafat: In the Eyes of the Beholder.* Rev. and updated ed. Secaucus, NJ: Carol Pub., 1997.

ARCHIMEDES

Born: c. 287 B.C.E.
Syracuse
Died: 212 B.C.E.
Syracuse
Greek mathematician

Archimedes is considered one of the greatest mathematicians of all time. He is also famed for his inventions and for the colorful—though unproven—ways he is believed to have made them.

Early life

Little is known about Archimedes's life. He probably was born in the seaport city of Syracuse, a Greek settlement on the island of Sicily in the Mediterranean Sea. He was the son of an astronomer (someone who studies outer space, such as the stars) named Phidias. He may also have been related to Hieron, King of Syracuse, and his son Gelon. Archimedes studied in the learning capital of Alexandria, Egypt, at the school that had been established by the Greek mathematician Euclid (third century B.C.E.). He later returned to live in his native city of Syracuse.

There are many stories about how Archimedes made his discoveries. A famous one tells how he uncovered an attempt to cheat King Hieron. The king ordered a golden crown and gave the crown's maker the exact amount of gold needed. The maker delivered a crown of the required weight, but Hieron suspected that some silver had been used instead of gold. He asked Archimedes to think about the matter. One day Archimedes was considering it while he was getting into a bathtub. He noticed that the amount of water overflowing the tub was proportional (related consistently) to the amount of his body that was being immersed (covered by water). This gave him an idea for solving the problem of the crown. He was so thrilled that he ran naked through the streets shouting, "Eureka!" (Greek for "I have discovered it!").

Archimedes.
Courtesy of the Library of Congress.

There are several ways Archimedes may have determined the amount of silver in the crown. One likely method relies on an idea that is now called Archimedes's principle. It states that a body immersed in a fluid is buoyed up (pushed up) by a force that is equal to the weight of fluid that is displaced (pushed out of place) by the body. Using this method, he would have first taken two equal weights of gold and silver and compared their weights when immersed in water. Next he would have compared the weight of the crown and an equal weight of pure silver in water in the same way. The difference between these two comparisons would indicate that the crown was not pure gold.

Archimedes also studied aspects of the lever and pulley. A lever is a kind of basic machine in which a bar is used to raise or move a weight, while a pulley uses a wheel and a rope or chain to lift loads. Such mechanical investigations would help Archimedes assist in defending Syracuse when it came under attack.

Wartime and other inventions

According to the Greek biographer Plutarch (c. C.E. 46–c. C.E. 120), Archimedes's military inventions helped defend his home city when it was attacked by Roman forces. Plutarch wrote that after Hieron died, the Roman general Marcus Claudius Marcellus (c. 268 B.C.E.–208 B.C.E.) attacked Syracuse by both land and sea. According to Plutarch Archimedes's catapults (machines that could hurl objects such as heavy stones) forced back the Roman forces on land. Later writers claimed that Archimedes also set the Roman ships on fire by focusing an arrangement of mirrors on them. Nevertheless, despite Archimedes's efforts, Syracuse eventually surrendered to the Romans. Archimedes was killed after the city was taken, although it is not known exactly how this occurred.

Perhaps while in Egypt, Archimedes invented the water screw, a machine for raising water to bring it to fields. Another invention was a miniature planetarium, a sphere whose motion imitated that of the earth, sun, moon, and the five planets that were then known to exist.

Contributions to mathematics

Euclid's book *Elements* had included practically all the results of Greek geometry up to Archimedes's time. But Archimedes continued Euclid's work more than anyone before him. One way he did this was to extend what is known as the "method of exhaustion." This method is used to determine the areas and volumes of figures with curved lines and surfaces, such as circles, spheres, pyramids, and cones. Archimedes's investigation of the method of exhaustion helped lead to the current form of mathematics called integral calculus. Although his method is now outdated, the advances that finally outdated it did not occur until about two thousand years after Archimedes lived.

Archimedes also came closer than anyone had before him to determining the value of pi, or the number that gives the ratio (relation) of a circle's circumference (its boundary line) to its diameter (the length of a line passing through its center). In addition, in his work *The Sand Reckoner,* he created a new way to show very large numbers. Before this, numbers had been represented by letters of the alphabet, a method that had been very limited.

For More Information

Bendick, Jeanne, and Laura M. Berquist. *Archimedes and the Door to Science.* Minot, ND: Bethlehem Books, 1997.

Ibsen, D. C. *Archimedes: Greatest Scientist of the Ancient World.* Springfield, NJ: Enslow Publishers, 1989.

HANNAH ARENDT

Born: October 14, 1906
Hanover, Germany

Died: December 4, 1975
New York, New York
German philosopher and writer

A Jewish girl forced to flee Germany during World War II (1939–45), Hannah Arendt analyzed major issues of the twentieth century and produced an original and radical political philosophy.

Early life and career

Hannah Arendt was born on October 14, 1906, in Hanover, Germany, the only child of middle-class Jewish parents of Russian descent. A bright child whose father died in 1913, she was encouraged by her mother in intellectual and academic pursuits. As a university student in Germany she studied with the most original scholars of that time: Rudolf Bultmann (1888–1976) and Martin Heidegger (1889–1976) in philosophy; the phenomenologist (one who studies human awareness) Edmund Husserl (1859– 1938); and the existentialist (one who studies human existence) Karl Jaspers (1883– 1969). In 1929 Arendt received her doctorate degree and married Gunther Stern.

In 1933 Arendt was arrested and briefly imprisoned for gathering evidence of Nazi anti-Semitism (evidence that proved the Nazis were a ruthless German army regime aimed at ridding Europe of its Jewish population). Shortly after the outbreak of World War II she fled to France, where she worked for Jewish refugee organizations (organizations aimed at helping Jews that were forced to flee Germany). In 1940 she and her second husband, Heinrich Blücher, were held captive in southern France. They escaped and made their way to New York in 1941.

Hannah Arendt.
Reproduced by permission of the Corbis Corporation.

Throughout the war years Arendt wrote a political column for the Jewish weekly *Aufbau,* and began publishing articles in leading Jewish journals. As her circle of friends expanded to include leading American intellectuals, her writings found a wider audience. Her first major book, *The Origins of Totalitarianism* (1951), argued that modern totalitarianism (government with total political power without competition) was a new and distinct form of government that used terror to control the mass society. "Origins" was the first major effort to analyze the historical conditions that had given rise to Germany's Adolph Hitler (1889–1945) and Russia's Joseph Stalin (1879–1953), and was widely studied in the 1950s.

Labor, work, and action

A second major work, *The Human Condition* (1958), followed. Here, and in a volume of essays, *Between Past and Future* (1961), Arendt clearly defined themes from her earlier work: in a rapidly developing world, humans were no longer able to find solutions in established traditions of political authority, philosophy, religion, or even common sense. Her solution was as radical (extreme) as the problem: "to think what we are doing."

The Human Condition established Arendt's academic reputation and led to a visiting appointment at Princeton University—the first time a woman was a full-time professor there. *On Revolution* (1963), a volume of her Princeton lectures, expressed her enthusiasm at becoming an American citizen by exploring the historical background and requirements of political freedom.

In 1961 Arendt attended the trial in Jerusalem of Adolf Eichmann (1906–1962), a Nazi who had been involved in the murder of large numbers of Jews during the Holocaust (when Nazis imprisoned or killed millions of Jews during World War II). Her reports appeared first in *The New Yorker* and then as *Eichmann in Jerusalem* (1964). They were frequently misunderstood and rejected, especially her claim that Eichmann was more of a puppet than radically evil. Her public reputation among even some former friends never recovered from this controversy.

Later career

At the University of Chicago (1963–1967) and the New School for Social Research in New York City (1967–1975), Arendt's brilliant lectures inspired countless students in social thought, philosophy, religious studies, and history. Frequently uneasy in public, she was an energetic conversationalist in smaller gatherings. Even among friends, though, she would sometimes excuse herself and become totally absorbed in some new line of thought that had occurred to her.

During the late 1960s Arendt devoted herself to a variety of projects: essays on current political issues, such as civil unrest and war, published as *Crises of the Republic* (1972); portraits of men and women who offered some explanation on the dark times of the twentieth century, which became *Men in Dark Times* (1968); and a two-volume English edition of Karl Jaspers's *The Great Philosophers* (1962 and 1966).

In 1973 and 1974 Arendt delivered the well-received Gifford Lectures in Scotland, which were later published as *The Life of the Mind* (1979). Tragically, Arendt never completed these lectures as she died of a heart attack in New York City on December 4, 1975.

Arendt was honored throughout her later life by a series of academic prizes. Frequently attacked for controversial and sometimes odd judgments, Hannah Arendt died as she lived—an original interpreter of human nature in the face of modern political disasters.

For More Information

Kristeva, Julia. *Hannah Arendt.* New York: Columbia University Press, 2001.

McGowan, John. *Hannah Arendt: An Introduction.* Minneapolis: University of Minnesota Press, 1998.

Jean-Bertrand Aristide

Born: July 15, 1953
Douyon, Haiti
Haitian president

A man of the people and loved by many in his home country, Jean-Bertrand Aristide was first elected president of Haiti by a large margin in 1990. He was removed from power in a military takeover in 1991, however. Aristide lived abroad until 1994, then a U.S. military occupation of Haiti restored him to power. In 1995 his hand-picked successor was elected president. In 2000 Aristide won his second term.

Early years and education

Jean-Bertrand Aristide was born on July 15, 1953, in Port-Salut, a small town along Haiti's southern coast. When Aristide was just three months old, his father passed away. His mother, who wanted to provide Jean and his sister with a better life, moved the family to Port-au-Prince, Haiti. Jean studied under the priests of the Society of St. Francis de Sales (or the Salesian Order) of the Roman Catholic Church. The Salesian Order, with European and American houses and members, focused on the religious instruction of Haiti's poor and orphaned children. Aristide received his early education in their schools and later attended their seminary (an institute for training priests) in Haiti. In 1979 he earned a bachelor's degree in psychology at the State University of Haiti. He was later sent to Israel, Egypt, Britain, and Canada for biblical studies. He learned to read and speak

Jean-Bertrand Aristide.
Reproduced by permission of AP/Wide World Photos.

French, Spanish, English, Hebrew, Italian, German, and Portuguese in addition to his native Creole, which is spoken by 90 percent of Haitians.

Religion and politics

Aristide became a priest in 1982. In 1988, however, he was expelled from the Salesian Order for preaching too politically and for what Aristide called his "fidelity [faithfulness] to the poor." The Vatican (the headquarters of the Roman Catholic Church) in Rome, Italy, and his local bishop had warned him to preach less radically, or less outside the mainstream, and to stop turning the members of his church against the Haitian state. From the time he became a priest, Aristide had condemned Haiti's lack of democracy. At the Church of St. Jean Bosco in the poorest part of Port-au-Prince he argued that only a religious and political cleansing could save the country.

For all but the first five years of Aristide's life, a harsh family dictatorship (a government in which power is controlled by one person or only a few people) led by François "Papa Doc" Duvalier (1907–1971) and his son, Jean-Paul "Baby Doc" Duvalier (1951–), had ruled Haiti. Human rights violations were common. Ordinary Haitians lived in fear of a violent group known as the "tonton macoutes," who terrorized the population. The ruling family and the state were one and the same, and the Duvaliers preyed viciously on the people. Corruption was everywhere.

Aristide's opposition to the dictatorship grew out of his religious beliefs and his feelings for the suffering Haitian people. He may have thought that the Duvalier dictatorship was crumbling. After months of popular protest, some of which was inspired by Aristide's preachings, Baby Doc fled from Haiti to France in early 1986.

The military groups that succeeded Baby Doc in power also oppressed the poor. Aristide criticized the reigns of both General Prosper Avril and Lieutenant General Henri Namphy. In revenge the tonton macoutes attacked the Church of St. Jean Bosco in revenge, killing thirteen members of Aristide's congregation in 1988. Two weeks later Aristide was expelled from the Salesian Order. The Roman Catholic Church ordered Aristide to Rome, but that resulted in one of the largest street demonstrations in Haitian history. Tens of thousands of Haitians angrily blocking Aristide's departure by air.

Aristide had not lost his power, despite his expulsion from the order. After 1988 he continued to work with Port-au-Prince's desperately poor. He ran a shelter for children living on the street and opened a medical clinic.

A presidency interrupted

When the United Nations (UN), the United States, and the Organization of American States finally persuaded the military men of Haiti to hold elections, Aristide was not an expected candidate. The character of the race for the presidency changed dramatically, however, when Aristide decided to run only a few months before the election in December 1990. His pledge for justice for victims of dictatorship and violence struck a chord among the poor, nearly all of whom would be voting for the first time in the nation's first free election. He also spoke harshly against the United States, both as a supporter of the Duvaliers and as an exploiter of the world.

Aristide soundly defeated his competition for the presidency. He won 67 percent of the popular vote, but his Lavalas (Avalanche) Party, which had had little time to organize, took only a relatively small percentage of the seats in the Haitian parliament. Before military men led by General Raoul Cedras overthrew Aristide on September 30, 1991, the new president had alarmed the commercial and old-line ruling classes of Haiti. Aristide had preached violence against macoutes and had gone after people suspected of being secret Duvalierists. His constructive accomplishments in office had been few, not all that surprising given that his power in parliament was small.

The free world rallies

Aristide lived first in Venezuela and later in the United States. Soon after he was removed from power, the United States, the Organization of American States, and the UN embargoed, or stopped, Haitian exports and attempted to cease shipping oil and other imports. But those efforts were only partially successful. The Haitian people suffered from these economic policies much more than the military leaders.

All three groups then attempted to bargain a settlement between Aristide and Cedras. Several agreements fell apart when Aristide changed his mind. Others failed because the military leaders were endlessly suspicious of Aristide's real intentions.

In mid-1993 the administration of President Bill Clinton (1946–) and the UN persuaded Aristide and Cedras to meet near New York. They were to make an agreement that would return Aristide to the Haitian presidency for the final twenty-seven months of his single, nonrenewable term, and to provide an amnesty, or group pardon, for the military. But powerful people in Haiti refused to put the agreement in place. President Clinton sent more than twenty-three thousand U.S. troops to Haiti. The task of this military mission was to ensure the safe and successful return of Aristide to power. The goal was accomplished, and Aristide completed his term. On December 17, 1995, a Haitian presidential election took place, and Rene Preval was elected to succeed Aristide.

Again the president

In 2000 Aristide's Lavalas Family Party won control of Haiti's Senate. On November 26 of that same year Aristide became a candidate for Haiti's national election. He faced four small-time candidates. The main opposition parties said they would not participate in the election, claiming Aristide wanted to return Haiti to a dictatorship. Many of his opponents thought that the parliamentary elections had not been fair, especially when Aristide won the presidential election. In his inaugural address, or first speech as new president, Aristide pledged to investigate the Senate elections. He also pledged to improve Haiti by, among other things, building more schools and bettering its healthcare system.

After the 2000 elections many foreign countries refused to give hundreds of millions of dollars in aid to Haiti until the disputes that arose as a result of the elections were settled. In December 2001 Aristide once again became the target of a group attempting to overthrow his government. But this time the attackers were defeated and Aristide remained in power. In 2002 Aristide promised to work at improving the political situation in Haiti.

For More Information

Aristide, Jean-Bertrand. *In the Parish of the Poor.* Edited by Amy Wilentz. Maryknoll, NY: Orbis Books, 1990.

Aristide, Jean-Bertrand, and Christophe Wargny. *Aristide: An Autobiography.* Maryknoll, NY: Orbis Books, 1993.

ARISTOPHANES

Born: c. 448 B.C.E.
Athens, Greece
Died: c. 385 B.C.E.
Athens, Greece
Greek writer

Aristophanes was the greatest of the writers of the original Greek comedy, which flourished in Athens in the fifth century B.C.E., and the only one with any complete plays surviving. He wrote at least thirty-six comedies, of which eleven still exist.

His life

Aristophanes was born in Athens between 450 and 445 B.C.E. into a wealthy family. He had an excellent education and was well versed in literature, especially the poetry of Homer (eighth century B.C.E.) and other great Athenian writers. His writings also suggest a strong knowledge of the latest philosophical theories.

All of Aristophanes' boyhood was spent while Athens was one of the two leading Greek political powers and the center of artistic and intellectual activity. Between the ages of seventeen and twenty-three Aristophanes began submitting his comedies for the annual Athens competition. His easy humor and good choice of words made most laugh and at least one politician take him to court. Whatever punishment resulted was mild enough to allow Aristophanes to continue his clever remarks at the leader's expense in his forthcoming comedies.

His plays

Aristophanes' special touch with comedy is best explained with a look at the original Greek comedy. The original Greek comedy, Old Comedy, was a unique dramatic mixture of fantasy, satire (literary scorn of human foolishness), slapstick, and obvious sexuality. Aristophanes used beautiful rhythmic poetry as the format for all of his comedy. He had a way of shrinking the self-importance of people involved in politics, social life, and literature, but above all he used his unlimited amount of comic invention and high spirits.

In one such comedy, *The Knights,* Aristophanes represented the local Athenian leader as the greedy and dishonest slave of a dimwitted old gentleman (the Athenian people come to life). The slave is his master's favorite until displaced by an even more rude and nasty character, a sausage seller. At the time the featured politician was at the height of his popularity, yet Athenian tolerance even in wartime allowed Aristophanes first prize in the competition for comedies.

Aristophanes.

Downfall and death

All of Aristophanes' comedies kept pace with the political climate of Athens. In peacetime he wrote an emotionally charged and rude celebration of favorite things to do during peacetime. In times of Athenian plots and prewar conflict, he wrote his own conspiracies, such as *Lysistrata,* a depiction of the women of Greece banding together to stop the war by refusing to sleep with their husbands. With such a plot the play was inevitably rude but Lysistrata herself is one of his most attractive characters, and his sympathy for the difficulty of women in wartime makes the play a moving comment on the foolishness of war.

The Peloponnesian war (431–404 B.C.E.) between Athens and the Spartans began in 431 B.C.E. The leaders of Athens decided to wage war from the sea only. Meanwhile the Spartans burned the crops of Athens. Then the plague (outbreak of disease) hit Athens in 430 B.C.E., killing many. As Athens faced her worst enemy—starvation—Aristophanes' comedy continued to be crisp and cutting. *Frogs* received the first time honor of the request for a second performance.

The long war finally ended, when the Athenians were starved into surrender in the spring of 404 B.C.E. This sad defeat broke something in the spirit of the Athenians, and though they soon regained considerable importance both in politics and in intellectual matters, they were never quite the same again. In the sphere of comedy the no-holds-barred rudeness of the Old Comedy disappeared and was replaced by a more cautious, refined, and less spirited New Comedy.

The political climate was uneasy with the Spartans lording over Athens. Aristophanes had to hold his tongue in his plays, no longer poking fun at leaders and politics. He died nine years after *Lysistrata,* which still exists, and three years after his play *Plutus.* Dates of death range from 385–380 B.C.E. but it is certain that Aristophanes died in his beloved city, Athens.

For More Information

Bloom, Harold, ed. *Aristophanes.* Philadelphia: Chelsea House, 2002.

David, E. *Aristophanes and Athenian Society of the Early Fourth Century* B.C. Leiden: E.J. Brill, 1984.

Russo, Carlo Ferdinando. *Aristophanes, an Author for the Stage.* New York: Routledge, 1994.

ARISTOTLE

Born: c. 384 B.C.E.
Chalcidice, Greece
Died: c. 322 B.C.E.
Chalcis, Greece
Greek philosopher and scientist

The Greek philosopher and scientist Aristotle created the scientific method, the process used for scientific investigation. His influence served as the basis for much of the science and philosophy of Hellenistic (Ancient Greek) and Roman times, and even affected science and philosophy thousands of years later.

Early life

Aristotle was born in the small Greek town of Stagiros (later Stagira) in the northern Greek district of Chalcidice. His father, Nicomachus, was a physician who had important social connections. Aristotle's interest in science was surely inspired by his father's work, although Aristotle did not display a particularly keen interest in medicine. The events of his early life are not clear. It is possible that his father served at the Macedonian court (the political leaders of Macedonia, an ancient empire) as physician to Amyntas II (died c. 370 B.C.E.) and that Aristotle spent part of his youth there.

At the age of seventeen Aristotle went to Athens, Greece, and joined Plato's (c. 428–c. 348 B.C.E.) circle at the Academy, a school for philosophers. There he remained for twenty years. Although his respect and admiration for Plato was always great, differences developed which ultimately caused a break in their relationship. Upon Plato's death Aristotle left for Assos in Mysia (in Asia Minor, today known as Turkey), where he and Xenocrates (c. 396–c. 314 B.C.E.) joined a small circle of Platonists (followers of Plato) who had already settled there under Hermias, the ruler of Atarneus. Aristotle married the niece of Hermias, a woman named Pythias, who was killed by the Persians some time thereafter.

In 342 B.C.E. Aristotle made his way to the court of Philip of Macedon (c. 382–c. 336 B.C.E.). There Aristotle became tutor to Alexander (c. 356–c. 323 B.C.E.), who would become master of the whole Persian Empire as Alexander the Great. Little information remains regarding the specific contents of Alexander's education at the hands of Aristotle, but it would be interesting to know what political advice Aristotle gave to the young Alexander. The only indication of such advice is found in the fragment of a letter in which the philosopher tells Alexander that he ought to be the leader of the Greeks but the master of the barbarians (foreigners).

Aristotle.

Peripatetic School

Aristotle returned to Athens around 335 B.C.E. Under the protection of Antipater (c. 397–c. 319 B.C.E.), Alexander's representative in Athens, Aristotle established a philosophical school of his own, the Lyceum, located near a shrine of Apollo Lyceus. Also known as the Peripatetic School, the school took its name from its colonnaded walk (a walk with a series of columns on either side). The lectures were divided into morning and afternoon sessions. The more difficult ones were given in the morning, and the easier and more popular ones were given in the afternoon. Aristotle himself led the school until the death of Alexander in 323 B.C.E., when he left Athens, fearing for his safety because of his close association with the Macedonians. He went to Chalcis, Greece, where he died the following year of intestinal problems. His will, preserved in the writings of Diogenes Laertius (third century C.E.), provided for his daughter, Pythias, and his son, Nicomachus, as well as for his slaves.

His writings

Aristotle produced a large number of writings, but few have survived. His earliest writings, consisting for the most part of dialogues (writings in the form of conversation), were produced under the influence of Plato and the Academy. Most of these are lost, although the titles are known from the writings of Diogenes Laertius and from others. Among these important works are *Rhetoric, Eudemus (On the Soul), On Philosophy, Alexander, Sophistes, On Justice, Wealth, On Prayer,* and *On Education.* They were a wide variety of works written for the public, and they dealt with popular philosophical themes. The dialogues of Plato were undoubtedly the inspiration for some of them, although the fall out between Plato and Aristotle reveals itself to a certain extent in these works, too.

A second group of writings is made up of collections of scientific and historical material, among the most important of which is the surviving fragment of the *Constitution of the Athenians.* This formed part of the large collection of *Constitutions,* which Aristotle and his students collected and studied for the purpose of analyzing various political theories. The discovery of the *Constitution of the Athenians* in Egypt in 1890 shed new light on the nature of the Athenian democracy (a government of elected officials) of Aristotle's time. It also revealed the difference in quality between the historical and scientific works of Aristotle and those that followed.

Theophrastus (c. 372–c. 287 B.C.E.) had kept Aristotle's manuscripts after the master's death in 322 B.C.E. When Theophrastus died Aristotle's works were hidden away and not brought to light again until the beginning of the first century B.C.E. They were then taken to Rome and edited by Andronicus (first century B.C.E.). The texts that survive today come from Andronicus's revisions and probably do not represent works that Aristotle himself prepared for publication. From the time of his death until the rediscovery of these writings, Aristotle was best known for the works that today are known as the lost writings.

Philosophical and scientific systems

The writings that did survive, however, are sufficient to show the quality of Aristotle's achievement. The *Topics and the Analytics* deal with logic (the study of reasoning) and dialectic (a method of argument) and reveal Aristotle's contributions to the development of debate. His view of nature is set forth in the *Physics and the Metaphysics,* which mark the most serious difference between Aristotelianism and Platonism: that all investigation must begin with what the senses record and must move only from that point to thought. As a result of this process of intellectualizing, God, who for Plato represents beauty and goodness, is for Aristotle the highest form of being and is completely lacking in materiality. Aristotle's God neither created nor controls the universe, although the universe is affected by this God. Man is the only creature capable of thought even remotely resembling that of God, so man's highest goal is to reason abstractly, like God, and he is more truly human to the extent that he achieves that goal.

Aristotle's work was often misunderstood in later times. The scientific and philosophical systems set forth in his writings are not conclusions that must be taken as the final answer, but rather experimental positions arrived at through careful observation and analysis. During the slow intellectual climate of the Roman Empire, which ruled over much of Europe for hundreds of years after Aristotle died, and the totally unscientific Christian Middle Ages (476–1453), Aristotle's views on nature and science were taken as a complete system. As a result, his influence was enormous but not for any reason that would have pleased him.

Aristotle shares with his master, Plato, the role of stimulating human thought. Plato had a more direct influence on the development of that great spiritual movement in late antiquity (years before the Middle Ages), and Aristotle had a greater effect on science. Antiquity produced no greater minds than those of Plato and Aristotle. The intellectual history of the West would be extremely different without them.

For More Information

Barnes, Jonathan. *Aristotle.* New York: Oxford University Press, 1982.

Dunn, John, and Ian Harris. *Aristotle.* Lyme, NH: Edward Elgar Pub., 1997.

Ross, W. D. *Aristotle.* 6th ed. New York: Routledge, 1995.

Louis Armstrong

Born: August 4, 1901
New Orleans, Louisiana
Died: July 6, 1971
New York, New York
African American jazz musician and singer

Louis Armstrong was a famous jazz trumpet player and singer. He is regarded as one of the most important and influential musicians in the history of jazz music.

Early life

Louis Daniel Armstrong was born in New Orleans on August 4, 1901. He was one of two children born to Willie Armstrong, a turpentine worker, and Mary Ann Armstrong, whose grandparents had been slaves. As a youngster, he sang on the streets with friends. His parents separated when he was five. He lived with his sister, mother, and grandmother in a rundown area of New Orleans known as "the Battlefield" because of the gambling, drunkenness, fighting, and shooting that frequently occurred there.

In 1913 Armstrong was arrested for firing a gun into the air on New Year's Eve. He was sent to the Waif's Home (a reform school), where he took up the cornet (a trumpet-like instrument) and eventually played in a band. After his release he worked odd jobs and began performing with local groups. He was also befriended by Joe "King" Oliver, leader of the first great African American band to make records, who gave him trumpet lessons. Armstrong joined Oliver in Chicago, Illinois, in 1922, remaining there until 1924, when he went to New York City to play with Fletcher Henderson's band.

Jazz pioneer

When Armstrong returned to Chicago in the fall of 1925, he organized a band and began to record one of the greatest series in the history of jazz. These Hot Five and Hot Seven recordings show his skill and experimentation with the trumpet. In 1928 he started recording with drummer Zutty Singleton and pianist Earl Hines, the latter a musician whose skill matched Armstrong's. Many of the resulting records are masterpieces of detailed construction and adventurous rhythms. During these years Armstrong was working with big bands in Chicago clubs and theaters. His vocals, featured on most records after 1925, are an extension of his trumpet playing in their rhythmic liveliness and are delivered in a unique throaty style. He was also the inventor of scat singing (the random use of nonsense syllables), which originated after he dropped his sheet music while recording a song and could not remember the lyrics.

By 1929 Armstrong was in New York City leading a nightclub band. Appearing in the theatrical revue *Hot Chocolates,* he sang "Fats" Waller's (1904–1943) "Ain't Misbehavin'," Armstrong's first popular song hit. From this period Armstrong performed mainly popular

Louis Armstrong.
Reproduced by permission of Schomburg Center for Research in Black Culture.

song material, which presented a new challenge. Some notable performances resulted. His trumpet playing reached a peak around 1933. His style then became simpler, replacing the experimentation of his earlier years with a more mature approach that used every note to its greatest advantage. He rerecorded some of his earlier songs with great results.

Later years

Armstrong continued to front big bands, often of lesser quality, until 1947, when the big-band era ended. He returned to leading a small group that, though it included first-class musicians at first, became a mere background for his talents over the years. During the 1930s Armstrong had achieved international fame, first touring Europe as a soloist and singer in 1932. After World War II (1939–45) and his 1948 trip to France, he became a constant world traveller. He journeyed through Europe, Africa, Japan, Australia, and South America. He also appeared in numerous films, the best of which was a documentary titled *Satchmo the Great* (1957).

The public had come to think of Louis Armstrong as a vaudeville entertainer (a light, often comic performer) in his later years—a fact reflected in much of his recorded output. But there were still occasions when he produced well-crafted, brilliant music. He died in New York City on July 6, 1971.

For More Information

Bergreen, Laurence. *Louis Armstrong: An Extravagant Life.* New York: Broadway Books, 1997.

Giddins, Gary. *Satchmo.* New York: Doubleday, 1988.

Jones, Max, and John Chilton. *Louis: The Louis Armstrong Story 1900–1971.* London: Studio Vista, 1971.

NEIL ARMSTRONG

Born: August 5, 1930
Wapakoneta, Ohio
American astronaut

The American astronaut Neil Armstrong was the first person to walk on the moon. In one of the most famous remarks of the twentieth century, he called his first movements on the moon "one small step for man, one giant leap for mankind."

Childhood interests

Neil Alden Armstrong was born on August 5, 1930, near Wapakoneta, Ohio. He was the eldest of three children of Stephen and Viola Engel Armstrong. Airplanes drew his interest from the age of six, when he took his first airplane ride. He began taking flying lessons at age fourteen, and on his sixteenth birthday he was issued a pilot's license. A serious pilot even at that age, Armstrong built a small wind tunnel (a tunnel through which air is forced at controlled speeds to study the effects of its flow) in the basement of his home. He also performed experiments using the model planes he had made. Through such activities he was preparing for what would be a distinguished career in aeronautics, or the design, construction, and navigation of aircrafts.

Armstrong was also interested in outer space at a young age. His fascination was fueled by a neighbor who owned a powerful telescope. Armstrong was thrilled with the views of the stars, the Moon, and the planets he saw through this device.

Years of training

Armstrong entered Indiana's Purdue University in 1947 with a U.S. Navy scholarship. After two years of study he was called to active duty with the navy and won his jet pilot wings at Pensacola Naval Air Station in Florida. At twenty he was the youngest pilot in his squadron. He flew seventy-eight combat missions during the Korean War, a civil war from 1950 to 1953 between North and South Korea in which China fought on the Communist North Korean side and the United States fought to assist South Korea.

After the war Armstrong returned to Purdue and completed a degree in aeronautical engineering in 1955. He immediately accepted a job with the Lewis Flight Propulsion Laboratory of the National Advisory Committee for Aeronautics (NACA) in Cleveland, Ohio. A year later he married Janet Shearon.

Aeronautical career

Shortly afterward Armstrong transferred to the NACA High Speed Flight Station at Edwards Air Force Base in California. Here he became a skilled test pilot and flew the early models of such jet aircraft as the F-100, F-101, F-102, F-104, F-5D, and B-47. He was also a pilot of the X-1B rocket plane, a later version of the first plane that broke through the sound barrier (the dragging effect of air on a plane as it approaches the speed of sound).

Armstrong was selected as one of the first three NACA pilots to fly the X-15 rocket-engine plane. He made seven flights in this plane, which was a kind of early model for future spacecraft. Once he set a record altitude of 207,500 feet and a speed of 3,989 miles per hour. Armstrong also received an invitation from the National Aeronautics and Space Administration's (NASA) American space-flight program, but he showed little enthusiasm for becoming an

Neil Armstrong.
Reproduced by permission of AP/Wide World Photos.

astronaut. His real love was flying planes. Largely because of his experience with the X-15, he was selected as a pilot of the *Dynasoar,* an experimental craft that could leave the atmosphere, orbit earth, reenter the atmosphere, and land like a conventional airplane.

Becoming an astronaut

In 1962 Armstrong decided to become an astronaut and applied for NASA selection and training. In September 1962 he became America's first nonmilitary astronaut. His first flight assignment as an astronaut was as a backup, or alternate, pilot for Gordon Cooper of the *Gemini* 5 mission. (Space programs created around a certain spacecraft type are given names such as Gemini or Apollo, while individual missions within these programs are numbered, such as *Gemini 5.*)

Armstrong continued his specialized training on the Gemini spacecraft and was selected as the command pilot for the *Gemini 8* mission. With copilot David Scott he was launched from Cape Kennedy (now Cape Canaveral), Florida, on March 16, 1966. The *Gemini 8* achieved orbit and docked as planned with another orbiting vehicle, but shortly afterward the *Gemini 8* went out of control. Armstrong detached his craft, corrected the problem, and brought *Gemini 8* down in the Pacific Ocean only 1.1 nautical miles from the planned landing point.

Armstrong's cool and professional conduct made a strong impression on his superiors as the training for the Apollo program was developing. During a routine training flight on the lunar (moon) landing research vehicle (a training device that permits astronauts to maneuver a craft in a flight environment similar to that in landing on the Moon), Armstrong's craft went out of control. He ejected (forced out) himself and landed by parachute only yards away from the training vehicle, which had crashed in flames. With his usual controlled emotions, he walked away and calmly made his report.

Apollo 11 mission

In January 1969 Armstrong was selected as commander for *Apollo 11,* the first lunar landing mission. On July 16 at 9:32 A.M. Eastern Daylight Time (EDT), Armstrong, with astronauts Michael Collins and Edwin Aldrin, lifted off from the Kennedy Space Center in Florida.

Apollo 11 passed into the gravitational influence (pull of gravity) of the moon on July 18 and circled the moon twice. Armstrong and Aldrin entered a lunar module (a small spacecraft) named the *Eagle,* which then disconnected from the larger command and service module named *Columbia.* As they descended toward the lunar surface, their computer became overloaded, but under instructions from the mission control center in Houston, Texas, Armstrong managed to land the module. At 4:17:40 P.M. EDT on July 20, a major portion of the Earth's population was listening to Armstrong's radio transmission reporting that the *Eagle* had landed. At 10:56 P.M. he set foot on the moon, saying, "That's one small step for man, one giant leap for mankind."

Armstrong and Aldrin spent nearly two and a half hours walking on the moon. The astronauts set up various scientific instruments on the surface and left behind a plaque (metal plate) reading, "Here men from the planet Earth first set foot upon the Moon. We came in peace for all mankind." Armstrong and Aldrin then returned to the *Eagle* and launched themselves to meet up again with Collins, who had been orbiting in the *Columbia* spacecraft. On July 24 *Columbia* returned to earth.

Career after NASA

Apollo 11 was Armstrong's final space mission. He joined NASA's Office of Advanced Research and Technology, where one of his main activities was to promote research into controlling high-performance aircraft by computer. In 1971 he began working at the University of Cincinnati in Ohio, where he spent seven years as a professor of aerospace engineering.

Armstrong did continue some government work. In 1984 he was named to the National Commission on Space, which completed a report outlining an ambitious future for U.S. space programs. He was also a leader of a government commission to investigate the disastrous explosion of the *Challenger* space shuttle that occurred in January 1986.

Armstrong has worked for several corporations since his astronaut days, including a position as chairman of AIL Systems, Inc., an aerospace electronics manufacturer. In 1999 he was honored at a ceremony at the National Air and Space Museum at the Smithsonian Institution in Washington, D.C., where he received the Langley Medal in honor of the thirtieth anniversary of the Apollo 11 mission. Armstrong also makes occasional public appearances at the Neil Armstrong Air & Space Museum in his hometown of Wapakoneta, Ohio.

For More Information

Aldrin, Buzz, and Malcolm McConnell. *Men From Earth.* New York: Bantam, 1989.

Connolly, Sean. *Neil Armstrong: An Unauthorized Biography.* Des Plaines, IL: Heinemann Library, 1999.

Kramer, Barbara. *Neil Armstrong: The First Man on the Moon.* Springfield, NJ: Enslow Publishers, 1997.

BENEDICT ARNOLD

Born: January 14, 1741
Norwich, Connecticut
Died: June 14, 1801
London, England
American military general

Although he fought with skill and courage in many campaigns during the American Revolution (1775–83), General Benedict Arnold is best known as the man who betrayed his country.

Youth and family

Benedict Arnold was born on January 14, 1741, in Norwich, Connecticut. He was one of only two of his mother's eleven children to survive into adulthood. His mother had been a prosperous widow before marrying Arnold's father, a merchant. However, Arnold's father did not manage the family's money well, and they were financially ruined when Arnold was thirteen. He was forced to leave school and go to work learning to be an apothecary, a position similar to that of a modern-day pharmacist.

As a young man, Arnold was a risk-taker who looked for outlets for his energetic and impulsive (taking action before thinking things through) nature. He volunteered for the French and Indian War (1754–63), a war fought between France and England in America for control of the colonial lands, but at eighteen he deserted in order to be with his mother, who was dying. In the 1760s he traded with Canada and the West Indies as a merchant and a sea captain. He took his hot-headed nature to sea with him, fighting at least two duels while on trading voyages. He was a financial success as a trader, but he was also accused of smuggling. In 1767 he married Margaret Mansfield, daughter of a government official in New Haven, Connecticut.

Joining the Revolution

News of the battles of Lexington and Concord (April 17, 1775) in Massachusetts, the first battles of the Revolution, reached Arnold in April 1775. Upon hearing of these events he set out as the head of a company of Connecticut militia for Cambridge, Massachusetts, where George Washington (1732–1799) was gathering an army to fight the British forces. Although he marched to Massachusetts without military orders to do so, Arnold was soon given an official mission. His first military engagement was the attack the next month on Fort Ticonderoga in northeastern New York, where the British had a supply of artillery, a type of large-caliber weaponry that includes cannons. The attack operation was successful, but Arnold got little of the credit for this success. Credit went mostly to Ethan Allen (1738–1789) and the troops Allen commanded, known as the Green Mountain Boys.

Arnold's second assignment was with an expedition against Canada. Leaving Cambridge on September 19, 1775, he led his troops north through Maine into Canada. By land and water and in snow and storms, he reached Quebec, Canada, in early November. There he was joined by another troop, led by General Richard Montgomery, which had come by way of Lake Champlain and Montreal, Canada. Together the two forces assaulted Quebec on December 31, but the attack failed; Montgomery lost his life and Arnold was left with a severe leg wound. Arnold next went to Lake Champlain to prevent the British from using it as a means of traveling from Canada to New York. He lost two naval battles on the lake in October 1776, but he had effectively delayed the British in their southward movement. In the same month Congress made Arnold a brigadier general (an army officer above a colonel).

Honor and accusations

The winter of 1776–77 was an unhappy one for Arnold. His hot temper, impulsiveness, and impatience had earned him many enemies who now made all sorts of charges against him. He was accused of misconduct (poor behavior) on the march through Maine, of incompetence (failure to successfully carry out a mission) on Lake Champlain, and more. Worse yet, in February 1777 Congress promoted five other brigadier generals, all Arnold's juniors, to the rank of major general (an army officer who is above a brigadier general). Only Washington's pleas kept Arnold from resigning from the army. Fortunately, the coming of spring gave him the chance for a successful operation. While visiting his home in New Haven, Arnold heard of a British attack on American supply stations in Danbury, Connecticut. He rounded up the local militia and raced to stop the enemy. Although he got there too late to prevent the destruction of the supplies, he did force the British to flee. A grateful Congress promoted him to major general on May 2, but he was still below the other five in rank. Meanwhile, he faced a formal charge of stealing goods and property from Montreal merchants during the Canadian campaign. He was cleared of the charge, but his anger at the accusation moved him to resign from the army in July 1777.

Once again Washington pleaded with him—this time to rejoin the army. Washington needed him for service in northern New York to block a bold British plan. The British hoped to split New England from the other colonies by sending General John Burgoyne from Fort Ticonderoga down the Hudson River to New York City. Burgoyne not only failed in his mission but also lost his whole army, which he surrendered at Saratoga, New York, in October 1777. Arnold played a major role in the two battles that led to the British defeat. Burgoyne himself said of Arnold that "it was his doing." Congress rewarded Arnold by restoring his position in rank above the other major generals.

Benedict Arnold.
Courtesy of the Library of Congress.

Arnold's next assignment was command of the military post at Philadelphia, Pennsylvania, which the British had left in June 1778. In April 1779 he married Margaret Shippen, the daughter of a wealthy Philadelphian. (His first wife had died in 1775.) Moving in wealthy social circles, Arnold lived expensively, spent beyond his means, and soon found himself heavily in debt. At the same time he was being charged with a number of offenses connected to using his military office for private gain. He demanded a trial in Congress, which began in May 1779. The verdict, or decision, handed down in December found him not guilty of most charges but ordered Washington to reprimand him. The general did this, but mildly, in April 1780.

End as a traitor

By this time Arnold had already started on the road to treason. Personally hurt by Congress's treatment and badly in need of money, he had begun to pass information on American troop movements and strength of units to the British in exchange for money as early as May or June of 1779. Early in the summer of 1780, he thought up a plan to turn over the important post at West Point, New York, to the English for the sum of ten thousand pounds. He persuaded Washington to place him in command there in order to carry out this scheme. However, Arnold's plan fell through when his contact, the British spy Major John André (1750–1780), was captured on September 21, 1780, with documents that showed Arnold was a traitor. André was hanged and Arnold fled to the British lines.

Arnold spent the rest of the war in a British uniform fighting his own countrymen. He went to London in 1781 and died there twenty years later on June 14, 1801, forgotten in England and despised in America. To this day, calling someone a "Benedict Arnold" in America is a way of saying that person has betrayed his or her side.

For More Information

Brandt, Clare. *The Man in the Mirror: A Life of Benedict Arnold.* New York: Random House, 1994.

Fritz, Jean. *Traitor: The Case of Benedict Arnold.* New York: B. P. Putnam's Sons, 1981.

Martin, James Kirby. *Benedict Arnold, Revolutionary Warrior: An American Warrior Reconsidered.* New York: New York University Press, 1997.

MARY KAY ASH

Born: c. 1916
Hot Wells, Texas
Died: November 22, 2001
Dallas, Texas
American businesswoman

Mary Kay Ash used her training in direct sales to create her own multimillion-dollar cosmetics firm and provide women with the opportunity for advancement.

Early years

Mary Kay Wagner Ash believed that "a lady never reveals her age," and therefore the exact year of her birth is unknown. It is estimated to be 1916. She was born to Edward and Lula Wagner in Hot Wells, Texas, the youngest of four children. Her mother, who had studied to be a nurse, worked long hours managing a restaurant. When Mary Kay was two or three, her father was ill with tuberculosis (an infection of the lungs). As a result, it was her responsibility to clean, cook, and care for her father while her mother was at work. She excelled in school, but her family could not afford to send her to college. She married at age seventeen and eventually had three children.

Working mother

During a time when few married women with families worked outside the home, Ash became an employee of Stanley Home Products in Houston, Texas. She conducted demonstration "parties" at which she sold company products, mostly to homemakers like herself. Energetic and a quick learner, Ash rose at Stanley to unit manager, a post she held from 1938 to 1952. She also spent a year studying at the University of Houston to follow her dream of becoming a doctor, but she gave it up and returned to sales work.

After Ash's marriage ended in 1952, she took a sales job at World Gift Company in Dallas, Texas. She began to develop her theory of marketing and sales, which included offering sales incentives (something that spurs someone to action) to the customer as well as the sales force. Ash was intelligent and hardworking, but, unlike men, women were given hardly any opportunities for advancement at the time. Tired of being passed over for promotions in favor of the men she had trained, she quit. She planned to write a book about her experiences in the work force.

Starts her own company

Instead, in 1963, Ash founded her own company (with an investment of five thousand dollars) to sell a skin cream to which she had purchased the manufacturing rights. She named her company "Beauty by Mary Kay." Ash was determined to offer career opportunities in her company to any woman who had the energy and creativity required to sell Mary Kay cosmetics. Before long she had a force of female sales representatives who were eager to prove themselves. Ash's second husband had died in 1963, a month before her company was established. Her oldest son helped guide her through the start-up phase of her company. Three years later she married Melville J. Ash, who worked in the wholesale gift business.

Mary Kay Ash.
Reproduced by permission of Halcyon Associates, Inc.

Believing it was important to reward hard workers, Ash gave away vacations, jewelry, and pink Cadillacs to her top performers. (By 1994 she had given away seven thousand cars valued at $100 million.) With goals such as these to shoot for, her salespeople made the company a huge success. Within two years sales neared $1 million. The company's growth continued, and new products were added. Every year since 1992 Mary Kay Cosmetics made *Fortune* magazine's list of five hundred largest companies. In addition the company was listed in a book entitled *The 100 Best Companies to Work for in America.* It now employs over 475 thousand people in over twenty-five countries.

Later years

Ash published her life story, *Mary Kay,* in 1981. It sold over a million copies, and she went on to write *Mary Kay on People Management* (1984) and *Mary Kay—You Can Have It All* (1995). In 1987 Ash became chairman *emeritus* of her company (meaning that she would hold the title of chairman even in her retirement). She helped raise money for cancer research after her third husband died of the disease. In 1993 she was honored with the dedication of the Mary Kay Ash Center for Cancer Immunotherapy Research at St. Paul Medical Center in Dallas. In 1996 the Mary Kay Ash Charitable Foundation was started to research cancers that mainly affect women.

Mary Kay Ash's health declined after she suffered a stroke in 1996. She died at her Dallas home on November 22, 2001. She was a tough businessperson with a thorough knowledge of marketing and sales. Through her belief in women's abilities and her willingness to give them a chance, she made the dream of a successful career a reality for hundreds of thousands of women worldwide.

For More Information

Ash, Mary Kay. *Mary Kay: You Can Have It All.* Rocklin, CA: Prima, 1995.

Stefoff, Rebecca. *Mary Kay Ash: Mary Kay, a Beautiful Business.* Ada, OK: Garrett Educational Corp., 1992.

ARTHUR ASHE

Born: July 10, 1943
Richmond, Virginia
Died: February 6, 1993
New York, New York
African American tennis player and activist

Arthur Ashe was the first African American player to compete in the international sport of tennis at the highest level of the game. After an early retirement from sports due to heart surgery, Ashe used his sportsman profile and legendary poise to promote human rights, education, and public health.

Early years

Arthur Robert Ashe Jr. was born on July 10, 1943, in Richmond, Virginia. He spent most of his early years with his mother, Mattie Cordell Cunningham Ashe, who taught him to read at age five. She died the next year of heart disease. Ashe's father, Arthur Ashe Sr., worked as a caretaker for a park named Brook Field in suburban North Richmond. Young Arthur lived on the grounds with four tennis courts, a pool, and three baseball diamonds. This was the key to his development as a future star athlete. His early nickname was "Skinny" or "Bones," but he grew up to be six feet one inch with a lean build.

Ashe began playing tennis at age six. He received instruction from R. Walter "Whirlwind" Johnson, an African American doctor from Lynchburg, Virginia, who opened his home in the summers to tennis prospects, including the great Althea Gibson (1927–). Johnson used military-style methods to teach tennis skills and to stress his special code of sportsmanship, which included respect, sharp appearance, and "no cheating at any time."

Arthur Ashe.
Reproduced by permission of AP/Wide World Photos.

An amateur tennis player

Ashe attended Richmond City Public Schools and received a diploma from Maggie L. Walker High School in 1961. After success as a junior player in the American Tennis Association (ATA), he was the first African American junior to receive a U.S. Lawn Tennis Association (USLTA) national ranking. When he won the National Interscholastics in 1960, it was the first USLTA national title won by an African American in the South. The University of California at Los Angeles (UCLA) awarded him a full scholarship.

In 1963 Ashe became the first African American player to win the U.S. Men's Hardcourt championships, and the first to be named to a U.S. Junior Davis Cup (an international men's tournament) team. He became the National College Athletic Association (NCAA) singles and doubles champion, leading UCLA to the NCAA title in 1965. After graduating with a bachelor's degree in business administration, Ashe served in the army for two years, during which he was assigned time for tennis competitions. In 1968 Ashe created a tennis program for U.S. inner cities. This was the beginning of today's U.S. Tennis Association/National Junior Tennis League program, with five hundred chapters running programs for 150 thousand kids.

As professional tennis player

Two events changed Ashe's life in the late 1960s. The first was the protest by African American athletes at the 1968 Olympic Games in Mexico City, Mexico, in opposition to separation based on race, or apartheid, in the Republic of South Africa. The second event was in tennis. He was the USLTA amateur champion and won the first U.S. Open Tennis Championship at Forest Hills. The USLTA ranked him co-number one (with Rod Laver). He became a top money-winner after turning professional in 1969. In 1972 he helped found the Association of Tennis Professionals (ATP).

In 1973 Ashe became the first African American to reach the South African Open finals held in Johannesburg, South Africa, and he was the doubles winner with Tom Okker of the Netherlands. Black South Africans gave Ashe the name "Sipho," which means "a gift from God" in Zulu. The year 1975 was Ashe's best and most consistent season. He was the first and only African American player to win the men's singles title at Wimbledon, beating the defending champion, Jimmy Connors. Ashe was ranked number one in the world and was named ATP Player of the Year.

In 1977 Ashe married Jeanne Moutoussamy, a professional photographer and graphic artist. The couple had a daughter, Camera Elizabeth. Ashe almost defeated John McEnroe (1959–) in the Masters final in New York in January 1979, and was a semi-finalist at Wimbledon that summer before a heart attack soon after the tournament ended his career. After heart surgery Ashe announced his retirement from competitive tennis.

As international role model

After retiring from competition, Ashe served as captain of the U.S. Davis Cup team and led it to consecutive victories (1981–82). Ashe received media attention for his Davis Cup campaigns, his protests against apartheid in South Africa, and his call for higher educational standards for all athletes. But he spent most of his time dealing quietly with the "real world" through public speaking, teaching, writing, business, and public service. Ashe helped develop: the ABC Cities program, combining tennis and academics; the Safe Passage Foundation for poor children, which includes tennis training; the Athletes Career Connection; the Black Tennis & Sports Foundation, to assist minority athletes; and 15-Love, a substance abuse program.

After heart surgery in 1983 Ashe became national campaign chairman for the American Heart Association and the only nonmedical member of the National Heart, Lung, and Blood Advisory Council. In the late 1970s he become an adviser to Aetna Life & Casualty Company. He was made a board member in 1982. He represented minority concerns and, later, the causes of the sick.

Ashe was elected to the UCLA Sports Hall of Fame, the Virginia Sports Hall of Fame, and the Eastern Tennis Association Hall of Fame. He became the first person named to the U.S. Professional Tennis Association Hall of Fame. He spent six years and $300,000 of his own money to write *A Hard Road to Glory: A History of the African-American Athlete,* a three-volume work published in 1988. Ashe won an Emmy Award for writing a television version of his work. He also worked as a broadcaster at tennis matches, sports consultant at tennis clinics, and columnist for the *Washington Post.*

Later years

After brain surgery in 1988 came the discovery that Ashe had been infected with the human immunodeficiency virus (HIV), the virus that causes acquired immune deficiency syndrome (AIDS, a fatal disease that attacks the body's immune system). Doctors traced the infection back to a blood transfusion he received after his second heart operation in 1983. After going public with the news in 1992, Ashe established the Arthur

Ashe Foundation for the Defeat of AIDS to provide treatment to AIDS patients and to promote AIDS research throughout the world. He rallied professional tennis to help raise funds and to increase public awareness of the disease. He addressed the General Assembly of the United Nations (UN) on World AIDS Day, December 1, 1992.

Arthur Ashe died on February 6, 1993, in New York City. As Ashe's body lay in state at the governor's mansion in Virginia, mourners paid their respects at a memorial service held in New York City and at the funeral at the Ashe Athletic Center in Richmond. In 1996 Ashe's hometown of Richmond announced plans to erect a statue in his honor. The following year a new stadium at the National Tennis Center in Flushing Meadows, New York, was named after him.

For More Information

Ashe, Arthur, and Arnold Rampersad. *Days of Grace: A Memoir.* New York: Alfred A. Knopf, 1993.

Lazo, Caroline. *Arthur Ashe.* Minneapolis: Lerner, 1999.

Martin, Marvin. *Arthur Ashe: Of Tennis & the Human Spirit.* New York: Franklin Watts, 1999.

ISAAC ASIMOV

Born: January 2, 1920
Petrovichi, Russia, Soviet Union
Died: April 6, 1992
New York, New York
Russian-born American writer

The author of nearly five hundred books, Isaac Asimov was one of the finest writers of science fiction in the twentieth century. Many, however, believe Asimov's greatest talent was for, as he called it, "translating" science, making it understandable and interesting for the average reader.

Early life

Isaac Asimov was born on January 2, 1920, in Petrovichi, Russia, then part of the Smolensk district in the Soviet Union. He was the first of three children of Juda and Anna Rachel Asimov. Although his father made a good living, changing political conditions led the family to leave for the United States in 1923. The Asimovs settled in Brooklyn, New York, where they owned and operated a candy store. Asimov was an excellent student who skipped several grades. In 1934 he published his first story in a high school newspaper. A year later he entered Seth Low Junior College, an undergraduate college of Columbia University. In 1936 he transferred to the main campus and changed his major from biology to chemistry. During the next two years Asimov's interest in history grew, and he read numerous books on the subject. He also read science fiction magazines and wrote stories. Asimov graduated from Columbia University with a bachelor's degree in chemistry in 1939.

Early influences

Asimov's interest in science fiction had begun as a boy when he noticed several of the early science fiction magazines for sale on the newsstand in his family's candy store. His father refused to let him read them. But

Isaac Asimov.
Reproduced by permission of AP/Wide World Photos.

when a new magazine appeared on the scene called *Science Wonder Stories,* Asimov convinced his father that it was a serious journal of science, and as a result he was allowed to read it. Asimov quickly became a devoted fan of science fiction. He wrote letters to the editors, commenting on stories that had appeared in the magazine, and tried writing stories of his own.

In 1937, at the age of seventeen, he began a story entitled "Cosmic Corkscrew." By the time Asimov finished the story in June 1938, *Astounding Stories* had become *Astounding Science Fiction.* Its editor was John W. Campbell, who would go on to influence the work of some of the most famous authors of modern science fiction, including Arthur C. Clarke (1917–), Poul Anderson (1926–2001), L. Sprague de Camp (1907–2000), and Theodore Sturgeon (1918–1985). Since Campbell was also one of the best-known science fiction writers of the time, Asimov was shocked by his father's suggestion that he submit his story to the editor in person. But mailing the story would have cost twelve cents while subway fare, round trip, was only ten cents. To save the two cents, he agreed to make the trip to the magazine's office, expecting to leave the story with a secretary.

Campbell, however, had invited many young writers to discuss their work with him. When Asimov arrived he was shown into the editor's office. Campbell talked with him for over an hour and agreed to read the story. Two days later Asimov received it back in the mail. It had been rejected, but Campbell offered suggestions for improvement and encouraged the young man to keep trying. This began a pattern that was to continue for several years, with Campbell guiding Asimov through his beginnings as a science fiction writer. His first professionally published story, "Marooned off Vesta," appeared in *Amazing Stories* in 1939.

Growing fame

During the 1940s Asimov earned a master's degree and a doctorate, served during World War II (1939–45) as a chemist at the Naval Air Experimental Station in Philadelphia, Pennsylvania, and became an instructor at Boston University School of Medicine. He also came to be considered one of the three greatest writers of science fiction in the 1940s (along with Robert

Heinlein and A. E. Van Vogt), and his popularity continued afterward. Stories such as "Nightfall" and "The Bicentennial Man," and novels such as *The Gods Themselves* and *Foundation's Edge,* received numerous honors and are recognized as among the best science fiction ever written.

Asimov's books about robots—most notably *I, Robot, The Caves of Steel,* and *The Naked Sun*—won respect for science fiction by using elements of style found in other types of books, such as mystery and detective stories. He introduced the "Three Laws of Robotics": "1. A robot may not injure a human being or, through inaction, allow a human being to come to harm. 2. A robot must obey the orders given it by human beings except where such orders would conflict with the First Law. 3. A robot must protect its own existence as long as such protection does not conflict with the First or Second Laws." Asimov said that he used these ideas as the basis for "over two dozen short stories and three novels . . . about robots." The three laws became so popular, and seemed so sensible, that many people believed real robots would eventually be designed according to Asimov's basic principles.

Also notable among Asimov's science fiction works is the "Foundation" series. This group of short stories, published in magazines in the 1940s and then collected and reprinted in the early 1950s, was written as a "future history," a story being told in a society of the future which relates events of that society's history. *Foundation, Foundation and Empire,* and *Second Foundation* were enormously popular among science fiction fans. In 1966 the World Science Fiction Convention honored them with a special Hugo Award as the best all-time science fiction series. Even many years after the original publication, Asimov's future history series remained popular—in the 1980s, forty years after he began the series, Asimov added a new volume, *Foundation's Edge.*

Branching out

Asimov's first works of fiction written mainly for a younger audience were his "Lucky Starr" novels. In 1951, at the suggestion of his editor, he began working on a series of science-fiction stories that could easily be adapted for television. "Television was here; that was clear," he said in his autobiography (the story of his life), *In Memory Yet Green.* "Why not take advantage of it, then?" *David Starr: Space Ranger* was the first of six volumes of stories involving David 'Lucky' Starr, agent of the outer space law enforcement agency called the Council of Science. The stories, however, were never made for television.

Asimov's first nonfiction book was a medical text entitled *Biochemistry and Human Metabolism.* Begun in 1950 it was written with two of his coworkers at the Boston University School of Medicine. His many books on science, explaining everything from how nuclear weapons work to the theory of numbers, take complicated information and turn it into readable, interesting writing. Asimov also loved his work as a teacher and discovered that he was an entertaining public speaker. Before his death in 1992, Asimov commented, "I'm on fire to explain, and happiest when it's something reasonably intricate [complicated] which I can make clear step by step. It's the easiest way I can clarify [explain] things in my own mind."

For More Information

Asimov, Isaac. *I. Asimov: A Memoir.* New York: Doubleday, 1994.

Asimov, Isaac. *It's Been a Good Life.* Edited by Janet Jeppson Asimov. Amherst, NY: Prometheus Books, 2002.

Boerst, William J. *Isaac Asimov: Writer of the Future.* Greensboro, NC: Morgan Reynolds, 1999.

FRED ASTAIRE

Born: May 10, 1899
Omaha, Nebraska
Died: June 22, 1987
Los Angeles, California
American actor, dancer, and choreographer

Fred Astaire was a famous dancer and choreographer (one who creates and arranges dance performances) who worked in vaudeville (traveling variety entertainment acts), musical comedy, television, radio, and Hollywood musicals.

Early years

Fred Astaire was born Frederick Austerlitz on May 10, 1899, in Omaha, Nebraska. His parents, Frederic E. and Ann Gelius Austerlitz, enrolled him in dancing school at age four to join his older sister Adele. The two Austerlitz children proved extraordinarily talented and the family moved to New York, where the children continued their training in singing, dancing, and acting. In 1905 Fred and Adele began performing in vaudeville. By 1917 they had changed their last name to Astaire and began performing in musicals. They appeared in successful productions on Broadway and in London, England, including the musical comedies *Lady, Be Good* in 1924, *Funny Face* in 1927, and a revue titled *The Band Wagon* in 1931.

When Adele retired from show business in 1932 to marry, Astaire sought to reshape his career. He took the featured role in the musical *Gay Divorce.* This show proved Astaire could succeed without his sister and helped establish the pattern of most of his film musicals: it was a light comedy, built around a love story for Astaire and his partner that was amusing, but basically serious—and featuring some great dancing, including routines Astaire was beginning to develop himself.

Astaire goes to Hollywood

In 1933 Astaire married Phyllis Livingston Potter and shortly afterward went to Hollywood. He had a featured part in *Flying Down to Rio* (1933). The film was a hit, and it was obvious that Astaire was a major factor in the success. *The Gay Divorcee* (1934), a film version of *Gay Divorce,* was the first of Astaire's major pictures with Ginger Rogers (1911–1995) and an even bigger hit. With seven more films in the 1930s (the most popular of which was *Top Hat* in 1935), Astaire and Rogers became one of the legendary partnerships in the history of dance, featuring high spirits, bubbling comedy, and romantic chemistry. By the end of the 1930s the profits from the Astaire-Rogers films were beginning to decline. Over the next few years

Astaire made nine films at four different studios and continued to create splendid dances, appearing with a variety of partners.

Other ventures

In 1946 Astaire retired from motion pictures to create a chain of successful dancing schools. In 1947 he returned to movies to make the highly profitable *Easter Parade* at Metro Goldwyn Mayer (MGM). Nine more musicals followed. Astaire's success was marred in 1954, however, when his beloved wife died from cancer.

By the mid-1950s the era of the Hollywood musical was coming to an end, and Astaire moved into other fields. On television he produced four award-winning musical specials with Barrie Chase as his partner. He also tried his hand at straight acting roles with considerable success in eight films between 1959 and 1982. Over the years he played a number of characters on television in dramatic specials and series. In 1980, as he entered his eighties, Astaire married Robyn Smith, a successful jockey in her mid-thirties. He died seven years later.

Ginger Rogers, Astaire's longtime dance partner, passed away in 1995. Rogers is often quoted as having said, "I did everything Fred did, only backwards and in high heels." Their partnership lasted sixteen years, from 1933 to 1949.

Looking back

Fred Astaire appeared in 212 musical numbers, of which 133 contain fully developed dance routines, many of which are of great artistic value. And, because he worked mainly in film, the vast majority of Astaire's works are preserved in their original form. Astaire's dances are a blend of tap and ballroom dancing with bits from other dance forms thrown in. What holds everything together is Astaire's class, wit, and apparent ease of execution.

Fred Astaire.
Reproduced by permission of the Corbis Corporation.

Astaire spent weeks working out his choreography. He also created an approach to filming dance that was often copied in Hollywood musicals: both camerawork and editing are used to support the flow of the dancing, not to overshadow it. Although his shyness and self-doubt could make him difficult to work with, Astaire was an efficient planner and worker. His courtesy, professionalism, and struggle for improvement earned him the admiration of his coworkers.

In January 1997, with Robyn Astaire's blessing, Astaire's image returned to television through special effects editing—Dirt Devil inserted its vacuum cleaners into dance scenes from Astaire's films for three of its commercials. The press criticized the commercials. The general feeling was that replacing Ginger Rogers with a vacuum cleaner was in poor taste.

For More Information

Adler, Bill. *Fred Astaire: A Wonderful Life.* New York: Carroll & Graf, 1987.

Gallafent, Edward. *Astaire & Rogers.* New York: Columbia University Press, 2002.

Mueller, John. *Astaire Dancing: The Musical Films.* New York: Knopf, 1985.

John Jacob Astor

Born: July 17, 1763
Waldorf, Germany
Died: March 29, 1848
New York, New York
German-born American businessman and industrialist

An American fur trader and businessman, John Astor used his profits from fur trading to invest in a wide range of business enterprises. By the time of his death he was the richest man in America.

Childhood poverty

John Jacob Astor was born in Waldorf, near Heidelberg, Germany, on July 17, 1763. He was named after his father Jacob Astor, a poor but happy butcher. His mother, Maria Magdalena Vorfelder, learned to be very careful with the little money the family had (a quality she passed on to her son). She died when Astor was three years old. Despite the family's poverty, Astor received a good education from the local schoolmaster. When he reached the age of fourteen he went to work as an assistant to his father. He did this for two years before striking out on his own in 1779. Astor joined one of his brothers in London, England, where he learned to speak English and worked to earn money to pay his way to America.

In 1783, after the peace treaty ending the American Revolution (1775–83; when the American colonies fought for independence from Great Britain) had been signed, Astor sailed for the United States to join another brother who had gone there earlier. The ship carrying Astor to America became stuck in ice before completing its voyage and remained there for two months. During this time, Astor met a German man on the ship who told him how much money there was to be made in fur trading. Astor finally landed at Baltimore, Maryland, in March 1784.

Success in fur trading

Astor soon joined his brother in New York and began to demonstrate his talent for business. He worked for several furriers and began buying furs on his own. In 1784 and 1785 Astor made trips to western New York to buy furs for his employers, purchasing some for himself at the same time. He acquired enough furs to make a trip to England profitable. In London he established connections with a well-known trading house, signed an agreement to act as the New York agent for a musical instrument firm, and used his profits from the furs to buy merchandise to use for trade with the Native Americans. Not yet twenty-two, he had already proved himself a shrewd and intelligent businessman.

Astor's early success convinced him that a fortune could be made in the fur trade. He began to spend more time managing and expanding his business. Between 1790 and 1808 his agents collected furs from as far west as Mackinaw, Michigan. The Jay Treaty of 1794, which led to the British leaving forts and trading posts in the Old Northwest, worked to Astor's advantage, and he expanded his operations in the Great Lakes region. Through an arrangement with the British Northwest Company, he purchased furs directly from Montreal, Canada. By about 1809 he was recognized as one of the leading fur traders in the United States.

John Jacob Astor.
Courtesy of the National Portrait Gallery.

Fur business grows

Following the Louisiana Purchase in 1803, which added land that contained part or all of thirteen more states to the union, Astor turned his attention to the fur trade in the Pacific Northwest. He obtained a charter (a grant of rights or privileges from the ruler of a state or country) for the American Fur Company and planned to establish a main fort at the mouth of the Columbia River, with subforts in the interior. His fleet of ships would collect the furs and sell them in China, where goods would be purchased for sale in Europe; in Europe merchandise could be bought to sell in the United States when the ships returned.

Although the town of Astoria was established on the Columbia, the company's operations were unsuccessful. After the War of 1812 Astor renewed his efforts to gain control of the fur trade in North America. Through influence in Congress he helped win passage of laws that banned foreigners from engaging in the trade (except as employees) and that eliminated the government's trading post serving independent traders. By the late 1820s he had sole control of the fur trade in the Great Lakes region and most of the Mississippi Valley. This put him into direct competition with the Rocky Mountain Fur Company and British fur interests in the Pacific

Northwest. However, by 1830 Astor's interest in the company had begun to decline.

Other importing

Through Astor's dealings in the fur trade he became involved in general merchandising. During the 1790s he had begun to import and sell a large variety of European goods. During this early period he showed little interest in establishing trade relations with China. Between 1800 and 1812, however, his trade with China expanded and became a large part of his business dealings in Europe. The War of 1812 temporarily disrupted his plans, but it also gave him an opportunity to purchase ships at a bargain price, since declining trade had made other merchants anxious to dispose of their fleets.

After the war Astor had a large fleet of sailing vessels and again became active in the China and Pacific trade. For a time he was involved in smuggling Turkish opium (an addictive drug) into China but found the profits were not worth the risk and abandoned this venture. Between 1815 and 1820 he enjoyed a commanding position in trade with China. Thereafter his interest declined, and he turned his attention to other business activities. One explanation for Astor's success as a merchant was that he had the money to buy quality merchandise at a low cost and a fleet of ships that could transport the goods to markets more quickly than his rivals.

Still dealing in later years

Astor retired from the American Fur Company and withdrew from both domestic and foreign trade in 1834. He turned to other investments, including real estate, moneylending, insurance companies, banking, railroads and canals, public securities, and the hotel business. The most important was real estate. He had invested some capital in land early in his career. After 1800 he concentrated on real estate in New York City. He profited not only from the sale of lands and rents but from the increasing value of lands within the city. During the last decade of his life his income from rents alone exceeded $1,250,000. His total wealth was estimated at $20–30 million (the greatest source being his land holdings on Manhattan Island) at his death on March 29, 1848, at the age of 84.

For More Information

Haeger, John D. *John Jacob Astor: Business and Finance in the Early Republic.* Detroit: Wayne State University Press, 1991.

Madsen, Axel. *John Jacob Astor: America's First Multimillionaire.* New York: John Wiley, 2001.

MARGARET ATWOOD

Born: November 18, 1939
Ottawa, Ontario, Canada
Canadian author, novelist, poet and cultural activist

One of Canada's best-known writers, Margaret Atwood is an internationally famous novelist, poet, and critic. She is also committed to positive change in our way of life.

Early freedom

Margaret Eleanor Atwood was born in Ottawa, Ontario, Canada, in 1939. She moved with her family to Sault Ste. Marie, Canada, in 1945 and to Toronto, Canada, in 1946. Until she was eleven she spent half of each year in the northern Ontario wilderness, where her father worked as an entomologist (insect scientist). Her writing was one of the many things she enjoyed in her "bush" time, away from school. At age six she was writing morality plays, poems, comic books, and had started a novel. School and preadolescence brought her a taste for home economics. Her writing resurfaced in high school, though, where she returned to writing poetry. Her favorite writer as a teen was Edgar Allan Poe (1809–1849), who was famous for his dark mystery stories.

Margaret Atwood.
Reproduced by permission of Mr. Jerry Bauer.

Atwood was sixteen years old when she made her commitment to pursue writing as a lifetime career. She studied at Victoria College, University of Toronto, where she received a bachelor's degree in 1961. Then she went on to complete her master's degree at Radcliffe College in Cambridge, Massachusetts, in 1962. Atwood also studied at Harvard University in Cambridge, Massachusetts, from 1962 to 1963 and from 1965 to 1967.

Honors and awards

Atwood has received more than fifty-five awards, including two Governor General's Awards, the first in 1966 for *The Circle Game,* her first major book of poems; the second for her 1985 novel, *The Handmaid's Tale,* which was made into a movie. In 1981 she worked on a television drama, *Snowbird,* and had her children's book *Anna's Pet* (1980) adapted for stage (1986). Her recognition is often reflective of the wide range of her work. She is also a major public figure and cultural commentator.

Most of Atwood's fiction has been translated into several foreign languages. A new Atwood novel becomes a Canadian, American, and international bestseller immediately. There is a Margaret Atwood Society, a *Margaret Atwood Newsletter,* and an ever-increasing number of scholars studying and teaching her work in women's studies courses and in North American literature courses worldwide.

Style and statement

Atwood has alternated prose (writing that differs from poetry due to lack of rhyme and closeness to everyday speech) and poetry throughout her career, often publishing a book of each in the same or consecutive years. While in a general sense the poems represent "private" myth and "personal" expression and the novels represent a more public and "social" expression, there is, as these dates suggest, continual interweaving and cross-connection between her prose and her poetry. The short story collections, *Dancing Girls* (1977), *Bluebeard's Egg* (1983), and especially the short stories in the remarkable collection *Murder in the Dark* (1983) bridge the gap between her poetry and her prose.

Atwood writes in an exact, vivid, and witty, style in both prose and poetry. Her writing is often unsparing in its gaze at pain and unfairness: "you fit into me / like a hook into an eye / a fish hook / an open eye" (from *Power Politics*) "Nature" in her poems is a haunted, clearly Canadian wilderness in which, dangerously, man is the major predator of and terror to the "animals of that country," including himself.

Atwood's novels are sarcastic jabs at society as well as identity quests. Her typical heroine is a modern urban woman, often a writer or artist, always with some social-professional commitment. The heroine fights for self and survival in a society where men are the all-too-friendly enemy, but where women are often participants in their own entrapment.

Atwood is also a talented photographer and watercolorist. Her paintings are clearly descriptive of her prose and poetry and she did, on occasion, design her own book covers. Her collages and cover for *The Journals of Susanna Moodie* bring together the visual and the written word.

Popular and accessible

Atwood is known as a very accessible writer. One of her projects, the official Margaret Atwood Website, is edited by Atwood herself and updated frequently. The Internet resource is an extensive, comprehensive guide to the literary life of the author. It also reveals a peek into Atwood's personality with the links to her favorite charities, such as the Artists Against Racism site, or humorous blurbs she posts when the whim hits. As well, the site provides dates of lectures and appearances, updates of current writing projects, and reviews she has written. The address is: http://www.owtoad.com

Margaret Atwood's contribution to Canadian literature was most recently recognized in 2000, when she received Britain's highest literary award, the $47,000 Booker Prize. Atwood donated the prize money to environmental and literary causes. Her generosity is not at all a surprising development to her many fans.

For More Information

Cooke, Nathalie. *Margaret Atwood: A Biography.* Toronto: ECW Press, 1998.

Howells, Coral Ann. *Margaret Atwood.* New York: St. Martin's Press, 1996.

VanSpanckeren, Kathryn, and Jan Garden Castro. *Margaret Atwood: Vision and Forms.* Carbondale: Southern Illinois University Press, 1988.

W. H. AUDEN

Born: February 21, 1907
York, England
Died: September 28, 1973
Vienna, Austria
English-born American poet

The English-born American poet W. H. Auden was one of the greatest poets of the twentieth century. His works center on moral issues and show strong political, social, and psychological (involving the study of the mind) orientations.

Early life

Wystan Hugh Auden was born on February 21, 1907, in York, England. He was the last of three sons born to George and Constance Auden. His father was the medical officer for the city of Birmingham, England, and a psychologist (a person who studies the mind). His mother was a devoted Anglican (a member of the Church of England). The combination of religious and scientific themes are buried throughout Auden's work. The industrial area where he grew up shows up often in his adult poetry. Like many young boys in his city, he was interested in machines, mining, and metals and wanted to be a mining engineer. With both grandfathers being Anglican ministers, Auden once commented that if he had not become a poet he might have ended up as an Anglican bishop.

Another influential childhood experience was his time served as a choirboy. He states in his autobiographical sketch, *A Certain World,* "it was there that I acquired a sensitivity to language which I could not have acquired in any other way." He was educated at St. Edmund's preparatory school and at Oxford University. At Oxford fellow undergraduates Cecil Day Lewis, Louis MacNeice, and Stephen Spender, with Auden, formed the group called the Oxford Group or the "Auden Generation."

At school Auden was interested in science, but at Oxford he studied English. He disliked the Romantic (nineteenth-century emotional style of writing) poets Percy Bysshe Shelley (1792–1822) and John Keats (1795–1821), whom he was inclined to refer to as "Kelly and Sheets." This break with the English post-Romantic tradition was important for his contemporaries. It is perhaps still more important that Auden was the first poet in English to use the imagery (language that creates a specific image) and sometimes the terminology (terms that are specific to a field) of clinical psychoanalysis (analysis and treatment of emotional disorders).

Early publications and travels

In 1928, when Auden was twenty-one, a small volume of his poems was privately printed by a school friend. *Poems* was published a year later by Faber and Faber (of which T. S. Eliot [1888–1965] was a director). The *Orators* (1932) was a volume consisting of odes (poems focused on extreme feelings), parodies (take offs) of school speeches, and sermons that criticized England. It set the mood for a generation of public school boys who were in revolt against the empire of Great Britain and fox hunting.

After completing school Auden traveled with friends in Germany, Iceland, and China. He then worked with them to write *Letters*

W. H. Auden.
Reproduced by permission of the Corbis Corporation.

from Iceland (1937) and *Journey To A War* (1939). In 1939 Auden took up residence in the United States, supporting himself by teaching at various universities. In 1946 he became a U.S. citizen, by which time his literary career had become a series of well-recognized successes. He received the Pulitzer Prize and the Bollingen Award and enjoyed his standing as one of the most distinguished poets of his generation. From 1956 to 1961 he was professor of poetry at Oxford University.

Poetic themes and techniques

Auden's early poetry, influenced by his interest in the Anglo-Saxon language as well as in psychoanalysis, was sometimes riddle-like and clinical. It also contained private references that most readers did not understand. At the same time it had a mystery that would disappear in his later poetry.

In the 1930s W. H. Auden became famous when literary journalists described him as the leader of the so-called "Oxford Group," a circle of young English poets influenced by literary Modernism, in particular by the artistic principles adopted by T. S. Eliot. Rejecting the traditional poetic forms favored by their Victorian predecessors, the Modernist poets favored concrete imagery and free verse. In his work Auden applied concepts and science to traditional verse forms and metrical (having a measured rhythm) patterns while including the industrial countryside of his youth. Coming to the United States was seen by some as the start of a new phase of his work. World War II (1939–45; a war in which France, Great Britain, the Soviet Union, and the United States fought against Germany, Italy, and Japan) had soured him to politics and warmed him to morality and spirituality.

Among Auden's highly regarded skills was the ability to think in terms of both symbols and reality at the same time, so that intellectual ideas were transformed. He rooted ideas through creatures of his imagining for whom the reader could often feel affection while appreciating the stern and cold outline of the ideas themselves. He nearly always used language that was interesting in texture as well as brilliant verbally. He employed a great variety of intricate and extremely difficult technical forms. Throughout his career he often wrote pure lyrics of grave beauty, such as "Lay Your Sleeping

Head, My Love" and "Look Stranger." His literary contributions include librettos (opera texts) and motion picture documentaries. He worked with Chester Kallmann on the librettos, the most important of which was T. S. Eliot's *The Rakes Progress* (1951).

Auden was well educated and intelligent, a genius of form and technique. In his poetry he realized a lifelong search for a philosophical and religious position from which to analyze and comprehend the individual life in relation to society and to the human condition in general. He was able to express his dislike for a difficult government, his suspicion of science without human feeling, and his belief in a Christian God.

Later works

In his final years Auden wrote the volumes *City without Walls, and Many Other Poems* (1969), *Epistle to a Godson, and Other Poems* (1972), and *Thank You, Fog: Last Poems* (1974), which was published posthumously (after his death). All three works are noted for their lexical (word and vocabulary relationship) range and humanitarian (compassionate) content. Auden's tendency to alter and discard poems has prompted publication of several anthologies (collected works) in the decades since his death on September 28, 1973, in Vienna, Austria. The multivolume *Complete Works of W. H. Auden* was published in 1989. Auden is now considered one of the greatest poets of the English language.

For More Information

Davenport-Hines, R. P. T. *Auden.* London: Heinemann, 1995.

Hecht, Anthony. *The Hidden Law: The Poetry of W. H. Auden.* Cambridge, MA.: Harvard University Press, 1993.

Smith, Stan. *W. H. Auden.* New York: Blackwell, 1997.

JOHN JAMES AUDUBON

Born: April 26, 1785
Les Cayes, Saint Dominigue (French colony)
Died: January 27, 1851
New York, New York
French-born American artist and ornithologist

American artist and ornithologist (one who studies birds) John James Audubon was a leading natural history artist who made drawings of birds directly from nature. He is mainly remembered for his *Birds of America* series.

Early life and move to France

John James Audubon was born in Saint Dominigue (now Haiti) on April 26, 1785. He was the son of Jean Audubon, a French adventurer, and Mademoiselle Rabin, about whom little is known except that she was a Creole and died soon after her son's birth. Audubon was an illegitimate child, meaning that his father was not married to his mother. Audubon's father had made his fortune in San Domingo as a merchant, a planter, and a dealer of slaves. In 1789 Audubon went with his father and a half sister to France, where they joined his father's wife. Their father and his wife adopted the children in 1794.

John James Audubon.
Courtesy of the Library of Congress.

Audubon's education was arranged by his father. He was sent to a nearby school and was tutored in mathematics, geography, drawing, music, and fencing. According to Audubon's own account, he had no interest in school, preferring instead to fish, hunt, and explore the outdoors. He was left with his stepmother most of the time while his father served as a naval officer. Audubon became a spoiled, stubborn youth who managed to resist all efforts to both educate him and keep him under control. When residence at a naval base under his father's direct supervision failed to have any effect, he was sent briefly to Paris to study art, but he disliked that also.

Business career in America

Audubon's father decided to send his son to America, where he owned a farm near Philadelphia, Pennsylvania. At first the boy lived with friends of his father. They tried to teach him English and other things, but after a time he demanded to live on his father's farm. There Audubon continued living the life of a country gentleman—fishing, shooting, and developing his skill at drawing birds, the only occupation to which he was ever willing to give effort. When Audubon began his work in the early nineteenth century, there was no such profession as a "naturalist" in America. The men who engaged in natural history investigations came from all walks of life and paid for their work—collecting, writing, and publication—from their own resources. Audubon developed a system of inserting wires into the bodies of freshly killed birds in order to move them into natural poses for his sketches.

In 1805 Audubon returned briefly to France after a long battle with his father's business agent in America. While in France he formed a business partnership with Ferdinand Rozier, the son of one of his father's associates. Together the two returned to America and tried to operate a lead mine on the farm. Then in August 1807 the partners decided to move west. There followed a series of business failures in various cities in Kentucky, caused largely by Audubon's preference for roaming the woods rather than keeping the store. During this period he married Lucy Bakewell. After the failures with Rozier, Audubon, in association with his brother-in-law, Thomas Bakewell, and others, attempted to start several more businesses, the last being a lumber mill in Henderson, Kentucky. In 1819 this venture failed and Audubon was left with only the clothes on his back, his gun, and his drawings. This disaster ended his business career.

"Birds of America"

For a time Audubon made crayon portraits (drawings of individual people) for $5 per portrait. Then he moved to Cincinnati, Ohio, where he became a taxidermist (one who stuffs and mounts the skins of animals) in the Western Museum that had been recently founded by Dr. Daniel Drake. In 1820 the possibility of publishing his bird drawings occurred to him. He set out down the Ohio and Mississippi rivers, exploring the country for new birds and paying his expenses by painting portraits. For a while he supported himself in New Orleans by tutoring and painting. His wife also worked as a tutor and later opened a school for girls. She became the family's main financial support while Audubon focused on publishing his drawings.

In 1824 Audubon went to Philadelphia to seek a publisher. He met with opposition, however, from the friends of Alexander Wilson (1766–1813), the other major American ornithologist with whom Audubon had begun a bitter rivalry in 1810. He finally decided to raise the money for a trip to Europe, where he felt he would find greater interest in his drawings. He arrived in Liverpool, England, in 1826, then moved on to Edinburgh, Scotland, and to London, England, signing up subscribers for his volumes in each city. Audubon finally reached an agreement with a London publisher, and in 1827 volumes of *Birds of America* began to appear. It took eleven years in all for the publication and reprintings of all the volumes.

The success of Audubon's bird drawings brought him immediate fame, and by 1831 he was considered the leading naturalist of his country, despite the fact that he possessed no formal scientific training. There was an intense popular interest in the marvels of nature during this era. Anyone who could capture the natural beauty of wild specimens was certain to take his place among the front ranks of those recognized as "men of science." Audubon had succeeded in giving the world the first great collection of American birds, drawn in their natural habitats as close to nature as possible.

Later years

With his great work finally finished in 1838, and the *Ornithological Biography* (a text-only book about birds) in publication, Audubon returned to America to prepare a "miniature" edition. He also began drawings for a new book (in collaboration with John Bachman), *Viviparous Quadrupeds of North America*, for which his sons contributed many of the drawings.

In 1841 Audubon bought an estate on the Hudson River and settled down to advise and encourage young scientists. It was during this period that the romantic picture of Audubon as the "American Woodsman," the great lover of birds, began to emerge. After several years of illness, Audubon suffered a slight stroke in January 1851, followed by partial paralysis and great pain. Audubon died on January 27, 1851.

For More Information

Blaugrund, Annette. *John James Audubon.* New York: Abrams, 1999.

Burroughs, John. *John James Audubon.* Woodstock, NY: Overlook Press, 1987.

Ford, Alice. *John James Audubon: A Biography.* Rev. ed. New York: Abbeville Press, 1988.

AUGUSTUS

Born: September 23, 63 B.C.E.
Rome (now in Italy)
Died: August 19, C.E. 14
Nola (now in Italy)
Roman emperor

Augustus was the first emperor of Rome. He established the principate, the form of government under which Rome ruled its empire for three hundred years. He had an extraordinary talent for statesmanship (the ability to take an active role in the shaping of a government) and sought to preserve the best traditions of republican Rome, the period in ancient Rome's history when governing power was in the hands of the Senate rather than the emperor.

Caesar's legacy

Augustus was born Gaius Octavius on September 23, 63 B.C.E., in Rome. His father had held several political offices and had earned a fine reputation, but he died when Octavius was four. The people who most influenced young Octavius were his mother, Atia, who was the niece of the Roman leader Julius Caesar (c. 100–44 B.C.E.), and Julius Caesar himself. Unlike Caesar, one of Rome's military heroes, Augustus was sickly as a young boy. Poor health troubled him throughout his life. Nevertheless his mother, who made sure the finest teachers tutored him at home, groomed him for the world of politics. By the age of sixteen he was planning to join his great-uncle and serve in Caesar's army.

At this time Rome and the areas it controlled were governed by the Senate, composed largely of members of a small group of upper class citizens who had inherited their positions. The generals who commanded the armies that conquered new territory for Rome's rule increasingly challenged the Senate's authority, however. One such general, Caesar, had basically become a dictator (someone who assumes absolute power) of Rome. The Senate strongly opposed Caesar, and in 44 B.C.E. conspirators (a group of people who plot in secret) assassinated (killed) him.

When Caesar's will was read, it revealed that Caesar had adopted Octavius as his son and heir. Octavius then set out to claim his inheritance in 43 B.C.E., changing his name to Octavian (Gaius Julius Caesar Octavianus in Latin).

Rise to power

Octavian's rival at this time was Mark Antony (c. 83–30 B.C.E.), who had taken command of Caesar's legions, the largest Roman military units. The two men became enemies immediately when Octavian announced his intention to take over his inheritance. Antony was engaged in war against the Senate to avenge Caesar's murder and to further his own ambitions. Octavian sided with the Senate and joined in the fight. Antony was defeated in 43 B.C.E., but the Senate refused Octavian the triumph he felt he was owed. As a result Octavian abandoned the senators and joined forces with Antony and Lepidus, another of Caesar's officers. The three men, who called themselves the Second Triumvirate (a group of three officials or government leaders in ancient Rome), defeated their opponents in 42 B.C.E. and assumed full governing power.

They then divided the empire into areas of influence. Octavian took the West; Antony, the East; and Lepidus, Africa. Over time Lepidus lost power, and it seemed impossible that Antony and Octavian could avoid clashing. In 32 B.C.E. Octavian declared war against Queen Cleopatra of Egypt, to whom Antony was romantically and politically tied. After a decisive naval victory in this conflict, Octavian was left as master of the entire Roman world. The following year Antony and Cleopatra committed suicide (killed themselves), and in 29 B.C.E. Octavian returned to Rome in triumph.

Augustus.
Reproduced by permission of the Corbis Corporation.

Political authority and achievements

Octavian's power was based on his control of the army, his financial resources, and his enormous popularity. The system of government he established, however, also recognized and made important compromises toward renewing republican feeling. In 27 B.C.E. he went before the Senate and announced that he was restoring the rule of the Roman world to the Senate and the people. To show their appreciation, the members of the Senate voted him special powers and gave him the title Augustus, indicating his superior position in the state. A joint government developed that in theory was a partnership. Augustus, however, was in fact the senior partner. The government was formalized in 23 B.C.E., when the Senate gave Augustus enormous control over the army, foreign policy, and legislation.

As emperor Augustus concerned himself with every detail of the empire. He secured its boundaries, provided for the defense of remote areas, reorganized the army, and created a navy. He also formed a large civil service department, which attended to the general business of managing Rome's vast empire. Augustus was also interested in encouraging a return to the religious dedication and morality of early Rome. His efforts included passing laws to regulate marriage and family life and to control promiscuity (loose sexual behavior). He made adultery (when a married person has a sexual relationship with someone other than his or her spouse) a criminal offense, and he encouraged the birthrate by granting privileges to couples with three or more children.

The succession

Augustus suffered many illnesses, but he outlived his preferred choices for legal heir. He was finally forced to appoint as his heir Tiberius, his third wife's son by her first marriage. Tiberius took power upon Augustus's death on August 19, C.E. 14.

For More Information

Jones, A. H. M. *Augustus.* New York: Norton, 1971.

Nardo, Don. *The Age of Augustus.* San Diego: Lucent, 1997.

Southern, Pat. *Augustus.* New York: Routledge, 1998.

AUNG SAN SUU KYI

Born: June 19, 1945
Rangoon, Burma (present-day Myanmar)
Burmese political leader

In 1988 Aung San Suu Kyi became the major leader of the movement toward the reestablishment of democracy in Burma (now Myanmar). In 1991, while under house arrest by the government for her activities, she was awarded the Nobel Peace Prize.

Early life

Aung San Suu Kyi was born in Rangoon, Burma, on June 19, 1945, the youngest of three children of Bogyoke (Generalissimo) Aung San and Daw Khin Kyi. (In Burma all names are individual and people do not have last names.) Her father is known as the founder of independent Burma in 1948 and is beloved in that country. He played a major role in helping Burma win independence from the British, and he was able to win the respect of different ethnic groups through the force of his personality and the trust he inspired. Her mother had been active in women's political groups before marrying Aung San, and the couple often hosted political gatherings in their home, even after the births of their children. In July 1947 Aung San, along with most of his cabinet, was assassinated by members of an opposing political group. He never saw his country become independent on January 4, 1948.

Aung San Suu Kyi spent her early years in Burma. She later joined her mother, who was appointed as Burmese ambassador (representative) to India in 1960. She was partly educated in secondary school in India and then attended St. Hugh's College, Oxford University, in England. While there, she studied politics, economics (the production, distribution, and use of goods and services), and philosophy (the study of ideas) and received her bachelor's and master's degrees. From her father she developed a sense of duty to her country, and from her mother, who never spoke of hatred for her husband's killers, she learned forgiveness. She also became influenced by the teachings of Indian leader Mohandas Gandhi (1869–1948), who was a believer in nonviolent civil disobedience.

For two years Aung San Suu Kyi worked at the United Nations (U.N.) in New York, New York. In 1972 she married Michael Vaillancourt Aris, a well-known scholar she had met while studying at Oxford. They had two sons and settled in England. Before they were married, Aung San Suu Kyi warned her fiancé that the people of Burma might need her one day and she would have to go back. She served as a visiting scholar at the Center for Southeast Asian Studies, Kyoto University, Japan, from 1985 to 1986 and at the Indian Institute of Advanced Studies in Simla, India, in 1987.

Government takeover and house arrest

After her mother suffered a stroke in 1988, Aung San Suu Kyi returned to Rangoon, Myanmar, to help take care of her. Later that year, there was a revolt against the overly strict administration associated with the militarily led Burma Socialist Party. This revolt started as a student brawl with no real political meaning. However, it was handled badly by the military and spread, becoming an expression of the unhappiness of the people that dated back to the last takeover in 1962. Unfortunately, the new group that took power, called the State Law and Order Restoration Council (SLORC), did not improve conditions in the country. In August 1988 Aung San Suu Kyi gained national recognition as the effective leader of the National League for Democracy (NLD), later opposed to the military-led SLORC. She became the general secretary of the NLD and was a popular and effective speaker in favor of democracy throughout the country. As a result she was placed under house arrest by the SLORC for attempting to split the army, a charge she denied.

Aung San Suu Kyi.
Reproduced by permission of AP/Wide World Photos.

Although Aung San Suu Kyi was not allowed to run for office in the May 1990 election, her party, the NLD, much to the surprise of the military, won 80 percent of the legislative seats. However, the winning candidates were never permitted to take office. For the first years of her house arrest Aung San Suu Kyi was not allowed to have any visitors, but later her immediate family was allowed to see her. In January 1994 the first visitor outside of her family, U.S. Congressman Bill Richardson, a Democrat from New Mexico, was allowed to meet with her. The United Nations called for her release, as did a number of other national and international groups, including Amnesty

International, the worldwide human rights organization. She won many awards for democracy and human rights, including the Sakharov Prize for Freedom of Thought (European Parliament, 1991), the Nobel Peace Prize (1991), and the International Simon Bolívar Prize (1992).

Restrictions continue

Aung San Suu Kyi remained under military watch and house arrest until July 1995. Afterward the government continued to restrict her movement both inside the country and abroad. During Aung San Suu Kyi's first year of freedom, she was only permitted to take short trips in and around her home city of Rangoon and did not travel outside Myanmar. She continued, however, to serve as the vocal leader of the NLD and push for democracy. The military government, meanwhile, closed schools, ignored the healthcare needs of the people, and forced many citizens into slave labor while torturing and imprisoning others.

In 1999 Michael Vaillancourt Aris, Aung San Suu Kyi's husband, died in England. He had been denied permission by the Myanmar government to visit his wife during the last year of his life. The government suggested she go to visit him, but she remained at home, fearing that if she left, she would not be allowed to reenter the country. In September 2000 she was again placed under house arrest after attempting to travel to rural areas outside Myanmar to meet with NLD members. In December of that year U.S. president Bill Clinton (1946–) awarded her the Presidential Medal of Freedom, the highest U.S. honor given to a civilian (nonmember of a military, police, or firefighting unit). The U.S. government also continued the ban on new investment in Myanmar and discouraged companies from doing business there as a protest against the military government's treatment of Aung San Suu Kyi and other citizens of Myanmar.

In December 2001, in Oslo, Norway, Nobel Prize winners gathered to protest Aung San Suu Kyi's continued detention and signed an appeal to the Myanmar government requesting that she and fifteen hundred other political prisoners be set free. In May 2002 Aung San Suu Kyi was finally released from house arrest. Once again free to move about the country, Aung San Suu Kyi drew large crowds wherever she spoke to her followers about freedom in Myanmar. "The NLD is working for the welfare of everyone in the country, not for NLD alone," she told an audience of supporters a few days after her release.

For More Information

Parenteau, John. *Prisoner for Peace: Aung San Suu Kyi and Burma's Struggle for Democracy* Greensboro, NC: Morgan Reynolds, 1994.

Stewart, Whitney. *Aung San Suu Kyi: Fearless Voice of Burma.* Minneapolis: Lerner, 1997.

Victor, Barbara. *The Lady: Aung San Suu Kyi, Nobel Laureate and Burma's Prisoner.* Boston: Faber & Faber, 1998.

JANE AUSTEN

Born: December 16, 1775
Steventon, England
Died: July 18, 1817
Winchester, England
English author, novelist, and writer

The English writer Jane Austen was one of the most important novelists of the nineteenth century. In her intense concentration on the thoughts and feelings of a limited number of characters, Jane Austen created as profound an understanding and as precise a vision of the potential of the human spirit as the art of fiction has ever achieved. Although her novels received favorable reviews, she was not celebrated as an author during her lifetime.

Jane Austen.

Family, education, and a love for writing

Jane Austen was born on December 16, 1775, at Steventon, in the south of England, where her father served as a rector (preacher) for the rural community. She was the seventh of eight children in an affectionate and high-spirited family. As one of only two girls, Jane was very attached to her sister throughout her life. Because of the ignorance of the day, Jane's education was inadequate by today's standards. This coupled with Mr. Austen's meager salary kept Jane's formal training to a minimum. To supplement his income as a rector, Mr. Austen tutored young men. It is believed that Jane may have picked up Latin from staying close to home and listening in on these lessons. At the age of six she was writing verses. A two-year stay at a small boarding school trained Jane in needlework, dancing, French, drawing, and spelling, all training geared to produce marriageable young women. It was this social atmosphere and feminine identity that Jane so skillfully satirized (mocked) in her many works of fiction. She never married herself, but did receive at least one proposal and led an active and happy life, unmarked by dramatic incident and surrounded by her family.

Austen began writing as a young girl and by the age of fourteen had completed *Love and Friendship.* This early work, an amusing parody (imitation) of the overdramatic novels popular at that time, shows clear signs of her talent for humorous and satirical writing. Three volumes of her collected young writings were published more than a hundred years after her death.

Sense and Sensibility

Jane Austen's first major novel was *Sense and Sensibility,* whose main characters are two sisters. The first draft was written in 1795 and was titled *Elinor and Marianne.* In 1797 Austen rewrote the novel and titled it *Sense and Sensibility.* After years of polishing, it was finally published in 1811.

As the original and final titles indicate, the novel contrasts the temperaments of the two sisters. Elinor governs her life by sense or reasonableness, while Marianne is ruled by sensibility or feeling. Although the plot favors the value of reason over that of emotion, the greatest emphasis is placed on the moral principles of human affairs and on the need for enlarged thought and feeling in response to it.

Pride and Prejudice

In 1796, when Austen was twenty-one years old, she wrote the novel *First Impressions.* The work was rewritten and published under the title *Pride and Prejudice* in 1813. It is her most popular and perhaps her greatest novel. It achieves this distinction by virtue of its perfection of form, which exactly balances and expresses its human content. As in *Sense and Sensibility,* the descriptive terms in the title are closely associated with the two main characters.

The form of the novel is dialectical—the opposition of ethical (conforming or not conforming to standards of conduct and moral reason) principles is expressed in the relations of believable characters. The resolution of the main plot with the marriage of the two opposites represents a reconciliation of conflicting moral extremes. The value of pride is affirmed when humanized by the wife's warm personality, and the value of prejudice is affirmed when associated with the husband's standards of traditional honor.

During 1797–1798 Austen wrote *Northanger Abbey,* which was published posthumously (after death). It is a fine satirical novel, making sport of the popular Gothic novel of terror, but it does not rank among her major works. In the following years she wrote *The Watsons* (1803 or later), which is a fragment of a novel similar in mood to her later *Mansfield Park,* and *Lady Susan* (1804 or later), a short novel in letters.

Mansfield Park

In 1811 Jane Austen began *Mansfield Park,* which was published in 1814. It is her most severe exercise in moral analysis and presents a conservative view of ethics, politics, and religion.

The novel traces the career of a Cinderella-like heroine, who is brought from a poor home to Mansfield Park, the country estate of her relative. She is raised with some of the comforts of her cousins, but her social rank is maintained at a lower level. Despite their strict upbringing, the cousins become involved in marital and extramarital tangles, which bring disasters and near-disasters on the family. But the heroine's upright character guides her through her own relationships with dignity—although sometimes with a chilling disdainfulness (open disapproval)—and leads to her triumph at the close of the novel. While some readers may not like the rather priggish (following rules of proper behavior to an extreme degree) heroine, the reader nonetheless develops a sympathetic understanding of her thoughts and emotions. The reader also learns to value her at least as highly as the more attractive, but less honest, members of Mansfield Park's wealthy family and social circle.

Emma

Shortly before *Mansfield Park* was published, Jane Austen began a new novel, *Emma,* and published it in 1816. Again the heroine does engage the reader's sympathy and understanding. Emma is a girl of high intelligence and vivid imagination who is also marked by egotism and a desire to dominate the lives of others. She exercises her powers of manipulation on a number of neighbors who are not able to resist her prying. Most of Emma's attempts to control her friends, however, do not have happy effects for her or for them. But influenced by an old boyfriend who is her superior in intelligence and maturity, she realizes how misguided many of her actions are. The novel ends with the decision of a warmer and less headstrong Emma to marry him. There is much evidence to support the argument of some critics that *Emma* is Austen's most brilliant novel.

Persuasion

Persuasion, begun in 1815 and published posthumously in 1818, is Jane Austen's last complete novel and is perhaps most directly expressive of her feelings about her own life. The heroine is a woman growing older with a sense that life has passed her by. Several years earlier she had fallen in love with a suitor but was parted from him because her class-conscious family insisted she make a more appropriate match. But she still loves him, and when he again enters her life, their love deepens and ends in marriage.

Austen's satirical treatment of social pretensions and worldly motives is perhaps at its keenest in this novel, especially in her presentation of Anne's family. The predominant tone of *Persuasion,* however, is not satirical but romantic. It is, in the end, the most uncomplicated love story that Jane Austen ever wrote and, to some tastes, the most beautiful.

The novel *Sanditon* was unfinished at her death on July 8, 1817. She died in Winchester, England, where she had gone to seek medical attention, and was buried there.

For More Information

Myer, Valerie Grosvenor. *Jane Austen, Obstinate Heart: A Biography.* New York: Arcade Pub., 1997.

Nokes, David. *Jane Austen: A Life.* New York: Farrar, Straus, and Giroux, 1997.

Tomalin, Claire. *Jane Austen: A Life.* New York: Knopf, 1997.

Tyler, Natalie. *The Friendly Jane Austen: A Well-Mannered Introduction to a Lady of Sense and Sensibility.* New York: Viking, 1999.

Baal Shem Tov

Born: c. 1700
Okopy, Poland
Died: c. 1760
Polish religious leader

The founder of modern Hasidism was the Polish-born Israel ben Eliezer, who is generally known as Baal Shem Tov.

Early life

Israel ben Eliezer was born to aged parents in Okopy, Poland, a small town that is now in the Ukraine, Russia. Most of what is known of his childhood is the product of legend and is difficult to verify. He was apprenticed (worked underneath someone in order to learn a trade from them) to the local teacher. Later he worked as an aid to the sexton (a person who looks after the grounds and building) of the synagogue (Jewish religious site), where he spent his nights studying the Cabala, or Jewish mystic lore.

Ben Eliezer married at the traditional age of eighteen, but his wife died shortly afterward. He then moved to Brody, in Galicia (a region of Eastern Europe), where he met and married the rabbi's sister. They moved to a distant village in the Carpathians (a mountain range in Eastern Europe). There Ben

Eliezer worked as a laborer, but he managed to devote considerable time to prayer and contemplation in the forest.

Becomes a religious leader

At this time Ben Eliezer learned the use of medicinal herbs for treating disease and became known as a healer and a worker of wonders. He was called the Baal Shem Tov, which means Good Master of the Name (of God). He ministered (treated) to his rural neighbors, both Christians and Jews, and performed miraculous cures of both body and soul. He is said to have undergone an important self-revelation at the age of thirty-six through the intervention of a divine spirit.

About 1740 the Besht (the common abbreviation of Baal Shem Tov) settled in Miedzyboz, Podolia. His kindliness and holiness attracted many followers, who were called Hasidim (the pious). The Besht's teachings emphasized spiritual communion (a meeting that takes place, not between physical bodies, but between spirits) with God, which was achieved not only in prayer but also in every aspect of everyday life. He taught that all man's deeds must express his worship of God. He disagreed with people who studied the Torah (Jewish religious writings) and worshipped as if it were a school lesson, precise and academic. He told his followers that worshipping should be done with a complete act of body, mind, and soul and should be joyous.

The Besht angered other Jews, who preferred to emphasize the rational discipline of prayer and study of the Torah. The Besht believed that he was a righteous person whose prayers opened the gates of heaven. He believed that others who had superhuman powers like him were born in every generation. He called these righteous leaders the tzaddikim (the "righteous ones"). His teaching especially appealed to those who were uneducated, because he said that the way to reach God did not require great learning. He used anecdotes (short, clever, or amusing stories) and parables (short stories told for the purpose of teaching a virtue or a religious idea) to illustrate his ideas. He criticized asceticism, the practice of denying oneself worldly pleasure in order to illustrate spiritual devotion. Instead he emphasized joy in observing Jewish law.

His followers, the Hasidim, changed many of the ways Judaism was traditionally practiced. For instance, they prayed in small rooms instead of in synagogues. This practice horrified other Jews, who felt it was too big a break with tradition.

Becomes a legend

Many legends grew up about the Besht. It was said he understood the language of plants and animals, and that he could walk on water. Some said that he talked to the Messiah (the king of the Jews who had been foretold by the prophets) on a regular basis. Still others believed that freedom would come to all Jews when the teachings of Baal Shem Tov were believed all over the world.

Baal Shem Tov wrote no works, but after his death his followers published compilations of his sayings and teachings. The Besht and the Hasidism had, and continue to have, a notable impact on Jewish life.

For More Information

Ben-Amos, Dan, and Jerome R. Mintz, eds. *In Praise of the Baal Shem Tov; the Earliest Collection of Legends about the Founder of*

Hasidism. Bloomington: Indiana University Press, 1970. Reprint, Northvale, NJ: Jason Aronson, 1993.

Buber, Martin. *The Legend of the Baal-Shem*. New York: Harper, 1955. Reprint, Princeton, NJ: Princeton University Press, 1995.

Heschel, Abraham J. *A Passion for Truth*. Woodstock, VT: Jewish Lights Pub., 1995.

Heschel, Abraham J. *The Circle of the Baal Shem Tov: Studies in Hasidism*. Edited by Samuel H. Dresner. Chicago: University of Chicago Press, 1985.

Klein, Eliahu. *Meetings with Remarkable Souls: Legends of the Baal Shem Tov*. Northvale, NJ: J. Aronson, 1995.

Rosman, Murray Jay. *Founder of Hasidism: A Quest for the Historical Baal Shem Tov*. Berkeley: University of California Press, 1996.

Charles Babbage

Born: December 26, 1791
London, England
Died: October 18, 1871
London, England
English mathematician and inventor

Charles Babbage was an English inventor and mathematician whose mathematical machines were based on ideas that were later put to use in modern computers. Indeed, Babbage is sometimes even called the inventor of the computer. He was also a pioneer in the scientific understanding of manufacturing processes.

A bright, curious child

Charles Babbage was born on December 26, 1791, in London, England. His father, Benjamin Jr., was a banker and merchant. One of his grandfathers, Benjamin Sr., had been mayor of Totnes, England. Babbage was always curious—when he would receive a new toy, he would ask his mother, Elizabeth, what was inside of it. He would then take apart the toy to figure out how it worked. Babbage was also interested in mathematics at a young age, and he taught himself algebra.

The Babbage family was wealthy, and Charles received much of his early education from private tutors. In 1810 he entered Trinity College at Cambridge University. He found that he knew more about mathematics than did his instructors. Very unhappy with the poor state of mathematical instruction there, Babbage helped to organize the Analytical Society, which played a key role in reducing the uncritical following of Sir Issac Newton (1642–1727; English scientist, mathematician, and astronomer) at Cambridge and at Oxford University.

In 1814, the same year of Babbage's graduation from Cambridge, he married Georgiana Whitmore. They had eight children together, but only three lived beyond childhood. Georgiana herself died in 1827.

Mathematical engines

In 1822 Babbage produced the first model of the calculating engine, which

Charles Babbage.
Courtesy of the Library of Congress.

would become the main interest of his life. The machine calculated and printed mathematical tables. He called it a "difference engine" after the mathematical theory upon which the machine's operation was based. The government was interested in his device and made a vague promise to fund his research. This encouraged Babbage to begin building a full-scale machine.

But Babbage had underestimated the difficulties involved. Many of the machine tools he needed to shape the wheels, gears, and cranks of the engine did not exist. Therefore, Babbage and his craftsmen had to design the tools themselves. The resulting delays worried the government, and the funding was held back.

Meanwhile, the idea for a far grander engine had entered Babbage's ever-active mind: the "analytical engine." This machine would be able to perform any mathematical operation according to a series of instructions given to the machine. Babbage asked the government for a decision on which engine to finish. After an eight-year pause for thought, the government decided that it wanted neither.

Other interests

Babbage managed to squeeze in an incredible variety of activities between dealing with the government and working on his engines. In addition to other subjects, he wrote several articles on mathematics, the decline of science in England, the rationalization of manufacturing processes, religion, archeology, tool design, and submarine navigation. He helped found the Astronomical Society, which later became the Royal Astronomical Society, as well as other organizations. He was Lucasian professor of mathematics at Cambridge for ten years. He was better known, though, for his seemingly endless campaign against organ-grinders (people who produce music by cranking a hand organ) on the streets of London.

He always returned to his great engines—but none were ever finished. He died on October 18, 1871, having played a major part in the nineteenth-century rebirth of British science.

For More Information

Campbell, Kelley Martin, ed. *The Works of Charles Babbage.* New York: New York University Press, 1988.

Collier, Bruce. *Charles Babbage and the Engines of Perfection.* Oxford, England: Oxford University Press, 1998.

Moseley, Maboth. *Irascible Genius: A Life of Charles Babbage, Inventor.* London: Hutchinson, 1964.

JOHANN SEBASTIAN BACH

Born: March 21, 1685
Eisenach, Germany
Died: July 28, 1750
Leipzig, Germany
German composer, organist, and musician

The works of the German composer and organist Johann Sebastian Bach are the utmost expression of polyphony (a style of musical composition in which two independent melodies are played side by side in harmony). He is probably the only composer ever to make full use of the possibilities of art available in his time.

Early life

Johann Sebastian Bach was born on March 21, 1685, in Eisenach, Germany, the youngest child of Johann Ambrosius Bach, a church organist, and Elizabeth Lämmerhirt Bach. There were musicians in the Bach family going back seven generations. The family was also devoutly Lutheran (a religion based on the faith of its believers that God has forgiven their sins). Bach received violin lessons from his father. He also had a beautiful voice and sang in the church choir. In 1694 his mother and father died within two months of each other. At age ten, Johann Sebastian moved to Ohrdruf, Germany, to live with his brother, Johann Christoph, who was the organist at St. Michael's Church. From him Johann Sebastian received his first instruction on keyboard instruments.

When an opening developed at St. Michael's School in Lüneburg in 1700, Bach was awarded a scholarship for his fine voice. After his voice changed, he was transferred to the orchestra and played violin. Bach often traveled to Hamburg, Germany, to hear other musicians. During this time he also began composing chorale preludes (organ compositions that were played before hymns sung in the Lutheran worship service). Bach graduated from St. Michael's School in 1702.

Develops organ skill

In 1703 Bach was hired as an organist in a church in Arnstad, Germany, which gave him time to practice on his favorite instrument and to develop his talent. He got into trouble on several occasions, once for fighting with a fellow musician and once for being caught entertaining a "strange maiden" in the balcony while he was practicing the organ. In 1705 Bach obtained a month's leave to visit a church in Lübeck, Germany, to hear the organist there. Bach was so impressed that he remained there for four months without sending word back to Arnstad about what he was doing. After returning to Arnstad, he began composing long organ preludes. After

Johann Sebastian Bach.
Courtesy of the Library of Congress.

people complained, he made the preludes extremely short. He also began changing and adding parts to the hymns that confused the churchgoers.

In 1707 Bach was appointed organist at a church in Mühlhausen, Germany, a larger and richer city than Arnstad. Later that year Bach married Maria Barbara Bach, his cousin. Bach wanted to present Mühlhausen with what he called "well-ordered church music." His pastor, Johann Frohne, liked both the mass and the music to be simple. The brilliant Cantata No. 71, *Gott ist mein König* (God Is My King), was written for the service at which new members were placed into the city council in February 1708. It so impressed the council that the music was printed and put into the city records. Still, the conflict between Bach's musical ideas and those of his pastor caused Bach to look elsewhere for a new position.

Working for royalty

Bach arrived in Weimar, Germany, in 1708 as court organist to Duke Wilhelm Ernst. His new position doubled his salary and allowed him to work in a stricter Lutheran environment. The years 1708 to 1710 saw an enormous output of original organ music by Bach. His reputation at the time, however, came mainly from his organ playing, not his compositions. Crown Prince Frederick of Sweden, who heard Bach play in 1714, was so astonished that he took a diamond ring from his finger and gave it to the organist.

In 1716 Bach became upset when he was not offered the opportunity to replace the duke's court conductor, who had died. At the same time Prince Leopold of Cöthen, Germany, heard of Bach and offered him a position. When Bach requested his release to go to Cöthen, Duke Wilhelm refused to accept such short notice. Bach, who had already accepted an advance in salary, became so angry that he was placed under arrest and jailed for almost a month. Bach began his duties at Cöthen after his release.

Prime of his life

In Cöthen Bach's prime responsibility was to conduct the court orchestra, in which the prince himself participated. In 1720 Bach's wife died, leaving him a widower with seven children. Late in 1721 he married Anna Magdalena Wülken, a twenty-year-old singer. She had to take over the difficult role of wife to a man of genius and also that of mother to his children, the oldest of whom was twelve years old. But she seems to have been equal to both tasks. In addition, during the next twenty years she presented Bach with thirteen more children.

Bach produced his greatest instrumental works during the Cöthen period. The other Cöthen musicians were all skilled performers, and their talent inspired Bach to write special music for them. Bach also wrote his major orchestral works during this period. He wrote many of his keyboard works for the instruction of his own children. However, after Prince Leopold married, he had less time for music, and the court orchestra had less to do. This decrease in importance, plus Bach's concern over his children's education, led him to look for another position in a strong Lutheran area. In 1723 he was named cantor (choir leader) of Leipzig, Germany, to replace the deceased Johann Kuhnau.

The Leipzig committee was reluctant to hire Bach. His reputation was mainly as an organist, not as a composer, and his ability as an organist was not needed since the cantor was not required to play at the services. His duties were primarily to provide choral music (designed for a choir) for two large churches, St. Thomas and St. Nicholas. In addition, special music was required on certain days of the church year and for other occasions such as funerals. Bach promised to perform not only the musical duties but also other responsibilities in connection with the St. Thomas School, such as teaching classes in music, giving private singing lessons, and even teaching Latin. While in Leipzig Bach composed the bulk of his choral music.

Later years

Bach gradually lost his eyesight during his final years, and he was totally blind the last year of his life. A few days before his death he read parts of the hymn *Vor deinen Thron tret' ich allhier* (Before Thy Throne I Stand) for his son-in-law to write down. Following a stroke and a high fever, Bach died on July 28, 1750. Four of his sons carried on the musical tradition of the Bach family. For Bach writing music was an expression of faith. Every composition was "in the name of Jesus" and "to the glory of God alone." His influence on music is well stated in the words of Johannes Brahms (1833–1897): "Study Bach: there you will find everything."

For More Information

Boyd, Malcolm. *J. S. Bach.* New York: Oxford University Press, 1999.

Eidam, Klaus. *The True Life of Johann Sebastian Bach.* New York: Basic Books, 2001.

Wolff, Christoph. *Johann Sebastian Bach: The Learned Musician.* New York: W. W. Norton, 2000.

FRANCIS BACON

Born: October 28, 1909
Dublin, Ireland
Died: April 28, 1992
Madrid, Spain
English painter and artist

Francis Bacon.
Reproduced by permission of the Corbis Corporation.

The English artist Francis Bacon was one of the most powerful and original figure painters in the twentieth century. He was particularly noted for the obsessive intensity of his work.

Early life

Francis Bacon was born in Dublin, Ireland, on October 28, 1909, to English parents. Raised with three siblings, Francis Bacon is a descendant of the sixteenth-century statesman and essayist of the same name. He left home at the age of sixteen and spent two years in Berlin, Germany, and Paris, France. In Paris he saw an art exhibit by the painter Pablo Picasso (1881–1973). Though he had never taken an art class, Bacon began painting with watercolors. He then settled in London, England, with the intention of establishing himself as an interior decorator and furniture designer. However, he soon turned to painting exclusively.

Bacon began oil painting in 1929. The few early paintings that survive (he destroyed most of them) show that he began as a late cubist (a twentieth-century movement that used geometric shapes). By 1932 he turned to a form of surrealism (using fantastic imagery of the subconscious) based partly on Pablo Picasso's works from about 1925 to 1928. Bacon began to draw attention in 1933 with his work *Crucifixion,* and the same year he took part in exhibitions in London.

Gains prominence after World War II

Bacon exhibited very rarely until 1945. It was only after World War II (1939–45; a war in which British, French, Soviet, and U.S. forces fought against Germany, Italy, and Japan) that his paintings became known outside his immediate circle of friends. At this time he also began to paint the human figure. The pictures that made his reputation are of such subjects as a melting head in front of a curtain and a screaming figure crouching under an umbrella. These extremely original works are impressive not only as powerful expressions of pain, but also for the magnificence of their presentation and professional quality.

By the early 1950s Bacon had developed a more direct treatment of the human figure, working almost always from photographs rather than from real life. Images taken from newspaper clippings or from the photographs of humans and animals by the nineteenth-century photographer Eadweard Muybridge were sometimes combined with images from the well-recognized paintings of the old masters. For instance, a series of paintings inspired by the portrait of Pope Innocent X by the Spanish painter Diego Velázquez (1599–1660) also uses a screaming face and eyeglasses that came from a close-up of a wounded nurse in Sergei Eisenstein's film *The Battleship Potemkin.* Such a combination of images drawn from completely unrelated sources is characteristic of Bacon's work.

Major themes and subjects

From the 1950s through the end of Bacon's painting career and life in the early 1990s, the consistent theme of his work was the isolation and pain of the individual, with a single figure (usually male) seated or standing in a small, windowless interior, as if confined in a private hell. His subjects were artists, friends, lovers, and even himself. His painting technique consisted of using rags, his hands, and dust along with paint and brush.

Bacon consistently denied that his paintings were used to explain his own life. The facts of his life, however, have tempted art critics and historians to draw links between his personal life and the subject matter of his paintings. One of the great tragedies of his life was the death of his longtime lover George Dyer, who apparently killed himself. Dyer's death occurred just before the opening of Bacon's major retrospective (a collection of the artist's work) in Paris, France, in 1971. Bacon's famous and moving *Triptych* (1973) was a three-paneled work of his dying friend hunched over a toilet, shadowed in a door frame and vomiting into a sink.

In a period dominated by abstract art, Bacon stood out as one of the few great representatives of the figure-painting tradition. During the last decade of his life major retrospective exhibitions were mounted at such sites as the Marlborough Gallery in New York, New York, in 1984, Moscow, Russia, in 1989, and the Museum of Modern Art in New York City in 1990. Bacon died of heart failure in Madrid, Spain, on April 28, 1992.

The year 1999 saw the release of the book *Francis Bacon: A Retrospective,* which analyzed the work of the artist. The book coincided with a national tour of many of Bacon's paintings.

For More Information

Farson, Daniel. *The Gilded Gutter Life of Francis Bacon.* New York: Pantheon Books, 1994.

Peppiatt, Michael. *Francis Bacon: Anatomy of an Enigma.* New York: Farrar, Straus, and Giroux, 1997.

Schmied, Wieland. *Francis Bacon: Commitment and Conflict.* Munich: Prestel, 1996.

ROGER BACON

Born: c. 1214
Ilchester, Somerset, England
Died: c. 1292
Oxford, England
English philosopher

Roger Bacon.
Reproduced by permission of Archive Photos, Inc.

The medieval English philosopher Roger Bacon insisted on the importance of a so-called science of experience. In this respect he is often thought of as a forerunner of modern science. Little is known for certain about the details of Roger Bacon's life or about the chronology of and inspiration for his major works.

Childhood, education, and university life

It appears that Bacon was born in Ilchester, Somerset, England. He was born into a noble family, although not a major one. In his youth he studied the works of the ancient Greeks as well as arithmetic, geometry, astronomy, and music. At thirteen years old he entered Oxford University, where he spent the next eight years. He eventually received an advanced arts degree.

In the 1240s, perhaps in the early years of the decade, Bacon lectured at the University of Paris, France, on the works of the ancient Greek philosopher Aristotle (c. 384–c. 322 B.C.E.). During this period he also wrote three works on logic, or the study of how to reason correctly. Within relatively few years there were three important events in Bacon's life: his return to England from France, the awakening of his scientific interests, and his entry into the Franciscan order, the Christian group founded by St. Francis of Assisi (1182–1226).

A universal science

Early on Bacon had the idea for a universal, or general, science that would promote the spread of Christianity, prolong life, aid health, and unite theology (the study of God and His ways) and the science of experience. He praised science as being "most beautiful and most useful." Bacon had other reasons for urging Christians to take up a science of experience. At the time there were many who believed that a struggle with the antichrist (or great evildoer whose arrival on Earth was predicted in the Bible) was near at hand. Bacon saw a science of experience as a Christian weapon for the fight.

It is quite likely that Bacon became a Franciscan in 1252. By Bacon's time the work begun by St. Francis had posed problems for his followers. Franciscans were required to take a vow of poverty, but their work had grown to such size and importance that it was impossible to continue it unless the order owned property and other possessions. The owning of property by the Franciscan order, however, was seriously questioned by a group of Franciscans. Bacon joined this group.

His works

About 1257 Bacon was taken from England to France and, for unknown reasons, underwent some kind of confinement, perhaps even an imprisonment, in a French monastery. One theory is that people questioned him because of his scientific interests, but it is more likely that his views on Franciscan life proved unpopular with some Franciscans in England.

During this period of confinement Bacon wrote his greatest works: *Opus majus* (major work), *Opus minus* (minor work), and *Opus tertium* (third work). Disagreements among scholars concerning the order and purposes of these works show once again the many unknowns concerning Bacon's life. In *Opus majus* he made use of scientific materials already written, added new material, and included a section on moral theory. With respect to the sciences, the overall tone of *Opus majus* is a plea, attempting to persuade the pope (the head of the Catholic Church) about the importance of experimental knowledge.

After the three works, Bacon wrote a great part of *Communium naturalium* (general principles of natural philosophy), one of his finest works. In 1272 he published another book on the study of philosophy in which the old, angry, argumentative Bacon reemerges. In it he claimed to see the presence of the antichrist in the then-warring Christian groups, and he took in general the extreme view of Franciscan life. It is also possible that an imprisonment in the final years of his life stems from this book.

Science's early friend

In many ways Bacon was ahead of his time. His works mention flying machines, self-driven boats, and an "instrument small in size, which can raise and lower things of almost infinite weight." He studied the heavens. He seems to have studied the refraction (bending) of light under experimental conditions. However, in his so-called science of experience he did not make any known advances in what is today called physics, nor did he make any known practical inventions. There is no evidence that Bacon made any important contribution to science, but there is much evidence that he was instead a reader, writer, and champion of science.

For More Information

Bridges, John Henry. *The Life and Work of Roger Bacon.* London: Williams & Norgate, 1914.

Easton, Stewart C. *Roger Bacon and His Search for a Universal Science.* Westport, CT: Greenwood Press, 1952.

Westacott, Evalyn. *Roger Bacon in Life and Legend.* Folcroft, PA: Folcroft Library Editions, 1974.

JOAN BAEZ

Born: January 9, 1941
Staten Island, New York
American musician, singer, and activist

American folk singer Joan Baez is recognized for her nonviolent, anti-establishment (against a nation's political and economic structure), and anti-war positions. She has used her singing and speaking talents to criticize violations of human rights in a number of countries.

Early life

Joan Baez was born on January 9, 1941, in Staten Island, New York. Her father, Albert V. Baez, was a physicist who came to the United States from Mexico at a very early age, and her mother was of western European descent. Joan inherited her father's dark complexion, and the occasional racial prejudice (hatred of a race) she suffered as a child probably led to her later involvement in the civil rights movement, a movement that called for equal rights for all races. Although as an adult she claimed not to share her parents' strict religious faith, it undoubtedly contributed to what some called her keen "social conscience."

Baez was exposed to an intellectual atmosphere with classical music during her childhood, but rejected piano lessons in favor of the guitar and rock and roll. Her father's research and teaching positions took the family to various American and foreign cities. When Joan was ten, she spent a year in Iraq with her family. There she was exposed to the harsh and intensely poor conditions of the Iraqi people, something that undoubtedly had an affect on her later career as a singer and activist. Baez went on to attend high school in Palo Alto, California, where she excelled in music more than in academic subjects. Shortly after her high school graduation in 1958, her family moved to Boston, Massachusetts, where Baez's interest in folk music surfaced after visiting a coffee shop where amateur folk singers performed.

From Boston coffeehouses to Newport, Rhode Island

Baez briefly attended Boston University, where she made friends with several semi-professional folk singers from whom she learned much about the art. In addition to simple folk songs, she began to sing Anglo American ballads, blues, spirituals, and songs from various countries. As she worked to develop her technique and range of songs, Baez began to perform professionally in Boston coffeehouses and quickly became a favorite of Harvard University students. She was also noticed by other folk singers, including Harry Belafonte (1927–), who offered her a job with his singing group.

In the summer of 1959 Baez was invited to sing at the Newport Folk Festival in Rhode Island. This performance made her a star—especially to young people—and led to friendships with other important folk singers such as the Seeger family and Odetta. Although the performance brought her offers to make recordings and concert tours, she decided to resume her Boston coffee shop appearances.

After Baez's second Newport appearance in 1960, she made her first album for Vanguard Records. Simply labeled *Joan Baez,* it was an immediate success. She was then such a "hot item" that she could choose her own songs and prop designs for her performances. In the following years Baez sang to capacity crowds on American college campuses and concert halls and on several foreign tours. Her eight gold albums and one gold single demonstrated her popularity as a singer.

Politics a source of controversy

While many critics agreed that Baez's untrained singing voice was unusually haunting, beautiful, and very soothing, they saw her spoken words, lifestyle, and actions as conflicting and sometimes anti-American. In the changing world of the1960s, Baez became a center of controversy (open to dispute) when she used her singing and speaking talents to urge nonpayment of taxes used for war purposes and to urge men to resist the draft during the Vietnam War (1965–73; when the United States aided South Vietnam's fight against North Vietnam). She helped block induction centers (which brought in new recruits) and was twice arrested for such violations of the law.

Baez was married to writer and activist David Harris in March 1968. She was pregnant with their son, Gabriel, in April 1969, and three months later she saw her husband arrested for refusing induction into the military forces. He spent the next twenty months in a federal prison in Texas.

In the early 1970s Baez began to speak with greater harshness. By the end of the decade she had offended dozens of her former peace-activist allies—such as Jane Fonda (1937–) and attorney William Kunstler—with her views on postwar Vietnam. As she had done in the case of Chile and Argentina (without public outcries from former associates), Baez called for human rights to be extended to those centers in the war-torn country.

Joan Baez.
Reproduced by permission of AP/Wide World Photos.

Baez's career through the 1980s and 1990s

In later years Baez's singing career faltered despite various attempts to revive it. Her 1985 effort featured a more conventional hairstyle and attire. Her supporters believed she would regain her prominence in the entertainment industry because her voice, although deeper, had the same qualities that made her so successful earlier. Meanwhile, she was quite busy throughout the world as the head of the Humanitas International Human Rights Committee, which concentrated on distracting (in any possible nonviolent way) those whom it believed exercised unauthorized power.

Baez has continued to make music and to influence younger performers. In 1987 Baez released *Recently,* her first studio solo album in eight years. She was nominated for a 1988 Best

Contemporary Folk Recording Grammy Award for "Asimbonanga," a song from the album. Also in 1988 Baez recorded *Diamonds and Rust in the Bullring* in Bilbao, Spain. The album was released the following April. In 1990 Baez toured with the Indigo Girls and the threesome were recorded for a Public Broadcasting Service (PBS) video presentation, "Joan Baez In Concert." In 1993 two more Baez recordings were released: *Play Me Backwards,* consisting of new material; and *Rare, Live & Classic,* a collection of her career from 1958 to 1989, featuring twenty-two previously unreleased tracks. Baez released *Gone from Danger* in 1997 and *Farewell Angelina* in 2002.

The singer's interest in politics and human rights has continued as well. In 1993 she was invited by Refugees International to travel to Bosnia-Herzegovina in order to help bring attention to the suffering there. In September of that same year Baez became the first major artist to perform in a professional concert on Alcatraz Island (the former Federal Penitentiary) in San Francisco, California. It was a benefit performance for her sister Mimi Farina's organization, Bread & Roses. She returned to the island for a second benefit in 1996 along with the Indigo Girls and Dar Williams. She has also supported the gay and lesbian cause. In 1995 she joined Janis Ian in a performance at the National Gay and Lesbian Task Force's Fight the Right fundraising event in San Francisco.

In 2001 Farrar, Straus, and Giroux released *Positively Fourth Street* by David Hajdu. The book is an intimate portrait that explores the relationships between Joan, Mimi Farina, Richard Farina, and fellow folkster Bob Dylan (1941–) during New York City's folk scene of the early 1960s.

For More Information

Baez, Joan. *And a Voice to Sing With.* New York: Summit Books, 1987.

Garza, Hedda. *Joan Baez.* New York: Chelsea House, 1991.

F. LEE BAILEY

Born: June 10, 1933
Waltham, Massachusetts
American attorney and author

F. Lee Bailey is a "superstar" lawyer and best-selling author. Bailey has been involved in a number of well-known cases, such as the trials of Patty Hearst, the Boston Strangler, and O. J. Simpson. Controversy has followed him throughout his career, often due to his willingness and ability to promote himself.

Early life and education

Francis Lee Bailey was born on June 10, 1933, in Waltham, Massachusetts. His mother was a teacher and nursery school director, and his father worked in newspaper advertising. Bailey grew up with two siblings. His parents divorced when he was ten years old. After attending Kimball Union Academy in New Hampshire, he entered Harvard University. An outstanding student, he nonetheless dropped out of Harvard to serve as a fighter pilot in the U.S. Marine Corps. Flying would be a lifelong passion. Bailey then went to law school at Boston University. Shortly after graduating in 1960, he married Florence Gott, but the two divorced in 1961.

The beginnings of stardom

Bailey was first noticed when he defended a doctor, George Elderly, who was charged with murdering his wife. The doctor—whose story served as the basis for the television series and film *The Fugitive*—was found not guilty. Soon thereafter, another doctor, Samuel H. Sheppard, who was also accused of murdering his wife, was found not guilty because of Bailey's defense. Bailey was on his way to stardom.

This new standout lawyer did not shy away from the spotlight. Indeed, Bailey drew criticism for appearing on television talk shows and discussing various cases. The Supreme Court of New Jersey even disallowed him from practicing in that state for a year. His second wife and former secretary, Froma, stood by while he was written about in magazines much the way a film star might be. He divorced Froma in 1972 and married Lynda Hart that same year.

Again Bailey used his stardom to further his career. He wrote *The Defense Never Rests* and *For the Defense,* as well as legal textbooks. Though Bailey lost his defense of Albert DeSalvo, a mental patient who admitted to being the Boston Strangler—a serial killer who had murdered thirteen women—the case did not damage Bailey's reputation.

Questions arise

The same could not be said, however, for the defense Bailey provided for Patty Hearst. The daughter of a publishing giant, Hearst claimed to have been kidnapped by a terrorist organization (an organization that achieves its ends by using violence) and forced to participate in a series of bank robberies. Bailey conducted a spirited defense, but Hearst was found guilty. She served twenty-two months in prison and eventually hired another lawyer, hoping for a second trial on the grounds that Bailey had not done his job well. Bailey's loss marked a turning point in the public's judgment of his courtroom abilities.

Bailey divorced Hart in 1980, then waited a full five years before getting married again, this time to flight attendant Patricia

F. Lee Bailey.
Courtesy of the Library of Congress.

Shiers. He continued to publish books, make speeches for $10,000 each, and speak regularly for a cause he cared a lot about: the necessity of reducing lawsuits.

Another strike against Bailey came when he represented the families of the passengers who had been on Korean Airlines flight 007, which was shot down over the Soviet Union in 1983. Though he made several public statements about his commitment to the case, his law firm put in a much smaller number of hours than did the two other law firms working on it.

In the mid-1990s Bailey was asked to join the defense team of O. J. Simpson, the football star turned actor who was accused (and later found not guilty) of murdering his ex-wife Nicole and her friend Ronald Goldman in Los Angeles, California. Bailey's questioning of Los Angeles police detective Mark Fuhrman was one of the most dramatic moments of the trial. Bailey, perhaps not surprisingly, gave himself high marks. "Other lawyers whom I respect told me that given what I had to work with, it was good." However, Edward Felsenthal of the *Wall Street Journal* said that "Americans who recently named F. Lee Bailey the most admired lawyer in the country might feel differently now that they have actually watched him in action in the O.J. Simpson case."

More troubles

In 1996 Bailey's reputation was questioned again. He was jailed after failing to hand over illegally obtained shares of stock and money from a former drug-dealer client to a court. Bailey was taken to court again in 1999 for refusing to give up $2 million from a jailed client. In 2001 the state of Florida prohibited Bailey from practicing law there.

In a television appearance Bailey argued that a person "in the business of defending criminal cases is going to live in controversy all of his or her life." Whether or not this is generally true, it certainly has been true for him. At the same time he has been a trailblazer for the superstar lawyers who have followed him.

For More Information

Bailey, F. Lee, and Harvey Aronson. *The Defense Never Rests.* New York: Stein and Day, 1971.

Whitten, Les. *F. Lee Bailey.* New York: Avon, 1971.

JOSEPHINE BAKER

Born: June 3, 1906
St. Louis, Missouri
Died: April 12, 1975
Paris, France
African American dancer and singer

Josephine Baker was an African American dancer and singer who lived in Paris, France, and was regarded as one of the most famous Americans living overseas.

Becoming Josephine Baker

Josephine Baker was born in a poor, black ghetto of St. Louis, Missouri, on June 3, 1906, to twenty-one-year-old Carrie MacDonald. Her mother hoped to be a music hall dancer but was forced to make a living as a laundress. Olive-skinned Eddie Carson, her father, was a drummer for vaudeville shows (theater that used a wide variety of acts) and was not seen much by his daughter. At the age of eight Josephine was hired out to a white woman as a maid. She was forced to sleep in the coal cellar with a pet dog and was scalded on the hands when she used too much soap in the laundry. At the age of ten she returned to school. Josephine witnessed the cruel East St. Louis race riot of 1917. She left the St. Louis area three years later.

From watching the dancers in a local vaudeville house, at age sixteen Josephine "graduated" to dancing in a touring show based in Philadelphia, Pennsylvania, where her grandmother lived. She had already been married twice: to Willie Wells (for a few weeks in 1919), and to Will Baker (for a short time in 1921). She took her second husband's name as her own—Josephine Baker.

In August 1922 Baker joined the chorus line of the touring show *Shuffle Along* in Boston, Massachusetts. Afterwards Baker was in New York City for the *Chocolate Dandies* (at the Cotton Club) and the floorshow at the Plantation Club in Harlem with Ethel Waters (c. 1900–1977). She drew the attention of the audience by clowning, mugging, and improvising. With her long legs, slim figure, and comic presence, her special style as an entertainer began to take shape.

Josephine Baker.
Reproduced by permission of the estate of Carl Van Vechten.

Baker goes to Paris

Baker went to Paris, France, for a top salary of $250 a week (more than twice what she was paid in New York) to dance at the Théâtre des Champs Elysées as a variety dancer in *La Revue Nègre.* With other African Americans, including jazz star Sidney Bechet, she introduced "le jazz hot" and went on to international fame on the wave of French intoxication for American jazz and exotic nudity. She quickly became the favorite of artists and left-intellectuals such as painter Pablo Picasso (1881–1973), poet E. E. Cummings (1894–1962), playwright Jean Cocteau (1889–1963), and writer Ernest Hemingway (1899–1961).

Baker survived a lawsuit regarding her abandoning Le Revue Nègre for a star billing at the Folies-Bergère in 1926. (The legal case was one of many in her life.) She was twenty when she was a sensation in the "jungle" banana dance: naked but for a string of rubber bananas around her waist. Soon banana-clad Josephine dolls were selling like hot cakes. Also, in 1926, she recorded her throaty voice for the first time. Magazine covers and posters added to her fame, and by 1936 Baker was one of the highest paid performers in the world.

A heroine in World War II

Baker married Jean Lion, a French industrialist, but the two were divorced by 1940, during the early months of World War II (1939–45; a war in which German-led forces fought against the United States and European nations). When Germany occupied Belgium, Baker became a Red Cross nurse, watching over refugees, or those forced to flee their own countries. When Germany finally occupied France itself, she worked for the French Resistance (the secret army that fought against the occupying German forces) as an underground courier, transmitting information "pinned inside her underwear" to Captain Jacques Abtey.

After spending years avoiding the United States, Baker returned in August 1963 to attend the civil rights march in Washington, D.C., a march that pushed for equal rights among all races. In October of that year she made a trip to Manhattan to sing, dance, and "fight bias," as *The New York Times* said. She flaunted her age: she would say she was sixty when she was really fifty-seven, but she seemed ageless to reporters.

Baker died in her sleep of a stroke on April 12, 1975. The Roman Catholic funeral service was held at the Church of the Madeleine in Paris, which was, after all, her true home. Josephine Baker will forever be remembered as someone who pulled herself out of poverty and the trauma of humiliation and made herself an international star, principally due to her love of dancing.

For More Information

Baker, Jean-Claude. *Josephine: The Hungry Heart.* New York: Random House, 1993.

Hammond, Bryan, and Patrick O'Connor. *Josephine Baker.* Boston: Little Brown, 1988.

Rose, Phyllis. *Jazz Cleopatra.* New York: Doubleday, 1989.

GEORGE BALANCHINE

Born: January 22, 1904
St. Petersburg, Russia
Died: April 30, 1983
New York, New York
Russian-born American choreographer

The Russian-born American choreographer George Balanchine formed and established the classical style (relating to music in the European tradition) of ballet in America.

Early life

George Balanchine was born Georgi Melitonovitch Balanchivadze in St. Petersburg, Russia, on January 22, 1904, the son of Meliton and Maria (Vassiliev) Balanchivadze. His father was a composer. Balanchine studied the piano as a child and considered a career in the military, which his mother encouraged. However, at the age of ten, he entered the Imperial Ballet School, where he learned the precise and athletic Russian dancing style.

After the Russian Revolution of 1917 (the rebellion of the Russian people against the ruler of Russia), Balanchine continued his training in a new government theater. In 1921 he entered the St. Petersburg Conservatory of Music to study piano while continuing work in ballet at the State Academy of Opera and Ballet. He used a group of dancers from the school to present his earliest choreographed works. One of the students was Tamara Gevergeyeva, whom Balanchine married in 1922. She was the first of his four wives, all of whom were dancers. In 1924, when the group traveled to Europe to perform as the Soviet State Dancers, Balanchine refused to return to the Soviet Union.

The manager of the Ballets Russes, Sergei Diaghilev (1872–1929), discovered Balanchine in 1925 in Paris, France. When Diaghilev's most famous choreographer, Nijinska, left the group, Balanchine took her place. At the age of twenty-one he became the main choreographer of the most famous ballet company (a group of ballet dancers who perform together) in the world. Balanchine did ten ballets for Diaghilev, and it was Diaghilev who changed the Russian's name to Balanchine. When Diaghilev died and the company broke up in 1929, Balanchine moved from one company to another until, in 1933, he formed his own company, Les Ballets.

George Balanchine.
Courtesy of the Library of Congress.

Work in America

Also in 1933 Balanchine met Lincoln Kirstein, a young, rich American, who invited him to head the new School of American Ballet in New York City. With the School of American Ballet and later with the New York City Ballet, Balanchine established himself as one of the world's leading classical choreographers. Almost single-handedly he brought standards of excellence and quality performance to the American ballet, which up to that point had been merely a weak copy of the great European companies.

In 1934 the American Ballet Company became the resident company at the Metropolitan Opera in New York. Audiences were treated to three new Balanchine ballets, *Apollo, The Card Party,* and *The Fairy's Kiss*—works that revolutionized American classical ballet style. Balanchine's style proved a bit too daring for the Metropolitan, leading to a conflict that ended the working relationship in 1938. Over the next several years he worked on Broadway shows and films and two ballets, *Ballet Imperial* and *Concerto Barocco,* which were created in 1941 for the American Ballet Caravan, a touring group.

In 1946, following Kirstein's return from service in World War II (1939–45), he and Balanchine established a new company, the Ballet Society. The performance of Balanchine's *Orpheus* was so successful that his company was invited to establish permanent residence at the New York City Center. It did so and was renamed the New York City Ballet. Finally Balanchine had a school, a company, and a permanent theater. He developed the New York City Ballet into the leading classical company in America—and, to some critics, in the world. Here he created some of his most enduring works, including his *Nutcracker* and *Agon.*

Keys to his success

Balanchine's choreography was not dependent on the ballerina's skills, the plot, or the sets, but on pure dance. The drama was in the dance, and movement was solely related to the music. For Balanchine the movement of the body alone created artistic excitement. He placed great importance on balance, control, precision, and ease of movement. He rejected the traditional sweet style of romantic ballet, as well as the more acrobatic style of theatrical ballet, in favor of a style that was stripped to its essentials—motion, movement, and music. His dancers became instruments of the choreographer, whose ideas and designs came from the music itself.

Balanchine died in New York City on April 30, 1983. Summing up his career in the *New York Times,* Anna Kisselgoff said, "More than anyone else, he elevated choreography in ballet to an independent art. In an age when ballet had been dependent on a synthesis (combination) of spectacle, storytelling, décor, mime, acting and music, and only partly on dancing, George Balanchine insisted that the dance element come first."

For More Information

Buckle, Richard, and John Taras. *George Balanchine, Ballet Master.* New York: Random House, 1988.

Kristy, Davida. *George Balanchine: American Ballet Master.* Minneapolis: Lerner, 1996.

McDonagh, Don. *George Balanchine.* Boston: Twayne, 1983.

JAMES BALDWIN

Born: August 2, 1924
New York, New York
Died: November 30, 1987
Saint-Paul-de-Vance, France
African American author and playwright

The author James Baldwin achieved international recognition for his expressions of African American life in the United States. During the 1960s he was one of the most outspoken leaders of the civil rights movement.

Early life

James Arthur Baldwin, the son of Berdis Jones Baldwin and the stepson of David Baldwin, was born in Harlem, New York City, on August 2, 1924. He was the oldest of nine children and from an early age loved to read. His father was a preacher in the Pentecostal church, and at the age of fourteen Baldwin also became a preacher. At eighteen he graduated from DeWitt Clinton High School, where he had written for a magazine put out by the school. Baldwin then realized that he wanted to write for a living.

In 1944 Baldwin met another writer named Richard Wright (1908–1960), who helped Baldwin secure a fellowship (a writing award) that provided him with enough money to devote all of his time to literature. By 1948 Baldwin had decided that he could get more writing done in a place where there was less prejudice, and he went to live and work in Europe with money from another fellowship. While overseas Baldwin completed the books *Go Tell It on the Mountain* (1953), *Notes of a Native Son* (1955), and *Giovanni's Room* (1956).

James Baldwin.
Reproduced by permission of Thomas Victor.

Spokesperson for civil rights movement

Returning to the United States after nine years overseas, Baldwin became known as the leading spokesperson among writers for the civil rights of African Americans. He gave popular lectures on the subject, and he quickly discovered that social conditions for African Americans had become even worse while he was abroad. As the 1960s began—and violence in the South increased—Baldwin grew increasingly angry. He responded with three powerful books of essays: *Nobody Knows My Name* (1961); *The Fire Next Time* (1963), in which he predicts future outbursts of black anger; and *More Notes of a Native Son.* These works were accompanied by *Another Country* (1962), his third novel. *Going to Meet the Man* (1965) is a group of short stories from the same period. During this time Baldwin's descriptions of Richard Avedon's photography were published under the title *Nothing Personal* (1964). Four years later came another novel, *Tell Me How Long the Train's Been Gone.*

In addition, the mid-1960s saw Baldwin's two published plays produced on Broadway. *The Amen Corner,* first staged in Washington, D.C., in 1955, was presented at New York City's Ethel Barrymore Theatre in April 1965.

Similar in tone to *Go Tell It on the Mountain,* it describes the strong religious feeling of the Pentecostal church. *Blues for Mr. Charlie,* which premiered at Broadway's ANTA Theatre in April 1964, is based on the case of Emmett Till, a fourteen-year-old African American from Chicago who was murdered by white people in Mississippi in 1955.

The assassinations of three of Baldwin's friends—civil rights marcher Medgar Evers (1926–1963), the Reverend Martin Luther King, Jr. (1929–1968), and the black Muslim leader Malcolm X (1925–1965)—destroyed any hopes Baldwin had that problems between the races would be solved in the United States, and he returned to France in the early 1970s. His later works of fiction include *If Beale Street Could Talk* (1974) and *Just Above My Head* (1979). Nonfiction writings of this period include: *No Name in the Street* (1972); *The Devil Finds Work* (1976), an examination of African Americans in the movie industry; and *The Evidence of Things Not Seen* (1985), a discussion of issues of race surrounding the child murders in Atlanta, Georgia, in 1979 and 1980. A volume of poetry, *Jimmy's Blues,* was issued in 1985.

Literary achievement

Baldwin's greatest achievement as a writer was his ability to address American race relations by discussing the effects of racism (unequal treatment based on race) on the mind. In his essays and fiction he considered the point of view of both the offender and the victim. He suggested that all people, not just one group of people, suffer in a racist climate. Baldwin's fiction and plays also explore the burdens society places on individuals. Two of his best-known works, the novel *Go Tell It on the Mountain* and the play *The Amen Corner,* were inspired by his years with the Pentecostal church in Harlem. In *Go Tell It on the Mountain,* for instance, a teenage boy struggles with a strict stepfather and experiences a religious awakening. Love in all of its forms became a key ingredient in Baldwin's writing. Later Baldwin novels deal honestly with homosexuality (sexual desire for members of the same sex) and love affairs between members of different races.

Baldwin's writing is noted for its beauty and power. His language seems purposely chosen to shock and shake the reader into a concerned state of action. His major themes are repeated: the terrible pull of love and hate between black and white Americans; the conflicts between guilt or shame and sexual freedom; the gift of sharing and extending love; and the charm of goodness versus evil. He describes the rewards of artistic achievement among the problems of modern life, including racism, industrialism (the influence of large corporations on everyday life), materialism (the pursuit of material wealth above all else), and a global power struggle. Everything that lessens or harms the human spirit is strongly attacked.

Final years

Baldwin remained overseas much of the last fifteen years of his life, but he never gave up his American citizenship. The citizens of France came to consider Baldwin one of their own, and in 1986 he was given one of the country's highest honors when he was named Commander of the Legion of Honor. He died of stomach cancer on November 30, 1987, in Saint-Paul-de-Vance, France, but he was buried in Harlem. One of his last works to see publication during his lifetime was a collection of essays called *The Price of the Ticket: Collected Nonfiction, 1948–1985.*

For More Information

Leeming, David Adams. *James Baldwin: A Biography.* New York: Knopf, 1994.

Washington, Bryan R. *The Politics of Exile: Ideology in Henry James, F. Scott Fitzgerald, and James Baldwin.* Boston: Northeastern University Press, 1995.

Weatherby, William J. *James Baldwin: Artist on Fire.* New York: D. I. Fine, 1989.

LUCILLE BALL

Born: August 6, 1911
Jamestown, New York
Died: April 26, 1989
Los Angeles, California
American actress and comedienne

The face of comedienne Lucille Ball, immortalized as Lucy Ricardo on the television program *I Love Lucy,* is said to have been seen by more people worldwide than any other. Known as "Lucy" to generations of television viewers who delighted at her rubber-faced antics and zany impersonations, she was a shrewd businesswoman, serious actress, and Broadway star as well.

A struggling star

Born Lucille Desiree Ball on August 6, 1911, she and her mother, DeDe, made their home with her grandparents in Celoron, outside Jamestown, New York. Her father died in 1915 of typhoid fever, a sometimes deadly disease that spreads through milk or water. Along with her brother, Lucille was then raised by her mother and grandparents, who took her to the theater and encouraged her to take part in her school plays.

Lucy's mother also strongly encouraged her daughter's love for the theater. The two were close, and DeDe Ball's laugh can be heard on almost every *I Love Lucy* sound track. But from Lucy's first unsuccessful foray to New York, New York, where she lost a chorus part in the musical *Stepping Stones,* through her days in Hollywood, California, as "Queen of the B's" (grade B movies were known for their lower production values), the road to *I Love Lucy* was not an easy one.

In 1926 Lucy enrolled at the John Murray Anderson/Robert Milton School of Theater and Dance in New York. Her participation there, unlike that of star student Bette Davis (1908–1989), was a terrible failure. The school's owner even wrote to tell Lucy's mother that she was wasting her money. Lucy went back to high school in Celoron.

After a brief rest, Lucy returned to New York City with the stage name Diane Belmont. She was chosen to appear in Earl Carroll's *Vanities,* for the third road company of Ziegfeld's *Rio Rita,* and for *Step Lively,* but none of these performances materialized. She then found employment at a Rexall drugstore on Broadway and later she worked in Hattie Carnegie's elegant dress salon, while also working as a model. Lucille Ball's striking beauty always set her apart from other comediennes. At the age of seventeen, Lucy was stricken with rheumatoid arthritis, a severe swelling of the joints,

Lucille Ball.
Courtesy of the Library of Congress.

and returned to Celoron yet again, where her mother nursed her through an almost three-year bout with the illness.

Returning to New York

Determined, Ball found more success in New York the next time, when she became the Chesterfield Cigarette Girl. In 1933 she was cast as a last-minute replacement for one of the twelve Goldwyn girls in the Eddie Canter movie *Roman Scandals,* directed by Busby Berkeley. (Ball's first on-screen appearance was actually a walk-on in the 1933 *Broadway Thru a Keyhole.*) During the filming, when Ball volunteered to take a pie in the face, the legendary Berkeley is said to have commented, "Get that girl's name. That's the one who will make it."

Favorable press from Ball's first speaking role in 1935 and the second lead in *That Girl from Paris* (1936) helped win her a major part in the Broadway musical *Hey Diddle Diddle,* but the project was dropped after the premature death of the male lead. It would take roughly another fifteen years for Ball to gain stardom.

Ball worked with many comic "greats," including the Three Stooges, the Marx Brothers, Laurel and Hardy, and Buster Keaton (1895–1966), with whom she developed her extraordinary skill in the handling of props. She gave a solid performance as a rising actress in *Stage Door* (1937), and earned praise from critic James Agee for her portrayal of a bitter, handicapped nightclub singer in *The Big Street* (1942).

Lucy goes red

Ball first acquired her flaming red hair in 1943, when Metro Goldwyn Mayer (MGM) officials signed her to appear opposite Red Skelton in Cole Porter's (1891–1964) *DuBarry Was a Lady.* (Throughout the years, rumors flew as to the color's origin, including one that Ball decided upon the dye job in an effort to somehow rival actress Betty Grable.)

It was on the set of a small film, *Dance, Girl, Dance,* that Lucille Ball first met her future husband, Cuban bandleader Desi Arnaz (1917–1986). Married in 1940, they were separated for much of the first decade of their marriage because of Desi's travels. The union, also plagued by Arnaz's work schedule, alcohol abuse, and outside affairs, dissolved in 1960.

I Love Lucy

Determined to work together and to save their marriage, Ball and Arnaz developed a television pilot (one show developed to sell to studios). Studio executives were not ready. The duo was forced to take their "act" on the road to prove its potential and to borrow five thousand dollars to found Desilu Productions. (After buying out Arnaz's share and changing the corporation's name, Ball eventually sold it to Gulf Western for $18 million.) It worked, and *I Love Lucy* premiered on October 15, 1951.

Within six months the show was rated number one. It ran six seasons in its original format and then evolved into hour-long specials. It won over twenty awards, among them five Emmys, the highest award for television programming.

The characters Lucy and Ricky Ricardo became household words, with William Frawley (1887–1966) and Vivian Vance (1909–1979) superbly cast as long-suffering neighbors Fred and Ethel Mertz. More viewers tuned in for the television birth of "Little Ricky" Ricardo than for President Dwight D. Eisenhower's (1890–1969) inauguration (swearing in as president). The show was the first in television history to claim viewing in more than ten million homes. It was filmed before a studio audience and helped revolutionize television production by using three cameras.

Lucy's legacy

The Lucy Ricardo character may be viewed as a downtrodden housewife, but compared to other situation comedy wives of television's "golden years," she was free of regular household duties. The show's premise was her desire to share the showbiz limelight with her performer husband and to leave the pots and pans behind. Later series featured Ball as a single mother and as a working woman "up against" her boss.

Following her retirement from prime time in 1974 Ball continued to make many guest appearances on television. Broadway saw her starring in *Mame* (1974), a role with which she identified. (Her other Broadway appearance after her career had "taken off" was in *Wildcat* in 1960.) Her last serious role was that of a bag lady in the 1983 made-for-television movie *Stone Pillow.*

Ball was married to comic Gary Morton from 1961 until the time of her death on April 26, 1989, eight days after open-heart surgery. She was survived by her husband, her two children by Arnaz, Luci and Desi Jr., and millions of fans who continue to watch her in reruns of *I Love Lucy.*

For More Information

Ball, Lucille, and Betty Hannah Hoffman. *Love, Lucy.* New York: Putnam, 1996.

Brady, Kathleen. *Lucille: The Life of Lucille Ball.* New York: Hyperion, 1994.

Morella, Joe, and Edward Z. Epstein. *Forever Lucy.* Secaucus, NJ: L. Stuart, 1986.

DAVID BALTIMORE

Born: March 7, 1938
New York, New York
American virologist

The American virologist David Baltimore was only thirty-seven years old when he received the Nobel Prize in Physiology and Medicine for his significant work in cancer research.

Early life and education

David Baltimore was born on March 7, 1938, in New York, New York, the son of Richard and Gertrude (Lipschitz) Baltimore. As a student Baltimore excelled in math, but quickly developed an intense interest in science. While still a high school student, he spent a summer at the Jackson Memorial Laboratory in Bar Harbor, Maine, experiencing biology under actual research conditions. This so affected him that upon entering Swarthmore College in 1956 he declared himself a biology major. Later he switched to chemistry to complete a research thesis (a research report, usually a requirement for graduation). He graduated in 1960 with a bachelor's degree with high honors. Between his sophomore and junior years at Swarthmore he spent a summer at the Cold Spring Harbor Laboratories. There the influence of George Streisinger led him to molecular biology, a branch of biology concerned with the structure and development of biological systems.

Baltimore spent two years doing graduate work at the Massachusetts Institute of Technology (MIT) in biophysics. He then left for a summer at the Albert Einstein Medical College and to take the animal virus course at Cold Spring Harbor under Richard Franklin and Edward Simon. In 1965 he became a research associate at the Salk Institute of Biological Studies, working in association with Renato Dulbecco. Here he met fellow scientist, Alice S. Huang, and the two were married on October 5, 1968. In 1972 Baltimore was appointed to a full professorship at MIT. In 1974 he joined the staff of the MIT Center for Cancer Research under Salvador Luria.

Received recognition

Baltimore received many awards for his work in cancer research. In 1971 he was the recipient of the Gustav Stern award in virology (the study of viruses), the Warren Triennial Prize, and the Eli Lilly and Co. award in microbiology (a type of biology that investigates microscopic life forms) and immunology (a branch of science that involves the study of the immune system). His most prestigious award came in 1975 when he shared the Nobel Prize in Physiology and Medicine with Howard M. Temin and Renato Dulbecco for research on retroviruses (types of viruses) and cancer. His research demonstrated that the flow of genetic information in such viruses did not have to go from DNA to RNA (deoxyribonucleic acid and ribonucleic acid, living cells that help define an individual's characteristics) but could flow from RNA to DNA, a finding that changed the central belief of molecular biology.

Baltimore's interests later took him further into the study of how viruses reproduce themselves and into work on the immune systems of animals and humans, where he concentrated upon the process of developing antibodies (proteins that help the immune system fight infection). Central to much of this work was DNA technology, in which he maintained an active interest.

Baltimore proved himself an effective educator, conducting seminars with graduate students as well as his peers. He also became successful at directing research rather than doing it himself, again working closely with students.

Research controversy

In 1989 Thereza Imanishi-Kari, with whom Baltimore coauthored a 1986 paper on immunology, was charged with falsifying data. Imanishi-Kari, an MIT assistant professor, was cleared in 1996 when a top government ethics panel (a group that judges behavior) declared they found no wrongdoing. Although Baltimore was never connected to any wrongdoing, the incident caused him to withdraw the paper. He was also pressured by colleagues to resign (quit) from his presidency at New York's Rockefeller University, which he did in 1991.

In 1998 Daniel Kevles, a humanities and scientific policy professor at the California Institute of Technology who had followed the case closely, wrote "The Baltimore Case: A Trial of Politics, Science, and Character." Kevles investigated the events and proposed that Imanishi-Kari and Baltimore were unjustly given a bad name.

Baltimore Chairs AIDS Vaccine Research Panel

Baltimore was an early supporter of government-sponsored research on acquired immune deficiency syndrome (AIDS, an incurable virus that attacks the body's immune system). In December 1996 Baltimore became the head of a new AIDS vaccine research panel for the Office of AIDS Research at the National Institute of Health. The panel was formed to step up the search for an AIDS vaccine. He also became the president of the California Institute of Technology in 1997.

David Baltimore.
Reproduced by permission of AP/Wide World Photos.

In 2000 President Bill Clinton (1946–) awarded Baltimore the National Medals of Science and Technology, the highest American award for science. He was honored for his discoveries in molecular biology, immunology, and virology.

Baltimore remains active in the scientific community. He is a strong supporter of the highly controversial issue of stem-cell research, a cancer research that takes cells from embryos. Baltimore argues that the study of such cells can greatly increase disease research. "Embryonic stem cells hold remarkable promise for reversing the devastation of human disease," Baltimore wrote in

The Wall Street Journal in 2002. "To refuse to allow [the country] to participate in this exciting research would be an affront [an offense] to the American people, especially those who suffer from diseases that could one day be reversed by these miraculous cells."

For More Information

Crotty, Shane. *Ahead of the Curve: David Baltimore's Life in Science.* Berkeley: University of California Press, 2001.

Sarasohn, Judy. *Science on Trial: The Whistle Blower, the Accused, and the Nobel Laureate.* New York: St. Martin's Press, 1993.

HONORÉ DE BALZAC

Born: May 20, 1799
Tours, France
Died: August 19, 1850
Paris, France
French novelist

The French novelist Honoré de Balzac was the first writer to use fiction to convey the social scene prevailing at a particular period in one country's history.

Childhood

Honoré de Balzac was born in Tours, France, on May 20, 1799, the eldest son of four children of Bernard François and Anne Charlotte Balzac. His mother was thirty-two years younger than his father, and the young Honoré was taken into another home and cared for until the age of four. His mother saw the birth of her son as her duty and treated him indifferently. Her lack of affection overshadowed his childhood. Sent to boarding school at the age of eight, Honoré sought a place to escape from the fierce school discipline. He found this place in books. But excessive reading eventually brought on a nervous condition, which affected his health, and he was brought home in 1813. The following year his family moved to Paris, France, where he completed his secondary education in law.

Adulthood

Rebelling against his parents, Balzac refused to enter the legal profession and instead declared writing as his profession. Despite disappointment, his father provided a small allowance with the understanding that he had to be financially independent within two years. Working together with friends, Balzac wrote several sensational (superficial, appealing to the senses) novels, none signed with his own name. These books were without literary merit, but he earned his living by them.

Searching for ways to make his fortune more rapidly, Balzac next entered a series of business ventures using borrowed funds. These commercial ventures were also failures, leaving him with very large debts.

Thereafter he published the first novel that he signed with his own name. *Le Dernier Chouan* was a historical novel. Since historical novels were the fashion, the book was well received. But real fame came to him two years later, when he published *La Peau de chagrin,* a fantasy that acts as an allegory (a symbolic representation) of the conflict between the will to enjoy and the will to survive.

Author and socialite

The constant struggle to earn enough to keep his creditors at bay drove him to a timetable of work that eventually ruined his health. He increased his hours from ten to fourteen or even eighteen a day, keeping himself awake with frequent cups of strong coffee. Whenever Balzac took a break from his writing, he would frequent fashionable salons (stylish lounges), where he was well received by female readers.

Honoré de Balzac.

The Human Comedy

Balzac's lifework consists of a series of some ninety novels and short stories collected under the title *La Comédie humaine* (*The Human Comedy*) in 1841. *The Human Comedy* was subdivided into smaller groups of novels: "Scenes of Private Life," "Scenes of Political Life," "Scenes of Parisian," "Provincial," and "Country Life." There was a separate group of "Philosophical Studies."

The novels were linked by both history and character. This practice enhanced the realistic illusion and also permitted Balzac to develop the psychology (involving the mind) of individual characters more fully than would have been feasible within the limits of a single novel.

Social and ethical assumptions

In a preface to his work in 1842, he defined his function as that of "secretary of French society." Accordingly, every class of people, from aristocrat to peasant, has a place in *The Human Comedy.*

Balzac often assigned the basest (lowest in value or quality) motivations to his characters. He once wrote that the lust for gold and the search for pleasure were the sole principles that ruled humanity. The monomaniac—the man obsessed by a purpose or passion, to the point of sacrificing his own comfort and the welfare of his dependents—is constantly encountered in Balzac's more impressive novels.

Balzac was writing in an age when the struggle for existence or social advancement among the poor was at its fiercest. Balzac himself disliked the disorderly individualism that he observed around him. Human nature, in his view, was basically depraved (morally wrong; evil); any machinery—legal, political, or religious— whereby the wickedness of men could be stopped, ought to be repaired and strengthened.

Marriage and death

During his last years Balzac suffered from poor health, and his morale had been weakened by the disappointments he endured in his one great love affair. In 1832 he had received his first letter from Madame Hanska, the wife of a Polish nobleman. Thereafter they kept up a correspondence, interrupted by occasional vacations spent together in different parts of Europe. In 1841 her husband died, but Madame Hanska obstinately refused to marry Balzac. Only when he fell gravely ill did she agree. The wedding took place at her home on March 14, 1850. The long journey back to France took a serious toll on Balzac's health, and he died on August 18, 1850.

For More Information

Keim, Albert, and Louis Lumet. *Honoré de Balzac.* New York: Haskell House, 1974.

Robb, Graham. *Balzac: A Life.* New York: Norton, 1994.

BENJAMIN BANNEKER

Born: November 9, 1731
Baltimore County, Maryland
Died: October 9, 1806
Baltimore County, Maryland
African American scientist and inventor

From 1792 through 1797 Benjamin Banneker, an African American mathematician and amateur astronomer, calculated ephemerides (tables of the locations of stars and planets) for almanacs that were widely distributed and influential. Because of these works, Banneker became one of the most famous African Americans in early U.S. history.

Early life

On November 9, 1731, Benjamin Banneker was born in Baltimore County, Maryland. He was the son of an African slave named Robert, who had bought his own freedom, and of Mary Banneky, who was the daughter of an Englishwoman and a free African slave. Benjamin grew up on his father's farm with three sisters. After learning to read from his mother and grandmother, Benjamin read the bible to his family in the evening. He attended a nearby Quaker country school for several seasons, but this was the extent of his formal education. He later taught himself literature, history, and mathematics, and he enjoyed reading.

As he grew into an adult, Banneker inherited the farm left to him by his grandparents. He expanded the already successful farm, where he grew tobacco. In 1761, at the age of thirty, Banneker constructed a striking wooden clock without having ever seen a clock before (although he had examined a pocket watch). He painstakingly carved the toothed wheels and gears of the clock out of seasoned wood. The clock operated successfully until the time of his death.

Interest in astronomy

At the age of fifty-eight Banneker became interested in astronomy (the study of the universe) through the influence of a neighbor, George Ellicott, who lent him several books on the subject as well as a telescope and drafting instruments (tools used in astronomy). Without further guidance or assistance, Banneker taught himself the science of astronomy. He made projections for solar (of the Sun) and lunar (of the Moon) eclipses and computed ephemerides for an almanac. In 1791 Banneker was unable to sell his observations, but these rejections did not stop his studies.

In February 1791 Major Andrew Ellicott (1754–1820), an American surveyor (one who maps out new lands for development), was appointed to survey the 10-mile square of the Federal Territory for a new national capital. Banneker worked in the field for several months as Ellicott's scientific assistant. After the base lines and boundaries had been established and Banneker had returned home, he prepared an ephemeris for the following year, which was published in Baltimore in *Benjamin Banneker's Pennsylvania, Delaware, Maryland and Virginia Almanack and Ephemeris, for the Year of Our Lord, 1792; Being Bissextile, or Leap-Year, and the Sixteenth Year of American Independence.* Banneker's calculations would give the positions of the planets and stars for each day of the year, and his almanacs were published every year from 1792 until 1797.

Benjamin Banneker.
Reproduced by permission of Fisk University Library.

Communications with Thomas Jefferson

Banneker forwarded a copy of his calculations to Thomas Jefferson (1743–1826), then secretary of state, with a letter criticizing Jefferson for his proslavery views and urging the abolishment (ending) of slavery of African American people. He compared such slavery to the enslavement of the American colonies by the British crown. Jefferson acknowledged Banneker's letter and forwarded it to the Marquis de Condorcet, the secretary of the Académie des Sciences in Paris. The exchange of letters between Banneker and Jefferson was published as a separate pamphlet, and was given wide publicity at the time the first almanac was published. The two letters were reprinted in Banneker's almanac for 1793, which also included "A Plan for an Office of Peace," which was the work of Dr. Benjamin Rush (1745–1813). The abolition societies of Maryland and Pennsylvania were very helpful in the publication of Banneker's almanacs, which were widely distributed as an example of an

African American's work and to demonstrate the equal mental abilities of the races.

The last known issue of Banneker's almanacs appeared for the year 1797, because of lessening interest in the antislavery movement. Nevertheless, he prepared ephemerides for each year until 1804. He also published a treatise (a formal writing) on bees and computed the cycle of the seventeen-year locust.

Banneker never married. He died on October 9, 1806, and was buried in the family burial ground near his house. Among the memorabilia preserved from his life were his commonplace book and the manuscript journal in which he had entered astronomical calculations and personal notations. Writers who described his achievements as that of the first African American scientist have kept Banneker's memory alive. Recent studies have proven Banneker's status as an extremely capable mathematician and amateur astronomer.

For More Information

Bedini, Silvio A. *The Life of Benjamin Banneker.* New York: Scribner, 1971.

Ferris, Jerri. *What Are You Figuring Now? A Story About Benjamin Banneker.* New York: Scholastic, 1988.

Pinckney, Andrea Davis. *Dear Benjamin Banneker.* San Diego: Harcourt Brace, 1994.

FREDERICK BANTING

Born: November 14, 1891
Alliston, Ontario, Canada
Died: February 21, 1941
Newfoundland, Canada
Canadian medical researcher and scientist

The Canadian medical scientist Frederick Banting was codiscoverer of insulin, a hormone that regulates the sugar in the blood and helps in the treatment of diabetes (a disorder that causes the body to have difficulty maintaining a healthy blood sugar level). Because of this discovery, Banting became the first Canadian to be awarded the Nobel Prize.

Childhood

Frederick Grant Banting was born in Alliston, Ontario, Canada, on November 14, 1891, to William Thompson Banting, a well-established farmer, and Margaret Grant Banting, who had moved to Canada from Ireland. The youngest of five children, Banting attended the local elementary schools before enrolling at the University of Toronto in 1911 in an arts course leading to theology (the study of religion).He decided, however, that he wanted to be a doctor, and in 1912 he registered as a medical student.

With World War I (1914–18, a war in which German-led forces fought for European control) under way, Banting left college in 1915 to join the medical corps as a private (the lowest military rank). Doctors were urgently needed, however, and he was sent back to finish his studies, graduating in 1916. Banting was commissioned (made an officer) in the Royal Canadian Army Medical Corps and left for England, where he received exceptional surgical experience in several army hospitals.

In 1920 Banting moved to London, Ontario, and opened a medical office. One evening he read an article dealing with new discoveries in fighting diabetes, a blood disorder. Banting's interest in diabetes stemmed from his school days when a classmate had died because of the disorder. This event affected him deeply, and now his mind eagerly looked for possibilities worthy of investigation.

Frederick Banting.
Courtesy of the Library of Congress.

Initiation of the insulin work

In 1920 Banting went to Toronto for an interview with the professor of physiology (the study of life systems) Dr. J. J. R. Macleod (1876–1902). Banting described his ideas and his desire to investigate the fluids released by the pancreas, a gland located near the stomach. He begged for an opportunity to try out his theories in the laboratory, but Macleod refused, for he knew that Banting had no training in research. Banting returned to Toronto several times to try to persuade Macleod. Finally, impressed by his enthusiasm and determination, Macleod promised Banting the use of the laboratory for eight weeks during the summer. Macleod knew that if Banting was to have any success, someone who knew the latest chemical techniques would have to work with him. Charles Best (1899–1978), completing courses in physiology and biochemistry (the study of biological processes), had been working on a problem related to diabetes in Macleod's department. Banting and Best met and decided that work would begin on May 17, 1921, the day following Best's final examination.

Discovery of insulin

The first attempts to produce a diabetic condition upon which to study the effect of pancreatic secretions were not successful. The observations were repeated time and again until, finally, there was convincing evidence that the fluids taken from the pancreas secretions did produce the dramatic effect that was being sought in animals lacking a pancreas.

As the material was extracted from the microscopic islands of Langerhans (cells of the pancreas, different from the majority, which are grouped together in tissue named after Paul Langerhans [1847–1888], the German physician who discovered them), it was called "isletin." Later the name was changed to "insulin," meaning island. Again and again the same successful results were obtained, and when Macleod returned to Toronto at the end of the summer, he was finally convinced that Banting and Best had captured the correct hormone (a substance produced by an organ) to prove Banting's theory.

On November 14, 1921, Banting and Best presented their findings before the Physiological Journal Club of the University of Toronto, and later that month a paper entitled "The Internal Secretion of the Pancreas" was submitted for publication in the *Journal of Laboratory and Clinical Medicine*. News of the discovery brought scientists from many parts of the world, as well as diabetics and their families, to Toronto.

Nobel Prize and other honors

In 1923 Banting received the Nobel Prize in Physiology or Medicine jointly with Macleod. With characteristic generosity he divided his share with Best. That year the university established the Banting and Best Department of Medical Research with a special grant from the Ontario Legislature. In 1934 Banting was made a knight commander of the British Empire and the following year was elected a fellow (associate) of the Royal Society of London.

Banting was killed in a plane crash on the coast of Newfoundland on February 21, 1941, while on a war mission to England. Because of his research and advancements, Banting has improved the lives of diabetics around the world.

For More Information

Bankston, John. *Frederick Banting and the Discovery of Insulin.* Bear, DE: Mitchell Lane, 2002.

Bliss, Michael. *Banting: A Biography.* Toronto, Ont.: McClelland and Stewart, 1984.

Shaw, Margaret Mason. *Frederick Banting.* Don Mills, Ont.: Fitzhenry & Whiteside, 1976.

KLAUS BARBIE

Born: October 25, 1913
Bad Godesberg, Germany
Died: September 25, 1991
Lyon, France
German military leader

Klaus Barbie, known as the "Butcher of Lyon," was a leader in the Nazi group called the SS, and was head of anti-Resistance operations in France during the German occupation of World War II (1935–45). As a war criminal (someone who commits crimes that violate the conventions of warfare during wartime) Barbie lived in Bolivia as Klaus Altmann for thirty years before he was arrested and returned to France for trial.

Shadow of war

Klaus Barbie was born October 25, 1913, in the town of Bad Godesberg, a few miles down the Rhine River from Bonn, Germany. The son of a schoolteacher, he spent an uneventful childhood as a good but not brilliant student with a gift for languages. His father had served and had been wounded in

World War I (1914–18). Klaus Barbie grew up in a Germany that had been bitterly humiliated by its defeat in the war.

Barbie's father died in 1932, leaving the family with little money. With no funds to go to college, he began working for the National Socialist Germany Workers Party (Nazi Party), the party that brought Adolf Hitler (1889–1945) to power in Germany.

A sinister career

Hitler became chancellor (head of the government) of Germany in 1933. Two years later, when Barbie was twenty-two, he joined the Shutzstaffel (SS), the Nazi Party's security squad that swore loyalty not to Germany but to Hitler. He served in the Sicherheitsdienst (SD), the intelligence and security branch of the SS, and was assigned to a number of posts in Europe for the next six years. During this time, as the German war machine swept westward, Barbie won a reputation as a shrewd, dedicated SS officer. He earned increases in his position, and admiring superiors expressed their approval of his performance.

After Germany invaded France in 1941, Barbie became head of operations to control the Resistance, the underground organization of French patriots resisting Nazi rule. He is widely believed to have been responsible for the torture and death of Jean Moulin (1899–1943), the secret head of France's anti-Nazi coalition. As head of the Gestapo security police in Lyon, Barbie also appears to have been responsible for a number of "actions" against innocent French Jews. Among them a raid on an orphanage in the town of Izieu, which sent over fifty boys and girls to the gas chambers at the concentration camp of Auschwitz in Poland.

Klaus Barbie.
Reproduced by permission of Archive Photos, Inc.

Postwar activities

When the war in Europe ended in spring 1945 with the Nazis' defeat, Barbie hid from the Allies (the nations allied against Germany, including Great Britain, the Soviet Union, and the United States) until April 1947. At this point he was recruited by the Counter Intelligence Corps of the U.S. Army in occupied Germany. Although the army had a warrant for Barbie's arrest as someone suspected of underground activities, the regional commander decided that his skills as an interrogator (someone who questions suspects or prisoners) made him more valuable as a spy than as a prisoner.

Over the next four years Barbie took on increasing responsibility for the army. At one time he ran a spy network that included scores of informants in East and West Germany and France. Barbie soon became one of the army's most trusted spies. In 1949, however, his presence became known to French war crimes investigators, who demanded that the "Butcher of Lyon" be turned over to them to stand trial for his crimes.

The U.S. army took a fateful step. It decided not to surrender Barbie to the French, fearing embarrassment by his service and worrying that he might disclose wide-ranging U.S. intelligence efforts to the French. With the aid of a Croatian priest, it delivered Barbie to Genoa, Italy, under the false name of "Klaus Altmann." There he and his wife and two young children boarded an Italian ship to Buenos Aires, Argentina. The "Altmann" family quickly moved to the mountainous city of La Paz, Bolivia, where Barbie supported himself as an auto mechanic.

Barbie's skills as a spy did not go unnoticed in the military government of Bolivia, and before long he became an associate of high-ranking generals. It is likely that he served as an adviser to Bolivia's secret security police. It is known that he became the director of Transmaritima Boliviana, a company organized to hire ships to bring supplies to land-locked Bolivia. He lived as any prosperous businessman might and was often seen in La Paz's cafes and restaurants.

True identity discovered

The past began to catch up with Barbie in 1971. Beate Klarsfeld, a German-born homemaker married to French lawyer Serge Klarsfeld, discovered from a German prosecutor's files that Barbie was living in Bolivia under the name of Altmann. In a dramatic move, she went to La Paz and chained herself to a fence, demanding that "Altmann" be tried for his crimes.

Although Klarsfeld's initial effort was unsuccessful, the spotlight of publicity was on Barbie to stay. For over a decade, "Altmann" denied that he was Barbie, but his identity was no secret to the regimes that had kept Bolivia under military rule. Finally, in 1982, a civilian government came to power. In February 1983 Barbie was arrested and turned over to French officials.

Barbie's return to France created tremendous publicity and soul-searching in the country, which had never fully come to terms with its mixed record of both collaboration with and resistance to the Nazis. Shortly after his return, the prosecutor in Lyon announced that Barbie would stand trial on several charges of "crimes against humanity." These events had consequences in America as well. Following a five-month investigation, the U.S. Department of Justice revealed Barbie's post-war role for U.S. intelligence and issued a formal apology to France for "delaying justice in Lyon" for nearly thirty-three years.

Justice served

Like nearly all the others who committed horrifying deeds under the Nazis, Barbie showed little remorse for his crimes. "There are no war crimes," he said. "There are only acts of war." When he was expelled from Bolivia, he seemed indifferent, saying, "I did my duty. I have forgotten. If they [the French] have not forgotten, that is their business."

The French had not forgotten. Nevertheless, three years after his return Barbie was still in a jail cell in Lyon, with no date set for his trial. The long awaited trial was again delayed in 1986, when the French Court of Indictments ruled that Barbie could be tried for crimes against Resistance fighters as well as for "crimes against humanity." Barbie was imprisoned for life in 1987 for crimes including the murders of at least four Jews and Resistance workers and fifteen thousand deportations to death camps. He was the last German war criminal of rank to be tried. Barbie died of cancer in a prison hospital in Lyon on September 25, 1991.

For More Information

Beattie, John. *The Life and Career of Klaus Barbie: An Eyewitness Record.* London: Methuen, 1984.

Murphy, Brendan. *The Butcher of Lyon: The Story of Infamous Nazi Klaus Barbie.* New York: Empire Books, 1983.

CHRISTIAAN BARNARD

Born: November 8, 1922
Beaufort West, South Africa
Died: September 2, 2001
Paphos, Cyprus
South African surgeon

The South African surgeon Christiaan Barnard performed the world's first human heart transplant operation in 1967 and the first double-heart transplant in 1974.

Childhood and education

Christiaan N. Barnard was born to Dutch descendants on November 8, 1922, in Beaufort West, South Africa. Barnard, along with his three brothers, grew up extremely poor and attended the local public schools. Barnard then went on to the University of Cape Town, where he received a master's degree in 1953.

Barnard worked for a short time as a doctor before joining the Cape Town Medical School staff as a research fellow in surgery. With the hope of pursuing his research interests and gaining new surgical skills and experiences, he enrolled at the University of Minnesota Medical School in 1955. After two years of study he received his Ph.D. (doctorate degree) and returned to his native country to embark upon a career as a cardiothoracic (heart) surgeon.

A distinguished surgeon

Before Barnard left for America, he had gained recognition for research in gastrointestinal pathology (intestinal diseases), where he proved that the fatal birth defect known as congenital intestinal atresia (a gap in the small intestines) was due to the fetus (undeveloped baby) not receiving enough blood during pregnancy. Barnard proved that this condition could be cured by a surgical procedure. Upon his return to South Africa, he introduced open-heart surgery to that country, designed artificial valves for the human heart, and experimented with the transplantation of the hearts of dogs. All of this served as preparation for his 1967 human heart transplant.

Although Barnard was a pioneering cardiac surgeon, his advances were based on

Christiaan Barnard.
Courtesy of the Library of Congress.

work that came before him. Of crucial importance was the first use of hypothermia (artificial lowering of the body temperature) in 1952, and the introduction in the following year of an effective heart-lung machine. These advances, combined with other techniques perfected in the 1960s, enabled a surgeon for the first time to operate upon a heart that was motionless and free of blood.

The first transplant

After a decade of heart surgery, Barnard felt ready to accept the challenge posed by the transplantation of the human heart. In 1967 he encountered Louis Washkansky, a fifty-four-year-old patient who suffered from extensive coronary artery disease (the arteries around the heart) and who agreed to undergo a heart transplant operation. On December 2, 1967, the heart of a young woman killed in an accident was removed while Washkansky was prepared to receive it. The donor heart was kept alive in a heart-lung machine that circulated Washkansky's blood until the patient's diseased organ could be removed and replaced with the healthy one.

In order to fool the body's defense mechanism that would normally reject a foreign organism, Barnard and his team of heart specialists gave the patient large doses of drugs, which allowed the patient's body to accept the new organ. Washkansky's body was not able to defend itself against infection, however, and he died on December 21, 1967, of double pneumonia, a disease effecting the lungs. Despite Washkansky's death, Barnard was praised around the world for his surgical feat. Within a year (January 1968) Barnard replaced the diseased heart of Philip Blaiberg, a fifty-eight-year-old retired dentist. This time the drug dosage was lowered, and Blaiberg lived for twenty months with his new heart. After Barnard's successful operations, surgeons in Europe and the United States began performing heart transplants, improving upon the procedures first used in South Africa.

Later career

Seven years after Barnard performed his first heart transplant, he made medical history once again when he performed a "twin-heart" operation on November 25, 1974. This time he removed only the diseased portion of the heart of fifty-eight-year-old Ivan Taylor, replacing it with the heart of a ten-year-old child. The donor heart acted as a booster and back-up for the patient's diseased organ. Although Barnard was optimistic about this new operation, which he believed was less radical than a total implantation, the patient died within four months.

Rheumatoid arthritis (a severe swelling of the joints), which had plagued Barnard since the 1960s, limited his surgical experimentation in later years. As a result, he turned to writing novels as well as books on health, medicine, and South Africa while also serving as a scientific consultant.

Barnard's advances in heart surgery brought him honors from a host of foreign medical societies, governments, universities, and philanthropic (charitable) institutions. He has also been presented many honors, including the Dag Hammarskjold International Prize and Peace Prize, the Kennedy Foundation Award, and the Milan International Prize for Science. Barnard died on September 2, 2001, while on vacation in Paphos, Cyprus. He was seventy-eight.

Shortly before Barnard's death, he spoke with *Time* magazine and left these inspiring words: "The heart transplant wasn't such a big thing surgically," he said. "The point is I was prepared to take the risk. My philosophy is that the biggest risk in life is not to take the risk."

For More Information

Bankston, John. *Christiaan Barnard and the Story of the First Successful Heart Transplant.* Bear, DE: Mitchell Lane, 2002.

Barnard, Christiaan, and Curtis B. Pepper. *One Life.* London: Harrap, 1970.

Clara Barton

Born: December 25, 1821
North Oxford, Massachusetts
Died: April 21, 1922
Glen Echo, Maryland
American humanitarian

A humanitarian works for the well-being of others. The American humanitarian Clara Barton was the founder of the American Red Cross. Her work helping people in times of war and times of peace made her a symbol of humanitarianism.

Early life and career

Clara Barton was born on December 25, 1821, in North Oxford, Massachusetts. She was the youngest child of Stephen Barton, a farmer and state law maker who had served in the American Revolution (1775–83), and his wife, Sarah. She later recalled that his tales made war familiar to her at an early age. Barton acquired skills that would serve her well when, at age eleven, she helped look after a sick older brother. In return her brother taught her skills that young women did not usually learn, such as carpentry.

The teenage Barton was very shy but was also well spoken and well read. Her mother suggested that she put her gifts to work by becoming a teacher. At age fifteen Barton began teaching at nearby schools. In 1850 she left to teach at Bordentown, New Jersey. Families in Bordentown were required to pay for children's schooling. Thus many children were unable to attend. Barton offered to teach without salary if children could attend for free. She

Clara Barton.
Courtesy of the Library of Congress.

later took pride in having established the first free school in New Jersey and in having raised enrollment from six to six hundred. However, when town officials decided to appoint a male principal over her, she resigned.

Civil War activities

Barton was working for the patent office in Washington, D.C., when the Civil War (1861–65) began. She decided to serve the Federal troops by personally collecting and storing supplies that people had given freely in support of the troops. In Washington she collected and stored food and medical supplies that could be distributed to the troops. In 1862 she was permitted to travel to places where the fighting was taking place. Barton was with Federal forces during the siege of Charleston, South Carolina, and also at battles in other areas.

Barton did not work primarily as a nurse during the war. She became increasingly skilled at obtaining and passing out supplies. However, her courage and concern for people made her presence strongly felt everywhere she went.

In 1865 Barton decided to begin the project of locating missing soldiers. With President Lincoln's approval, she set up the Bureau of Records in Washington and traced perhaps twenty thousand men.

Franco-Prussian War

Barton suffered from periods of poor health. In 1869 she went to Geneva, Switzerland, hoping to improve her condition through rest and change. There she met officials of the recently organized International Red Cross, a group that worked to help victims of war. They urged her to seek U.S. agreement to the Geneva Convention, a treaty that permitted medical personnel to be treated as neutral parties who could aid the sick and wounded during wars. Before Barton could turn to this task the Franco-Prussian War (1870–71), a war in which France was defeated by a group of German states led by Prussia, began.

Barton helped organize military hospitals during this war. Her most original idea was to put needy women in Strasbourg, France, to work sewing garments for pay. She also introduced this work system in Lyons, France. In 1873 she was awarded the Iron

Cross of Merit by the German emperor, William I (1797–1888). It was one of many such honors for Barton.

American Red Cross

Barton then returned to the United States and settled in Danville, New York. In 1877 she wrote to a founder of the International Red Cross and offered to lead an American branch of the organization. Thus, at age fifty-six she began a new career. In 1881 Barton incorporated the American Red Cross; that is, she organized it as a legal corporation. The American Red Cross was devoted to helping people in need during peacetime as well as wartime. She herself served as its president. A year later her extraordinary efforts brought about U.S. agreement to the Geneva Convention.

In 1883 Barton also served as superintendent of the Women's Reformatory Prison in Sherborn, Massachusetts. However, she remained devoted to her major cause. In 1882 she traveled as a Red Cross worker to assist victims of fires in Michigan and earthquake victims in Charleston, South Carolina. In 1884 she brought supplies to flood victims along the Ohio River. Five years later she went to Johnstown, Pennsylvania, after it suffered a disastrous flood. Barton also traveled to Russia and Turkey to assist those in need. As late as 1900 she visited Galveston, Texas, to supervise assistance after a tidal wave.

Retirement and death

In 1900 Congress reincorporated the Red Cross and demanded a review of its funds. Soon public pressures and conflict within the Red Cross itself became too much for Barton. She resigned from the organization in 1904. By this point Barton was a figure of international fame. She retired to Glen Echo, Maryland, and died there on April 12, 1912.

For More Information

Burton, David H. *Clara Barton: In the Service of Humanity.* Westwood, CT: Greenwood Press, 1995.

Dubowski, Cathy East. *Clara Barton: Healing the Wounds.* Englewood Cliffs, NJ: Silver Burdett Press, 1991.

Oates, Stephen B. *A Woman of Valor: Clara Barton and the Civil War.* New York: Free Press, 1994.

COUNT BASIE

Born: August 21, 1904
Red Bank, New Jersey
Died: April 26, 1984
Hollywood, Florida
African American bandleader and musician

Count Basie was an extremely popular figure in the jazz world for half a century. He was a fine pianist and leader of one of the greatest jazz bands in history.

Early years

William Basie was born in Red Bank, New Jersey, on August 21, 1904. His parents, Harvey and Lillian (Childs) Basie, were both musicians. Basie played drums in his school band and took some piano lessons from his

Count Basie.
Reproduced by permission of AP/Wide World Photos.

mother. But it was in Harlem, New York City, that he learned the basics of piano, mainly from his sometime organ teacher, the great Fats Waller (1904–1943).

Basie made his professional debut playing piano with vaudeville acts (traveling variety entertainment). While on one tour he became stranded in Kansas City, Missouri. After working briefly as house organist in a silent movie theater, he joined Walter Page's Blue Devils in 1928. When that band broke up in 1929, he Bennie Moten's band hired him. He played piano with them, with one interruption, for the next five years. It was during this time that he was given the nickname "Count."

After Moten died in 1935, Basie took what was left of the band, expanded the personnel, and formed the first Count Basie Orchestra. Within a year the band developed its own variation of the Kansas City swing style—a solid rhythm backing the horn soloists, who were also supported by sectional riffing (the repeating of a musical figure by the non-soloing brass and reeds). This familiar pattern was evident in the band's theme song, "One O'Clock Jump," written by Basie himself in 1937.

Success in the swing era

By 1937 Basie's band was, with the possible exception of Duke Ellington's (1899–1974), the most famous African American band in America. Basie's band regularly worked some of the better big city hotel ballrooms. With many of the other big bands of the swing era he also shared the less appealing one-nighters (a series of single night performances in a number of small cities and towns that were traveled to by bus).

Many of the band's arrangements were "heads"—arrangements worked out without planning in rehearsal and then written down later. The songs were often designed to showcase the band's brilliant soloists. Sometimes the arrangement was the reworking of a standard tune—"I Got Rhythm," "Dinah," or "Lady, Be Good." Sometimes a member of the band would come up with an original, written with a particular soloist or two in mind. Two of Basie's earliest favorites, "Jumpin' at the Woodside" and "Lester Leaps In," were created as features for saxophonist Lester Young. They were referred to as "flagwavers," fast-paced tunes designed to excite the audience. The swing era band (1935–45) was unquestionably Basie's greatest. The superior arrangements (reflecting Basie's good taste) and the skilled performers (reflecting Basie's sound management) gave the band a permanent place in jazz history.

Later years

The loss of key personnel (some to military service), the wartime ban on recordings, the 1943 musicians' strike, the strain of one-nighters, and the bebop revolution of the mid-1940s all played a role in the death of the big-band era. Basie decided to form a medium-sized band in 1950, juggling combinations of all-star musicians. The groups' recordings were of the highest quality, but in 1951 Basie returned to his first love—the big band—and it thrived. Another boost was provided in the late 1950s by the recording of "April in Paris," which became the trademark of the band for the next quarter of a century.

A stocky, handsome man with heavy-lidded eyes and a sly smile, Basie was a shrewd judge of talent and character, and he was extremely patient in dealing with the egos of his musicians. He and his band recorded with many other famous artists, including Duke Ellington (1899–1974), Frank Sinatra (1915–1998), Ella Fitzgerald (1917–1996), and Sarah Vaughan (1924–1990). Perhaps the most startling of the band's achievements was its fifty-year survival in a culture that experienced so many changes in musical fashion, especially after the mid-1960s, when jazz lost much of its audience to other forms of music.

In 1976 Basie suffered a heart attack, but he returned to the bandstand half a year later. During his last years he had difficulty walking and so rode out on stage in a motorized wheelchair. He died of cancer in Hollywood, Florida, on April 26, 1984. His wife, Catherine, had died in 1983. They had one daughter. The band survived Basie's death, with trumpeter Thad Jones directing until his own death in 1986.

For More Information

Basie, Count. *Good Morning Blues: The Autobiography of Count Basie.* New York: Random House, 1985.

Dance, Stanley. *The World of Count Basie.* New York: C. Scribner's Sons, 1980.

Kliment, Bud. *Count Basie.* New York: Chelsea House, 1992.

Volume numbers are in *italic;* page numbers for main entries are in **boldface;** "(ill.)" following a page number indicates an illustration on the page.

A

B

C

D

E

F

G

H

I

J

K

L

M

N

O

P

Q

R

S

T

U

V

W

X

Y

Z